SCHOLARLY
REPRINT
PUBLISHING
IN THE UNITED STATES

SCHOLARLY REPRINT PUBLISHING

IN THE UNITED STATES

CAROL A. NEMEYER

R. R. BOWKER COMPANY, New York & London, 1972

To my husband Sheldon, and
my mother, Betty Anmuth Rosalin

Published by R. R. Bowker Co. (a Xerox company)
1180 Avenue of the Americas, New York, N.Y. 10036

Copyright © 1972 by Carol A. Nemeyer

Printed and bound in the United States of America.

Library of Congress Cataloging in Publication Data
Nemeyer, Carol A   1929–
    Scholarly reprint publishing in the United States.
    Bibliography: p.
    1. Scholarly publishing—United States. 2. Reprints (Publications) I. Title.
Z479.N44   070.5'73   74-163901
ISBN 0–8352–0485–5

Contents

Preface

With this book I try to offer readers a broad picture of the current reprint industry, as well as an account detailed enough to capture the fast-moving reprint scene from various viewpoints.

The research study upon which this book is based was accepted as a doctoral dissertation by the School of Library Service, Columbia University, in June 1971. When the study was proposed in the latter part of 1968, some people said, "They will not talk." "They" referred to reprint publishers, generally described as secretive, hotly competitive, and distrusting. A few publishers seem to fit this bill, but the majority of the 300 publishers I was able to identify as reprinters cooperated in providing factual information and opinions. What these people said, what they do, and how they do it form the core of this book.

I interviewed many kinds of publishers, some with large reprint programs, others with relatively few titles on their lists. Most of them accepted the fact that I was not advocating a particular position, but rather was trying to collect heretofore ungathered data in order to offer them and their customers a much-needed overview of the industry. I listened without threat or promise, and learned a great deal. One ground rule I followed carefully was a promise I made to myself not to disclose to any one publisher the information collected from others, but to provide the same report for all. This book is that promise kept. I hope the results will encourage open discussion and will increase the level of understanding among publishers, other bookmen, and the librarians who are the industry's major customers. It is my further hope that the reprint industry can continue to offer good old wine in new bottles.

In order to portray the current reprint scene it seemed necessary and interesting to look backward in history, to see where reprinting made its first noticeable marks. Thus, the opening chapters provide historical perspective for the book's major focus—reprint publishing in the 1960s. Indeed, during the sixties and into the early seventies, reprint publishing has experienced a period of tremendous growth, change, and turmoil. Reprint publishing has emerged as a significant sector of the publishing industry in terms of the number of publishers involved and the vast quantity and variety of titles they reprint.

While hardcopy and microform republication programs are examined here, the main focus is on hardcopy, small edition, facsimile reprinting. The primary goal of this normative survey has been to discover and report the overall dimensions and the particular characteristics of the reprint industry in this country. A general overview and details of the industry's procedures, programs, problems, and relationships with libraries are presented.

Publishers' survey responses have been supplemented by factual information and opinions gathered from the industry's suppliers and customers, and by documentary analysis. The Directory of Reprint Publishers (Appendix E) and its accompanying Index to Subject Specialties (Appendix F) should prove particularly useful to all who deal with reprinters, since they represent the most comprehensive and up-to-date compilation of such information currently available. The study's findings should have significant implications for publishers, librarians, printers, and booksellers, and scholars—the ultimate users of new copies of scarce and out-of-print titles produced by reprint publishers.

I am grateful to Professor Oliver L. Lilley of Columbia University for his assistance as my doctoral advisor, and to Jack Dalton, recently retired Dean of the School of Library Service, who encouraged me to enter the doctoral program and who administered the Title IIB fellowship I received under the U.S. Office of Education's Higher Education Act of 1965. The significance of this generous grant far exceeds the monetary value. The fellowship of people, the deep commitment of each recipient to help improve the profession of librarianship—*these* are the rewards and responsibilities of a Title IIB fellow.

I am privileged also to acknowledge receipt of an officer's grant from the Council on Library Resources, Inc. My particular thanks are extended to Dr. Fred C. Cole, President, and Mr. Foster E. Mohrhardt, Senior Program Officer, for this support.

I am indebted to Dean Richard L. Darling, Professor Theodore C. Hines, Mr. Dan M. Lacy, and Professor Thomas P. Fleming for reading and correcting the original manuscript, and to Dr. Luther M. Evans, who reviewed the chapter on World War II.

I deeply appreciate Professor Maurice F. Tauber's friendly counsel, always generously given, and thank Professor Ray Trautman for unselfishly sharing his knowledge of the book trades.

Mr. Andrew Bernstein bore the major responsibility for the production of a computerized version of the directory of reprint publishers in the original thesis. He did his work well, with good will and with but small reward. The cooperation of the administration and staff of the Columbia University Computer Center is also gratefully acknowledged.

I also acknowledge Dr. Jessica Harris' help with subject headings selection, and thank Mrs. Ruth H. Hines for preparing the book's index.

I greatly appreciate the help given me by Mrs. Jean A. Guasco, Chief Librarian, McGraw-Hill, Inc., who provided materials and information, but most important, professional interest and friendship. I thank Mrs. Ruth Cangialosi, McGraw-Hill's Senior Reference Librarian, for trusted companionship in the years we worked together and for generous help since then.

My appreciation goes to Mr. Alfred H. Lane, Head of Gifts and Exchange at Columbia University Libraries and Chairman of the ALA Reprinting Committee, for helping me to keep up with the rapidly changing reprint scene, and to Dr. Felix Reichmann, formerly Assistant Director, Cornell University Libraries, for his continuing "alerting" service and for sharing his outstanding scholarship.

I am deeply grateful to Miss M. Ann Heidbreder, formerly Senior Associate, Association of American Publishers, Inc., for reviewing and helping to edit the original report, and to Mrs. Joan Lehn for help in searching the literature and for other deeds of friendship.

Chapter 1

Background and Nature of Reprint Publishing

The modern reprint industry has been described as "a revolution," "a jungle," and "a racket." Why? One reason might be that the industry has developed largely outside the spotlight of objective inquiry. Occasional voices have been raised in praise of specific reprints and in dismay over others, but factual information about a large number of the industry's publishing projects and participants has not previously been gathered and made available.

In the latter part of 1968, when this survey was begun, reprint publishing was found to be plagued by, and partly responsible for, serious information gaps which cloaked the industry with a veil of mystery. Plaintively people asked, "How do you find out if a particular title has been reprinted? By which publisher? In what format? At what price?" The lack of reliable, consistently reported reprint information seemed to be a deterrent to cooperative relations among reprinters and between them and their prospective customers, most of whom were believed to be librarians.

Yet, persons who would make more informed professional judgments about the reprint industry—those who make decisions about the selection, acquisition, preservation, and use of reprinted scholarly materials—need access to factual reprint information. How many people try to find this kind of data and are frustrated by its unavailability is a moot question. It is difficult for anyone to assess the extent of the industry's overall achievements or its deficiencies, however, in a partial void. Piratical practices and seemingly unethical business behavior have been the most newsworthy features of the industry to date. Even *Publishers' Weekly*, the "Bible" of the book trade, apparently had trouble gathering credible facts for its December 30, 1968, review of "Facsimile Reprinting: The Newest Revolution," for the article could only provide guesses, some of which were later contested in conversations with reprint publishers. Perhaps negative criticism of the industry is warranted. If so, the critics must be fair, specific and aware of the truth. Anything less is rumor.

The primary goal of the research survey reported in this book was to discover the size of the U.S. reprint industry and to identify and describe the particular characteristics of this sector of the publishing industry. An effort was made to identify all active reprint publishers in this country. The search became a Sherlock Holmesian pursuit for clues in published and unpublished documents; a large number of reprinters were discovered through word-of-mouth leads. Originally it was planned to schedule personal interviews with each publisher and with others in the book trades to collect factual data about the size and nature of each firm. These data would be tabulated for machine manipulation where feasible, then synthesized and analyzed, and the findings systematically reported.

Theory clashed with reality as it became apparent that simply identifying reprint publishers posed serious problems because of the lack of available reference tools and because the universe of publishers never was static. Probably the reader is aware of the dynamic nature of the publishing industry, knowing that statistical data about it must be subject to continuous revision. This fact need not detract from the usefulness of collected statistics as industry indicators. Any industry that stood still awaiting a recapitulation of where it was even a year or two ago would be a dull and static mass, probably unworthy of serious study.

Early on, it was found that there was no association of reprint publishers to provide overall industry information, to field questions about individual firms, or to recommend or enforce standards of performance. There was no comprehensive, enumerative list of reprinted titles, current or retrospective. There was no published list of titles that are out-of-print (OP), out-of-stock, or works in the public domain (i.e., unprotected by copyright in this country). Some of these gaps, which caused difficulties throughout the survey, remained troublesome at the end of 1971, creating tensions within the industry that exceed those normal in other competitive businesses, wasting time and money for publishers and librarians alike.

As the reprint story unfolds in the following chapters, we shall see that certain of the voids are lessening. It is hoped that one major need is met by the presentation of a reasonably complete and accurate identification and description of reprint firms in the Directory of Reprint Publishers compiled for this study (Appendix E).

The survey was conducted by means of documentary analysis, personal interviews, and mailed questionnaires. During the period of pre-research it became clear that, since the mid-1960s, the sea of scholarly materials surging into the nation's libraries has been heavily freighted with republished works. Mostly these are newly manufactured copies of OP books, periodicals, and government documents. These replicated works may be reprints on paper (i.e., hardcopies) bound in hardcovers or paper bindings, or microfilmed copies in any of a variety of microforms discussed in the Terminology section of the following chapter.

In order to cast a wide net this broad working definition of a *scholarly reprint publisher* was formulated:

> A scholarly reprint publisher is one who assumes the responsibility for the selection, production and sale of new copies of scholarly works that were available at some earlier date from another publisher or institution. The reprints are generally (but not exclusively) produced by a photographic process, and are intended to satisfy a relatively small, specialized market.

Nearly 300 U.S. reprint publishers have been identified. For some firms, reprinting is a primary business; in other organizations, reprinting activity is considered a sideline. It is important to keep the diversified structure of the reprint industry in mind, for it helps to explain some of the scattered findings. With this background, the reader is invited to share the results of a research survey of an ongoing publishing industry phenomenon—reprinting in the United States.

COLLECTING THE DATA

Personal interviews were conducted with about ninety publishers and other persons in the book trades and library world (see Appendix C). Thirty-seven publishers were found to be involved in the kinds of scholarly reprint programs within the survey's scope. Personal interviews were deliberately loosely structured. Some questions were open-ended to encourage publishers to provide additional information, to suggest or expand upon general industry problems, and to discuss their firms and problems from their own viewpoints. Face-to-face communication with the publishers proved a great aid to understanding the industry, and was enjoyable as well.

But the reprint industry boomed throughout 1969, when many of the interviews were conducted. New firms appeared unexpectedly and older firms created a plethora of new imprints. Near the year's end it was clear that a personal interview with each publisher was no longer practical. The geographical spread of the firms was wider than anticipated. Therefore, a 29-item questionnaire form (Appendix D) was constructed, pretested and mailed to 250 additional firms believed to be reprint publishers.

Questionnaire forms were returned by 159 firms, a gratifying 63.6 percent response from an industry known to be highly competitive and disorganized. Of these respondents 31 were eliminated from further study because the publishers felt their programs were out of scope or because the returns came back stamped "current address unknown." These firms are identified in the Directory so that others who might seek this information will avoid the same dead-end route.

About 68 percent of the 274 reprint publishers identified by the end of 1969 provided direct input. Additional firms located since then are also listed in the Directory, which is believed to include all of the industry's most active reprint publishers. Selected data about a large number of the nonrespondents were retrieved from secondary sources; these too appear in the Directory and, where feasible, the data are included in the overall findings reported.

Collected data were machine manipulated, where appropriate, for synthesis and analysis. The use of Columbia University's IBM 360/75 computer provided an efficient means to record changes, to count frequency of occurrence of selected data, to correlate data by a variety of surrogates, and to prepare a working copy of the Directory and its indexes. The programming language was SNOBOL4, developed by Bell Telephone Laboratories.

MAJOR GROWTH FACTORS

Two major factors influenced the tremendous growth of the industry in the sixties. These are (1) technological innovations and improvements in offset printing, small-edition binding and micropublishing processes, with resulting economies that make small pressruns of specialized titles feasible to produce and sell, and (2) the increasing market for previously OP rare and scarce textually significant works created by the expansion and upgrading of libraries at all educational levels, particularly at colleges and universities. Monumental federal aid-to-education programs were implemented during the 1960s. These programs injected large amounts of money into libraries where considerable amounts were invested in building and maintaining collections that could support the changing character of American education. Libraries needed many older scholarly titles, but found either that their demand for original copies exceeded the supply available through normal book trade channels or that they did not have staff with the know-how or time to search the OP market effectively. The infusion of government funds into libraries thus sparked and helped to nourish the fledgling reprint publishing industry.

THE SOURCE OF THE PROBLEMS

The copying concept threads through much of publishing history. The practice of mass-produced, machine-aided reprinting was born with the invention of printing more than 500 years ago, for many of the products of the early presses were typeset representations of previously prepared manuscripts.

By the late 1920s, a small number of firms, including Peter B. Smith and the F. S. Crofts Company, had begun to produce reprint editions of scholarly materials needed only in small quantities. Probably Peter Smith, still actively publishing, is the most durable of the independent specialist reprint publishers. His long and devoted attention to reproducing good books for libraries at reasonable prices has earned him deserved praise and the affectionate title, "Granddaddy of the reprint industry." Generally these early reprints were issued as a sideline to another primary business, most often by antiquarian booksellers or back-issue periodicals dealers. Scholarly reprinting has close bonds to the antiquarian book trade. The reader's attention is called to writings on the early book trades by the indefatigable Dr. Felix Reichmann, who retired as assistant director of Cornell University Libraries in 1971, and to his 1967 article in *Library Resources & Technical Services* (hereafter cited as *LRTS*), one of the few good published overviews of the current reprint industry.[1]

Though obviously not devoid of self-interest, many booksellers have immeasurably aided scholarship by recommending or reproducing scarce scholarly works. Continuing evidence appears in *Antiquarian Bookman*, published and edited by Sol and Mary Ann Malkin. It is, in fact, Sol M. Malkin, whom Helen Tuttle recently dubbed the "informer to and chronicler extraordinary of the antiquarian book trade,"[2] who deserves credit for coining the useful phrase "specialist reprint trade." In the 1969 *AB Bookman's Yearbook* Malkin sketched some of the problems arising from the early endeavors of bookmen-turned-publishers:

> They were the ones who would catalog a rare o.p. item and receive dozens of orders, not only from libraries but also from collectors and fellow dealers. . . . Advertising and searching might scare up a couple of copies a year, far too little to satisfy the demand.
>
> Thus it was that, after WWII, we saw too many poorly bound offset reprints from booksellers who had to learn the hard way the many pitfalls in successful publishing. Most learned and survived, some were swallowed up by other more knowledgeable dealers, and then, as was inevitable, a few enterprising major publishers and printers—and binders—entered the field with considerable success.[3]

These early "occasional reprinters" were primarily in the business of selling old copies of old books. Today's specialist reprint publishers, as Belzer points out, are engaged in the business of selling *new* copies of old books.[4]

In 1938 Harrison Craver, then president of the American Library Association, wrote to Dr. F. P. Keppel, president of the Carnegie Corporation, longtime benefactor of American libraries, requesting a grant of $10,000 to help libraries overcome some of their OP book problems. The grant was approved and an Out-of-Print Books Committee was appointed by the ALA to carry out the project. Essentially the plan was for the committee to receive suggestions of OP book titles from librarians, these to be reprinted by a publisher of "experience and repute," Peter B. Smith. From 1939 through 1950 only four titles were brought back into print, in no way a reflection on the publisher's capability and willingness; but certainly an indication of a lack of sustained interest and support from the library world. There is no need to provide further details here, but it should be noted that in 1950 the committee, under the chairmanship of Mrs. Edith A. Busby, felt that libraries needed to take another look at the OP book situation.

Thus, the funds remaining in the original Carnegie grant were re-assigned for an out-of-print book survey conducted by G. William Bergquist. The Bergquist report, now 20 years old, remains insightful.[5] Bergquist, concerned mostly with OP books for students, reference workers and the general public, excluded reprints of really rare books, incunabula, first editions, and other collector's items, presuming that such works would be reprinted and distributed by interested societies or groups without concern for profit. Bergquist found that general publishers were not keeping their titles in print as long as they once had, nor were they anxious to reprint their backlist titles. Increasing costs and financial risks involved in bringing out new editions made it difficult for large publishing houses to reprint editions of less than 4,000–5,000 copies.

The exigencies of World War II had created unusual and wide-spread pressures for libraries and the book trade to supply copies of works then unavailable but urgently needed for immediate and future scientific and scholarly research. We shall see that the U.S. Office of the Alien Property Custodian was extensively involved in reprint programs which focused on reprinting scientific periodicals from enemy countries. The custodian licensed such firms as Edwards Brothers, Johnson's Academic Press, Stechert-Hafner (then G. E. Stechert & Co.) and University Microfilms, all at the forefront of wartime republishing programs.

Concurrently, microfilming was increasingly utilized for copying research materials, proving especially useful for the preservation and storage of long backruns of periodicals and newspapers, materials which might otherwise have been destroyed or unavailable for use during and after the war years. Filming also made it possible to disseminate copies of current periodicals not generally available through normal trade channels.

The use of photographic copying techniques was not then new to the American library world. As Lawrence Thompson reminds us, photography has been used in libraries in this country since 1912, when a photostat machine was installed in the Library of Congress, and micro-filming has been adapted to library needs since the 1930s. By the end of the thirties, according to Thompson, "virtually every American research library had collections on 35mm film."[6]

Micropublishing already has a vast literature and it is rapidly expanding. In 1969, Sullivan noted trends emerging from a "review of the avalanche of current developments relating to the production of library materials and graphic communications."[7] His salient comments about major microform projects and vexing copyright problems recommend this article. Publications of the National Microfilm Association and titles concerning micropublishing included in the Bibliography of this book are also recommended.

After World War II, from 1945 until the early 1960s, the helter-skelter growth of the reprint industry went largely unheeded by the general publishing industry, then under its own mounting pressures to publish new works for a growing reading public and ever-larger numbers of educational institutions. We mentioned above some library efforts in the OP book field, but reprinting did not really receive coordinated, effective attention from the library world until the 1960s, when it became increasingly evident, as Tuttle so well describes, that the ". . . lively reprinting industry makes cooperation useful for both the book trade and library world," because:

> Librarians are able to suggest titles for reprinting, provide some indication of potential sales, offer a ready market for many titles to provide a partial underwriting of the costs of production, and often supply the copy from which the reprint is made. In return, the reprinters bring back into print some of the titles which the library needs.[8]

In Chapter 8 we shall discuss in detail problems librarians have in dealing with the reprint industry and examine the efforts of the ALA Reprinting Committee and other concerned library groups to improve library-publisher relations.

THE REPRINTER UNIVERSE

In 1968, estimates of the number of active reprint publishers ranged from about 20 to 100 publishers. The fact that almost 300 U.S. reprint publishers have been identified is evidence that the reprint tribe continues to increase. Earlier we noted that there are reprint specialists and other kinds of reprint programs. Some of the latter have been initiated by general publishing houses, either as coventures (e.g., McGraw-Hill with Chelsea House or Arno Press) or solo (e.g., J. & J. Harper Editions); and by non-book-oriented firms such as INSILCO (International Silver Company), which acquired Kennikat Press in 1969, and IT&T, which bought the Gregg Press in 1971. Mergers and acquisitions between publishing houses and "hardware" firms have also spawned new reprint programs. Obvious examples include Xerox–University Microfilms–Bowker; and National Cash Register–Microcard Editions.

Many university presses now conduct significant reprint programs, yet a considerable number of their titles appear on commercial reprint lists. For reasons not altogether clear, many university presses let their titles go OP or out of copyright years ago. Thus many important university press titles are in the public domain; these may be republished by any firm that selects the titles for their own list. Some reprinters' catalogs bear long lists of press titles (e.g., AMS Press, Kraus and Johnson Reprint). Some reprinters pay royalties or other fees for these titles; others do not. University presses with sizable reprint programs of titles not from their own backlists (e.g., Bison Books from University of Nebraska Press) are included in this survey, but no claim is made that all these programs have been found. Certain aspects of reprint publishing are more akin to university press publishing than to any other sector of the publishing industry, but the relationships between the two frequently create unwilling bedfellows. One might read Chester Kerr's classic study of university press publishing, the 1949 *Report on American University Presses*, and his "Revisit" to gain insight into small-edition, specialized publishing for limited audiences.[9]

THE PUBLISHING EXPLOSION

That books are pouring off the world's presses at unprecedented rates is a fact often alluded to as a flood that is inundating libraries and the book trades. Bowker's *Books in Print 1971* listed approximately 335,000 titles, but not all reprint titles are listed in *BIP*.

In the United States, 301,615 new titles and new editions were published from 1960 through 1970.[10] The publishing industry has not distinguished between scholarly reprints and regular trade reprints in reporting annual title-output statistics (they should), nor is the meaning of "new editions" clear. A former Bowker senior editor defined "new books" as first editions of new works and "new editions" as a second or third edition of a work usually with something new added, i.e., new illustrations, foreword, etc.[11] There are many discomforting gaps in statistics about the book trades generally, but the reprint sector fares worst—it has no statistical summary or trend reports based on factual evidence.

How many of the new titles published are scholarly reprints? Nobody knows with certainty.[12] How many titles have ever been printed? How many are out of print? These are questions that can never be answered certainly. Various estimates have been made, but these must be taken as opinion.

Frederick G. Melcher once said that the flow from in-print to out-of-print is the foundation of the conduct of the book business. He estimated that in each of the ten years prior to 1958, over 10,000 titles had gone OP, most of which he believed would never be reprinted.[13] Ten years later, reprinter Burt Franklin suggested that maybe fifteen million titles have been published since the invention of printing and that fifteen thousand titles (he put it as "1/1000 of 1 per cent") have been reprinted.[14] In an interesting *Times Literary Supplement* article about the reprint industry, Pafford guessed "there may be fifty million titles out-of-print and some two million in print."[15]

What makes this arithmetic guessing game important is the fact that there obviously are huge numbers of OP titles. Many of these, though certainly not all, would make significant contributions to current scholarship if reprinted. As Howard Mumford Jones wisely noted in discussing the annual output of thousands of ephemeral novels, children's books, mediocre poems, and the like, "Some are of no concern to humanistic scholarship, though at some later date their pitiful remnants invariably become so."[16]

NATURE OF THE PROBLEMS STUDIED

Preliminary investigative discussions with librarians and bookmen revealed the existence of two major clusters of problems. These may be categorized as reprint purchaser problems and reprint publisher problems. There is also a prodigious, though repetitious, literature from which the problems outlined below were culled and synthesized. Dahl-Hansen and Dougherty stated the overall problem from the library viewpoint: "If there is one issue causing concern to acquisition librarians, it is the uncertainty associated with the selection and acquisition of reprints and microform publications."[17]

Other librarians have suggested that once the decision to purchase materials is made, there is no essential difference in library procedures for acquiring reprints and general current books. Reichmann holds this view,[18] as does Catherine Maybury Seelye, Collections Development Officer at the University of Connecticut at Storrs, who states that the difference in dealing with reprinters and general publishers is mostly one of different library "attitudes," but that procedures remain quite similar.[19]

Thus, the grievances listed below are the expressions of many people; none is the voice of one offended soul. This record is not intended to minimize the valuable contribution to scholarship made by the many responsible members of the reprint industry. The intertwined problems of purchasers (here mostly librarians) and publishers recalls more of Burt Franklin's words. Speaking of the amazing growth and acceptance of reprint publishing, he said, "Those who may not want to live with it may nevertheless not be able to live without it."[20]

PURCHASER-USER'S PROBLEMS

Reprint purchasers frequently are dissatisfied with:

1. Publishers who announce titles prior to publication without specifying or meeting promised publication dates. This practice relates to late

or no delivery of materials, with a possible library loss of encumbered funds, and to bibliographic access problems.

2. Publishers who select titles that some people regard as unworthy of reprinting because the works are not now, or perhaps never were considered significant works of scholarship.

3. Publishers who change the titles of reprints without identifying the original materials precisely. A title that may have appeared originally as a monograph, or in a differently named series, may be hidden by incorporation into a newly named series. The practice of assigning new series titles or incorporating works that previously were separates may lead to unintended purchases and unwanted multiple copies.

4. Publishers who change the contents of reprints without explicitly noting variations from the originals. Criticism of this practice ranges from disgust over "padding" reprints with unsubstantial new matter to the serious charge that essential information in the original, such as maps, front matter, or illustrations, has been suppressed. The omission of original publication date and place from the reprint edition and the exclusion of contemporary advertisements are criticized practices.

5. Publishers who do not add indexes to certain works that might thus be substantially enhanced and made more useful to modern scholarship.

6. Publishers who price reprints too high. Critics of pricing practices use descriptive terms such as "outrageously high" and "scandalous." Some critics have questioned why certain titles, issued by more than one publisher (known in the trade as "rival editions") are sold at widely variant prices.

7. Publishers who do not produce a good physical quality product or, at least, a product that measures up to what has been advertised.

8. Publishers who borrow originals for copying, from librarians or book collectors, and do not properly care for the materials, are lax in returning them, do not honor requests to provide copies of reprint editions, or balk at the payment of borrowing fees.

9. Publishers who seem unconcerned about the effect their reprint editions might have on the secondhand book market or on library budgets. Booksellers and collectors have noted that original copies of some titles are readily available on the used-book market, often at a lower price than the reprint.

Some of these questions call forth value judgments and cannot be resolved by generalizations. Counterarguments and explanations are offered in subsequent chapters.

PUBLISHERS' PROBLEMS

Reprint publishers have two major kinds of problems. The first are internal, or problems inherent in the diversified structure and the economics of the reprint industry. Problems of this kind include the selection, production, and marketing of reprints; business ethics, royalty payments for public domain materials; and questions related to the need for a reprint publishers' association.

This present study moved ahead on the theory that the highly competitive nature of the industry and the relatively small potential market for reprints have created most of these difficulties.

It might be useful to note here that the economics of small-edition publishing was believed to have a significant effect upon publishing decisions related to the selection of titles, and to estimating the size of the market and hence the number of copies to be manufactured. This last item, the size of the print order, is a major determinant of unit manufacturing costs. What it costs each publisher to produce his copies obviously influences the selling price he establishes for his product.

The second set of publishers' problems is external, or problems that relate to the publisher's need to know—to really understand—his markets. He must be astute (or hire the talent to tell him) about which titles and publishing procedures will attract and satisfy prospective customers. Librarians will recognize the queries below as basic elements of library selection and acquisition policies. There is almost a direct match with the points Wilson and Tauber deem essential for effective development of university library collections.[21] Publishers may need to read more of what librarians write. Perhaps librarians may be of service to the publishing community by preparing lists of suggested bibliographic aids and specialized readings.

During this survey, a large number of publishers have asked these questions:

1. How do librarians select reprint titles for purchase?
2. Which kinds of personnel, in various types of libraries, are responsible for the selection and acquisition of reprints, and who in the library hierarchy might be the most effective recipients of publisher-produced catalogs and other mailings?
3. What kinds and amount of descriptive information do librarians want publishers to provide, in the reprints and in advertising and promotional literature? In a related vein, do librarians want publishers to supply Library of Congress cards; and if so, what charges (if any) are considered appropriate for publisher-supplied LC cards? Toward the completion of this survey, publishers began to ask if they should participate in the Library of Congress Cataloging in Publication (CIP) Program, and why?
4. What is the preferred arrangement of contents and frequency of issue of publishers' catalogs? Do librarians really *read* catalogs, some publishers asked.
5. What factors influence the purchase of titles that are produced in more than one format; for instance, in microform and hardcopy, or in the same format by more than one publisher?

After listening to these questions for several years (the interviewer often became the interviewee), it was remarkable to come upon Harry M. Lydenberg's comment that critics of libraries consider them to be "somewhere between a nuisance and a luxury." As director of the New York Public Library, he was concerned with librarian-publisher relations in the field of out-of-print books and reprints, so he added, "We have talked about this often, with little tangible results so far."[22] He said that in 1935!

Chapter 2

The Design of the Survey

What is the nature and extent of the current scholarly reprint publishing industry? Inherent in this broad question are a host of corollary concerns: What features will describe the "nature" of the industry? How might the "extent" be measured reliably? To what extent and in what ways might firms that began publishing reprints in or after 1960 differ from longer-established firms? Do microfilming programs differ from hardcopy reprint programs primarily in physical format, or are there other essential differences? In what ways do microrepublished and hardcopy reprint programs complement or compete with each other?

From this welter of problems, the following were selected for investigation. The study was designed to:

1. Determine the extent of the current reprint industry by identifying reprint publishers and their programs.

2. Describe the nature of current scholarly reprint programs in terms of the forms of original materials reprinted, reprint formats, and subject specializations.

3. Identify production methods commonly utilized by reprint publishers and describe general production problems that reprinters claim affect their publishing programs.

4. Seek and report factual data about the governing economics of the industry to the extent that reliable data might be made available, and to attempt to relate these findings to industry pricing practices and to the intentional or unintentional republication of the same title by more than one firm.

(It should be noted that the present study was not conceived or designed as an economic survey of the industry, though an up-to-date

13

"Cheney Report" would be welcomed. Questions about publishers' sales, production and distribution costs, inventory write-offs and profit margins would provide valuable information useful to many competitive publishers, but this is proprietary information, by nature generally confidential and carefully guarded.)

5. Determine the criteria that publishers proclaim to apply to the selection of titles for reprinting.

6. Identify and describe the nature of bibliographic controls imposed upon reprint editions.

(It was guessed that the bibliographic apparatus that exists to control reprints is inadequate and poorly organized to meet the legitimate information needs of reprint publishers, prospective customers, and others seeking publication facts and descriptions of scholarly reprints.)

7. Identify and report emerging trends that might signal the future direction of the reprint industry.

8. Suggest, on the basis of the findings, possible approaches to solving expressed problems—between reprinters and their customers and within the industry itself.

To gather factual evidence and reliable opinions from industry participants, the questions listed in the questionnaire (Appendix D) were formulated.

SCOPE AND LIMITATIONS
Reprint Publishers

It was impossible to say how many publishers would finally fall into the study's scope, but all U.S. publishers of small-edition, scholarly reprints, in all formats, who could be identified and located were considered for inclusion. Major attention was given to publishers of hardcopy reprints, the kinds of books Hayward Cirker, president of Dover, calls "paper objects" to distinguish them from microforms.[1] As noted earlier, hardcopy reprints include casebound and paperbound books.

It is seldom easy and not always possible to distinguish clearly one kind of publishing house from another. This is increasingly true of the reprint sector, for, in the words of the sagacious Reichmann, "The dividing line between reprint houses and regular publishers is a very thin one."[2] It is essential to note, therefore, that publishers whose reprint programs consist primarily of titles from their own backlists are not knowingly a part of this survey.

Based on the educated guess that the largest market for scholarly reprints is institutional, the search was made for publishers who specialize in the republication of books of scholarship and other OP materials intended for sale primarily, but not exclusively, to libraries and other educational institutions. "Scholarly" is a devilish word to define in this context, for "The Rover Boys" could be "scholarly works" for one studying children's books. "Scholarly" is meant to imply works of interest to scholars and other serious readers.

Micropublishers

The original research proposal included a plan to survey the micropublishing industry comprehensively. This ingenuous (in retrospect) idea had to be modified as it became more and more evident that the industry was growing vast and changing so rapidly that it required a separate study.[3] In view of the study's intent to provide a picture of the overall reprint scene, however, it was not possible to exclude all microfilming activities, for many film projects are designed to bring older materials to the market again, in microform. Microrepublishing (producing and selling microform copies of previously published works) differs from microform publication of unpublished original materials and obviously differs from photo-offset reprinting, not only technologically, but in publishing attitudes, rationale, and operational procedures. But there is an overlapping gray area where the microform and hardcopy reprint industry seem inseparable and sometimes are even mutually influential.

For example, as shown in the Directory, there are firms that republish some titles in hardcopy and others in microform, and selected titles in both formats (i.e., dual formats). The practice of publishing in more than one format is increasing, especially for long serial runs, where a complete run of a title may be put onto film, and special issues and indexes reprinted in hardcopy as well.

There is another distinction among micropublishers. Some produce editions; others produce only single filmed copies to meet a specific demand. Robert F. Asleson, president of University Microfilms, stressed this difference when he pointed out the variation in controlling economics, noting, "In demand publishing we make no attempt to determine what the size of the market is in advance. We produce what people tell us they want produced. We define an edition as NCR does in its *Guide to Reprints*, i.e., titles that are reproduced in an edition size of at least 200 copies."[4]

For the present survey it was not always possible to determine, before questioning a firm, whether it was essentially a micropublisher or *microrepublisher*. After a publisher was queried and useful factual data were collected, it seemed helpful to include *microrepublishing* specialists in this report and in the Directory, but no claim is made that all such firms were identified.

While these complex issues were being considered, it was learned that Reichmann had begun a study of the bibliographic control of microforms, a project sponsored by the Association of Research Libraries.[5]

With this study in view, further limitations to the present survey seemed appropriate.

It was decided not to study the huge microfilming systems operated by scientific, governmental, banking, and business services agencies whose primary purpose is the duplication and dissemination of film copies of current materials. Also excluded were firms that primarily produce films on a custom-contract basis (i.e., film manufactories). Out of scope, for example, are the massive filming and distribution projects of the Defense Documentation Center, the National Technical Information Service (formerly the Clearinghouse for Federal Scientific and Technical Information), Leasco Data Processing's filming of the Securities and Exchange Commission Reports, and McGraw-Hill's Information Systems Company DODGE/SCAN Microfilm Systems.

Examples of microfilm firms included in the study are such diversified micropublishers as University Microfilms, Readex Microprint, NCR Microcard Editions, and Bell & Howell's Micro Photo Division; and microrepublishing specialists such as MikroBuk and Research Publications, Inc.

Trade Publishers and the Reprinting Processes

Reprinting is a technological process utilized by general (trade) houses to keep their titles in print or to produce more copies when inventories are low and future markets are anticipated. This kind of "reprinting" is more precisely another or a new printing, and is not discussed in this study. The essential differences in purpose, edition size, and distribution methods help to distinguish trade reprinting from specialist reprint publishing.

Photo-offset is the most usual but not the exclusive reproduction method utilized by the reprint firms surveyed.[6] Photo-offset is a "method of offset printing in which images are photographically transferred to metal plates or paper mats from which inked impressions are made on a rubber roller, and thence to paper."[7] Reprints may also be reset into type (in whole or in part, as done, for example, by Ye Galleon Press), reprinted from standing type or existing plates (infrequently), or reproduced by xerographic or other electrostatic printing processes.

Any microform was considered for inclusion: 16mm and 35mm roll film, microfiche (sheets of film generally 4 × 6 inches)[8] and high-density ultrafiche (a transparency as small as 2 × 2 inches which can contain images of more than 9,000 pages of printed matter), and micro-opaque forms, including Microprint® and Microcards®. Microprint, a proprietary trademark of Readex Microprint Corporation, is produced on paper card stock, 6 × 9 inches, with each card usually containing 100 pages, reduced 12 to 18 diameters.[9] Microcard, registered trademark of the Microcard Corporation, is an opaque card 75mm × 125mm.

Whether titles are custom mandated or reproduced as an edition did not influence a firm's inclusion in this study.

Mass-Market Paperback Publishers

In 1966, Dan Lacy, then Managing Director, American Book Publishers Council, commented that "Paperbound books, once almost solely a vehicle for light recreational reading, have been a mainstay of education."[10] He added, "The more than 35,000 titles in print [in 1966] include substantially all the world's standard literature." By March 1971, according to *Paperbound Books in Print* (Bowker), the number of paperbound titles had increased to 88,500. However, publishers of mass-market paperback reprints were not studied because, although many mass-market paperback titles are similar to titles republished by specialist reprinters, again, the publishing concept, target audiences, and distribution methods differ significantly from specialist reprint publishing.

Frank L. Schick described the mass-market paperback industry up to 1957 in *The Paperbound Book in America* (Bowker, 1958). Hayward Cirker's "The Scientific Paperback Revolution" (*Science*, May 10, 1963), shows clearly how that sector's startling growth relates to scholarly reprinting; but to be certain that the delimitation for this survey was justified, in 1969 an interview was conducted with Michael deForrest, editor of Award Books, a mass-market paperback publisher.[11] The firm, which he described as a "quiet giant," first published reprints in 1963, with most first printings in editions of 75,000 to 100,000 copies. Most titles are reset into type, with offset lithography only occasionally used for special photographic problems. Apparently it is more economical to reset the type for editions that range in these large sizes. Most reprints are from the firm's own backlist, and seldom, according to the editor, does the firm reprint a public-domain title that would have mass-market appeal. These factors, which appear to be generally applicable to mass-market paperback publishing, reinforced the decision to exclude such programs from this survey.

International Aspects

Reprint publishing is very definitely an international phenomenon. Reichmann's perceptive overview of the industry encourages awareness of the international aspects of the reprint business.[12] Important reprint activity is underway especially in Great Britain, West Germany, The Netherlands, Italy, Japan, and South Africa. Since 1967, the German periodical *Borsenblatt für den Deutschen Buchandel* (Frankfurt) has issued annual selected reviews and lists of reprint titles under the heading, "Sondernummer Reprints." Most titles are from European publishers. Several foreign bibliographies (listed in the Bibliography of this book) are important to worldwide reprinting; but, for practical reasons only, the present study has focused on reprint publishing in the United States. American firms that operate joint ventures abroad are included, but no effort was made to contact foreign firms directly or to report their indigenous reprint programs.

A serious study of worldwide reprint activities was highly recommended by Sir Frank Francis, K.C.B., consultant on foreign library developments to the Council on Library Resources, Inc., and by other members of the Council who emphasized this point at the time the Council awarded an officer's grant for the present study. Because of this major delimitation of scope, the results of the present study should not be extended to the foreign reprint scene without validation.

Subject Fields

Books reprinted in all subjects and in all languages were studied, and the subject index to the Directory (Appendix F) reveals a range of about 250 subjects published by some 200 of the firms listed. No attempt was made to evaluate the content or scholarship of reprint editions, nor to judge the edition of a particular work the reprinter selected. To do so one would indeed need to be the Renaissance man. Some attention has been given to the statements and evaluative opinions made by scholars in published reviews of reprints, and their involvement as consultants to the industry will be discussed further.

Manuscript Copying

Special manuscript copying projects have been noted only peripherally. The brilliant republication of "Magellan's Voyages" by Yale University Press, for example, or George Braziller's "Ovid Metamorph. English'd by Caxton 1480," are rightly acclaimed as projects of great significance. Because these republishing projects appear to be atypical of the publisher's regular business, the firms were not included. Manuscripts reproduced by specialist reprint publishers, such as those in the music field, and in the study of medieval sources, are included.

Although details cannot be given here, attention is drawn to the Monastic Manuscript Microfilm Library at Saint John's University, Collegeville, Minnesota, where the library's curator, Julian G. Plante, is preparing an "Inventory of Medieval Manuscript Photocopy Repositories."[13] The Monastic Manuscript Microfilm Project is an attempt to secure the preservation of all handwritten manuscripts and documents dating before the year 1600 still extant in European monastic libraries, and to make copies of these works available to scholars in a single American center. The 1966 floods in Florence, Italy, and other disasters have made such projects invaluable to scholarship everywhere.

Large Print Books

Since 1965 when Keith Jennison began printing editions for the visually handicapped in enlarged type, other trade publishers have initiated similar programs (e.g., Walker, Prentice-Hall, Macmillan, Viking, and Scribner's), but most of these titles are photographically enlarged texts from the firm's own backlists.[14] A small number of firms, such as Dakota and Lanewood are included in this survey, for they also engage in other kinds of scholarly reprinting and do not generally reprint from their own backlists. The decision not to attempt to include all "large print" publishers was influenced also by the following: (a) in 1969 a special study group directed by Professor Ray Trautman (Columbia University) began its "Study on the Production of Reading Materials for Blind and Handicapped," in order to establish and recommend standards;[15] (b) a bibliography is now available that lists and identifies large print titles and publishers;[16] and (c) many titles in large print programs do not classify as "scholarly" materials in the traditional sense of the word, however broadly construed.

Reprint Terminology

Any search for standard terminology in the reprint field is frustrated by a large body of literature written about the problem and few accepted solutions. The lack of standard terminology has been a persistent problem in communicating the purpose and findings of this study.

The terms *reprint, facsimile, reissue, replica, type facsimile, straight reprint, textual reprint, shortrun printing, republishing,* and the like, are so variously assigned that redefinition by each writer considering the reprint field is necessary—a practice wasteful of individual effort, troublesome to readers and an obstacle to a clear view of the industry.

"What is an edition?" Symons pleaded in 1932, noting that "so far back as 1898 the Publishers' Association commented on the 'inconvenience caused by the existing want of precision and uniformity of practice' in stating bibliographical details," and that "the want of precision is now more marked than it was thirty years ago."[17] According to Symons, "edition" indicated a new setting of type, since the early printers necessarily distributed standing type after each printing. A "new edition" then meant only that new type was set. It was to differentiate "mere reprints" from original settings that various definitions were conjured.

Freedman's recent question, "What is a reprint and when is a reprint a reprint?" is as justifiably posed now as Symons' was 38 years ago.[18] As Mason has pointed out, "The term *reprint* has in the past been utilized in the book field to describe a number of different and totally exclusive concerns."[19]

Although Pollard, Greg, Esdaille, McKerrow, and other eminent bibliographers have been concerned with the problems for lo, these many years, questions persist. Specifically, is there a significant difference between a reprint and a facsimile edition? What properties define a type facsimile, a straight reprint, a textual reprint, a photomechanical reprint? Does it matter if an original edition is photographically copied or reproduced from newly set type? To whom might it matter, and why? Should a reprint edition made by collating parts of various copies of a work be defined differently than a reprint made from a single original? Are printed copies of manuscripts "reprints" or are they "primary" publications?

The literature was searched for definitions and ways to resolve these questions. Excerpts of variant definitions are given in Appendix A, for three reasons. First, it is hoped the display itself will suggest remedial action to some standards group (e.g., the appropriate Z39 Subcommittee of the American National Standards Institute); next, listing the definitions chronologically reveals that part of the terminology problem stems from the practice of assigning new meanings to old words; and last, the annotated list provides a historical view of changing copying practices.

Rowland, in an insightful outline for a proposed survey of the reprint industry, noted that no study should be restricted for the purpose of delimiting definitions.[20] In agreement with this dictum, a deliberate effort has been made in the present study to create broad working definitions.

Reprint editions may be macroreprints, defined as text printed on paper for eventual binding as casebound or paperbound books, or microreprints, in any microformat. Microreprints imply a reduction in type size and hence a need for machinery to read and/or reproduce the text.

Shortrun printing has been variously defined as a printrun (the number of copies run through the press at one time) of less than 50,000, less than 10,000, several thousand, a few hundred, and for microprinting, even a single copy. For this study, a short printrun refers to a print order generally not exceeding 1,500 copies. A majority of firms reprint far fewer copies; a few considerably more. Shortrun printers specialize in handling relatively small orders from many publishers. The shortrun printing business is influenced by available equipment, staff capabilities, and workload scheduling that permits "gang" runs of sheets of the same size. Shortrun printers operate in ways quite distinctive from large commercial printing firms. The latter produce many thousands of duplicate copies of a title in a single run, with all the implied benefits and drawbacks of a large-scale printing operation. Shortrun reprinting has unusual problems (e.g., scheduling, costs) but offers special benefits to reprinters who specialize in small editions.

The distinction between "reprinting" and "reprint publishing" is implicit in the literal meaning of the terms. Reprinting is a machine process—the means by which materials are reproduced. The term *reprinting* is frequently used as a synonym for reprint *republishing*. It should be emphasized that republishing includes the totality of efforts involved in bringing new life to works that existed in some form before. Republishing introduces new copies of older titles—works that probably had lapsed from popularity—to the market. As Grannis suggests, "Publishing implies the whole intellectual business procedure of selecting and arranging to make a book and of promoting its ultimate use."[21] Republishers have only some of these responsibilities.

Facsimile, in this report, describes unaltered copies of manuscripts (i.e., photographic copies of writings that appear holographically in the reprint edition) and unaltered copies of previously printed editions. (Freedman recommends that "facsimile" should define only a republication of a primary source. In his field, music, this generally would mean a manuscript.)[22] Minimal use is made of "facsimile" in this book because the term tends to confuse and is easily misinterpreted. In much of the published literature, "facsimile" and "reprint" are used interchangeably.

Reissue is another confusing term which some reprint publishers use synonymously for "reprint." Others imply *another* reprinting or a return to press for additional copies in order to keep their reprints in print. In some cases a reprint may be numerically designated (i.e., a second or third reprinting) in order to avoid the absurdity of re-re-reprinting to indicate a work thrice dead and born again.

Photographic printing terms are defined in many graphic arts dictionaries and need not be reviewed here. It is of interest, however, that under the heading "Photographic and Other Reproductions," in the 1967 *ALA Anglo-American Cataloging Rules*,[23] it is stated that:

> Photographic techniques may be used to make a single copy or multiple copies of a work, in microform or in macroform. They may be used as a method of production for original publication, for facsimile editions, or for reprint editions. In some cases the fact the a work is a photoreproduction or a facsimile is of significance for cataloging purposes.

The rules provide that:

> The use of photographic (indicative of "any process of reproduction involving the use of radiant energy") techniques is ignored for cataloging purposes in the case of reissues by the same publishers, reprint editions issued for new or changed title pages, and original editions in macroform produced from copy or assembled specifically for the purpose of the edition. Such publications are cataloged under the general rule for monographs, serials, music, etc.

Rule 190, "Facsimile Editions" provides that:

These rules apply to editions the chief purpose of which is to provide replicas that reproduce as closely as possible the original publication, manuscript, etc., that has been copied.

Blessed be the catalogers who recognize the use of "radiant energy" and who are able to determine the "chief purposes" of the copies being cataloged.

Chapter 3

The Copying Industries from Early Times into the Twentieth Century

Before splashdown into the sea of current scholarly reprints, it may be informative and interesting to review features of republishing in past years.

Modern scholarly reprint publishing is essentially a twentieth-century phenomenon, camera-born and nurtured by institutional funds. Yet the republishing industry bears characteristic traits inherited from an ancestral line of booksellers, printers, publishers, and librarians.

Older works of scholarship were copied for contemporary use centuries before the bookseller-printer-publisher triumvir separated into distinctive industries—in Europe in about the sixteenth century and during the nineteenth century in America.

It is a curious thought that no comprehensive account of the long history of republishing has been written; curious, that is, until the inseparability of republishing from overall publishing and printing history is understood. To write the history of republishing would be to rewrite much of the history of the book trades. No such effort is made here.

Rather, this chapter identifies selected copying concepts and past practices from the annals of the book trades. These will serve as the historical rim that binds the spokes of the modern reprint industry.

COPYING BEFORE PRINTING

Historically, the way in which the written word has been preserved, reproduced, and made public has been determined largely by the materials and technology available and by the extent of interest evidenced in the marketplace.

At least since the first Assyrian booksellers prepared and peddled copies of clay tablets in the public square, a variety of means has been utilized to duplicate and disseminate ideas.

Until the modern development of film and plastics, the most satisfactory writing surfaces were stone, papyrus, vellum, and paper. But stone was not easily portable or workable; papyrus suffered when rolled and was adversely affected by climatic conditions; and vellum was generally expensive. Recent studies of the permanence and durability of paper indicate that this material too does not have ideal lasting properties, particularly paper manufactured from wood pulp in the late nineteenth and early twentieth centuries. And the physical characteristics of microforms, the long-range endurance of film stock and processing procedures, are currently under investigation.

In Roman and Greek classical cultures, many persons gained their subsistence by copying books. Although Isaac Taylor stated that "for those with leisure it was not a wasted labor, since the high price of books made the collection of a library by purchase scarcely practicable, except for the most opulent,"[1] more recent scholarship shows that not all books were highly priced. Reichmann, in his 1938 *Library Quarterly* article, showed that some books sold during the Roman Empire were inexpensive enough for people living below the subsistence level.

Searching the annals of antiquity, Mumby found it disconcerting that the first bookseller about whom there appears to be definite information was an undertaker—an Egyptian who dispersed copies of the *Book of the Dead* for preservation in the grave. (Eugene B. Power, retired chairman of the board of University Microfilms, gets a twinkle in his eye when he recalls that *his* first commercial microphotographic work began in the quarters of a funeral parlor in Ann Arbor, Michigan. While Power is deeply concerned with the preservation of library materials, the analogy obviously stops there.) According to Mumby, "bookselling does not seem to have had any tangible existence as a trade in Greece until the fifth century B.C., and did not grow to considerable dimensions until the reign of Alexander the Great."[2]

SCRIBAL COPYING

Long before Gutenberg's mid-fifteenth-century invention of printing from movable metal type, manuscript copies of scrolls and codexes were produced by "the painful penmen of the scriptoria."[3] Extant manuscripts from monastic and secular scribal cultures provide a written heritage astounding in quality and quantity. Under noble patronage and with support from the Church, the great monasteries, those of the Benedictines and Cistercians for example, provided their users with copies of works of older scholarship. Scholarly research has always benefited by the existence of bibliophiles and the willingness of book collectors to support the book trades. The Abbot Paul (d. 1093), we are told, was such a devoted bookman that a "wealthy Norman surrendered the tithes from his land to the abbey so that it should have books, and these were copied by professional scribes."[4]

Monasteries were the centers of bookmaking and book collecting from the sixth through the twelfth centuries. Concerned chiefly with education and the transmission of learning, monasticism developed an efficient and highly competitive book production industry. Special scribal book-art talents developed. These skills encouraged a division of labor within the scriptoria. The scribal copying industry greatly influenced the structure and techniques of the early printing-publishing trades.

Scholars often traveled great distances to locate, borrow, exchange, and sell manuscripts and copies of manuscripts. Writings worthy of reproduction were copied "in house" to build local collections.

Condensations, excerpts, epitomes, and abridgements had their origin in scribal republishing business practices. Scribes who wrote swiftly with reed, stylus, or pen, developed techniques for condensing the bulk of large original manuscripts, sometimes altering copies they reproduced for sale. Scribal booksellers competitively sought markets for copies of their works, which they attempted to sell before rival copies became available. Scribes reproduced copies quickly and inexpensively, with quality sometimes sacrificed for quantity and speed of production.

The average size for an edition of a book printed in the fifteenth century has been estimated at about 200 copies by the printing historian, S. H. Steinberg. Earlier monastic and commercial scriptoria issued works in editions as large as 500 to 1,000 copies. The size of these scribal editions, it is interesting to note, is roughly equivalent to the number of copies printed by many reprint publishers in the 1970s. Then as now, the number of copies reproduced determined the unit production cost, affecting, in turn, the ultimate selling price of each copy.

Early scribal copyists reproduced works for which there was a known demand, or titles recommended by scholarly advisers. Consultants advised on such matters as the scholarly value of a text. They suggested titles that could be altered and improved by condensation. Scholarly consultants also determined which titles were needed only in a single copy for archival storage. Title selection is an ages-old publishing problem.

Space required to store the written words was a problem in libraries and archives long before the advent of mechanical printing. Large, cumbersome scrolls gave way at first to smaller rolls and then to the codex book format. The transition from roll to book format took place gradually from the second to the fourth centuries. By A.D. 400, the parchment codex had become the predominant book form.

Some 1,500 years have elapsed since the birth of the book format we know today. Yet the question is currently asked: Is the book being superseded by the "new" formats of rolls and reels?

EARLY LIBRARIES AND PUBLISHING

Libraries have always had a direct and mostly a mutually rewarding relationship with the publishing world. Library histories frequently begin with a description of the urbane library and book world of Egyptian Alexandria, although, as Richardson points out, "at least twenty-one librarians lived before Ashurbanipal, King of Assyria (669–626 B.C.), patron of the famed royal library at Nineveh."[5]

"A big book is a big nuisance," Callimachus, the innovative librarian of the Alexandrian Library, is supposed to have said. Coming to grips with library space and accessibility problems, and concerned with conservation and preservation of resources, Callimachus communicated library needs to the book trades. In his role as librarian-adviser to the trade, Calllimachus had much to do with the shape of books to come.

In Alexandria from the fourth century B.C., the bibliomaniacal Ptolemaic kings encouraged the copying of Greek literature. Library collections grew. Schools opened, many with on-site copying facilities for the production of student copies of needed works. Callimachus' library, housed in a one-time grain elevator called the Brucheion, contained, according to Raymond Irwin, some several hundred thousand volumes at an early stage of its growth.[6] The library maintained copying facilities for the production of volumes in its own scriptorium. Irwin estimates that four fifths of the rolls in the collection were "composite, or mixed," similar to medieval books; and, it might be added, much like the "new" massive reprint programs sold today in hardcopy and microform "packages." Composite rolls contained collections of miscellaneous, unrelated pieces added at random to complete a roll. Unmixed rolls, Irwin conjectures, were probably those that had been edited, recopied, and rearranged.

A 120-volume book catalog describing the Alexandrian Library collections was prepared by Callimachus, attesting to what Gudeman calls "a practically exhaustive cyclopedia of Greek literature."[7]

The copying of classical literature and older works of scholarly importance was extensive at an early date. In the fourth century A.D., the library and literary traditions of Alexandria passed to the Greeks at Constantinople, the city Irwin calls "the flower and source of scholarship in the Eastern Empire for over a thousand years."

MOVABLE TYPE AND REASONABLE FACSIMILES THEREOF

The prerequisites for a successful printing trade already existed when Johann Gutenberg was financed (and later forced out of business) by Fust and Schoeffer in the 1450s. The term "printer" was not firmly established for some time after the invention of printing; some printers called themselves scribes, as successors of the "scriptor" or "scriba," the earlier producers of books.[8]

The following factors, Wells suggests, gave support to the early printing trade: a continuously growing audience of interested readers and book buyers; the existence of a well-organized international publishing trade; the emergence of specialist booksellers; and the large corpus of works available for printing, i.e., copies of earlier manuscripts or new literary and scholarly works. The advent of printing offered "vital advantages to authors and scholars: economy of production and the exact duplication of established texts."[9]

In the fifteenth century, scholarly conclaves became the locus for university development in Oxford, and in Paris, Bologna, and Cologne. Stationers set up shop nearby to supply scholars with the books they needed, selling manuscripts or renting them for a copying fee. Stationers were the ancestors of the first university printers who, in turn, stimulated the growth of university presses. The first university press, Oxford, was established in 1478; the second, Cambridge, in 1521.

Early printers entered the business with varying backgrounds, as Hirsch reveals so interestingly. Some were concurrently scribes; others came from book-connected trades, having been rubricators, illustrators, artists, letter writers, educators, authors, and the like. Mostly literate, the early printers still remained dependent upon others for advice about the existence of manuscripts worth printing, and for estimates of their sales potential.

Anyone with the desire and necessary funds to become a printer could do so, as Hirsch describes, because of the absence of legal restraints. Although printers were free of guild restrictions, printing soon developed the kind of ruthless competition which spelled failure for many. Book prices were undercut. The very freedom to print that encouraged entrance into the trade lured the "unqualified and the unscrupulous, the mere adventurers and speculators to enter the field of printing and publishing."[10]

By the time a large number of printing presses were operational, the most practical way for a newcomer to enter the printing business was to buy out an established press. Before then, Hirsch notes, marrying into the family of a printer or marrying the widow of a printer was a frequent method of acquiring equipment, or at least a way to gain important personal and business connections.

Those bygone weddings bring to mind the more recent spate of publishing industry acquisitions and mergers. With his customary acuity and wit, Curtis G. Benjamin, former president and chairman of the board of McGraw-Hill Book Company, suggests that the marriages of "hardware grooms" and "software brides" of the 1960s "though widely celebrated and greatly feared, have been tried and found wanting." Benjamin concludes that, while the marriages have provided many publishing houses with more adequate working capital and more progressive management, perhaps the 1970s will bring about some "annulments or spin-off divorces."[11]

WHAT WILL SELL

Printing was from the start a commercial enterprise, and "however often printers and publishers have lost their money in the past five centuries," E. Ph. Goldschmidt has aptly noted, "there has never been a book that went to press unless the printer rightly or wrongly believed he would who stated, "Reprinting is as old as printing itself."[13]

Many of the early printers were also booksellers who sought to reproduce the kinds of materials they anticipated would sell well. They sent book scouts throughout Europe, Western Asia, and Africa to collect manuscripts to keep their presses busy. The primary productions of the early printers were sacred and liturgical texts, law codes, dictionaries, school books, calendars, indulgences, and broadsides serving political controversy. The customers for these works were mostly clergymen, teachers, students, and as Hirsch calls others, "an undefined medley of townspeople" who represented a broad segment of the population.

In the cradle days of printing, scholar-printers were the ones most likely to be drawn away from reprinting older works to concentrate on the production of new works needed in their own subject specialties. The merchant-printers, the artisans and craftsmen, relied more upon advisers for title suggestions or concentrated on reprinting previously acclaimed works of scholarship.

It has been estimated that in the 60 to 80 years after printing was invented, most of the classical works now known were committed to the press. Publishing historians would generally agree with Lehmann-Haupt, who stated, "reprinting is as old as printing itself."[13]

Most specialists agree, Hirsch notes, that the presses of the fifteenth century produced about 40,000 titles (books and broadsides), amounting to about 10 million pieces, the majority of which were produced during the last quarter of the century. By the late fifteenth century, a sufficient quantity of each title had been produced to encourage a systematic retail trade. Book stores began to flourish as separate outlets, although the early shops were an adjunct to the printing shop or the publishing office.

Scribes did not vanish with the coming of mass-production printing processes. Many joined the ranks of the printers. During the sixteenth century, due to the lack of Greek type fonts, it remained more economical to produce volumes of Greek text in manuscript. The limited market, the lack of familiarity of many printers with the Greek language, and the difficulty of gauging the potential sale of specialized works persuaded many printers to leave these works to the scribes who continued to produce copies on demand.[14] Since the early printers aimed at "perfect imitation of the existing manuscripts," as Plant notes, there was a continuing demand for scribal skills . . . a practice that continued for the first twenty years after typography was introduced.[15]

Histories of the book trades reveal that, to the extent that scholars need specialized works in relatively small numbers of copies, their needs have generally been best served by a segment of the book trade geared specifically to satisfying this need.

LITHOGRAPHY: THE NEW TECHNOLOGY

Only brief mention will be made of the significant technological breakthrough that occurred in the printing industries in 1798, when the Bavarian, Alois Senefelder, invented and began to perfect the lithographic technique of printing. In 1846 this transfer printing process was introduced in America. Its early applications were for the reproduction of illustrations in books and periodicals, and for printing music.

Further lithographic refinements, among them the use of the steam press and the introduction of zinc, and more recently, plastic plates accelerated the use of the lithographic production process.

Details of the development of the now very large photo-offset industry are outside the scope of this brief review, but it should br noted that technological changes provided the impetus and the means for reprinting to become the considerable enterprise it is today.

PIRATICAL PUBLISHING

In modern times, the cry of "Pirate!" is still occasionally heard in bookland, evoking an image of swashbuckling, self-interested skulduggery.

Book pirating gained impetus from monopolistic book publishing practices in sixteenth- and seventeenth-century England. Titles frequently were stolen and illicitly printed without payment or permission. Prices were undercut so drastically that profitable returns were diminished for each rival printer. It should be recalled that, in sixteenth-century England, printing had only recently spun off into a commercial trade separate from bookselling. Because the trade was still without legal restrictions, the number of printers steadily increased. British rulers became increasingly afraid that the growing literate public might be politically and socially persuaded because they had easy access to supposedly heretical and seditious books and pamphlets that were streaming onto the market. In an effort to control the contents of printed materials, the British government imposed a grant system, giving crown patents to so-called privileged printers.

But the underground press was at work. Any printer with type at hand and an eye on the market could, as many did, produce copies without privilege. Titles produced by one printer were easily reprinted by another. Book production increased so rapidly in the sixteenth century that, according to Roberts, "each successive Parliament and sovereign was caused consternation and alarm."[16]

Competition within the trade made it difficult for all printers to remain in business successfully. Joined by their colleagues from allied book trades, some of the well-to-do printers requested and received a government charter, granted in May 1557, to form a kind of "trade association" which they called the Stationers' Company. In her description of the company, Plant notes that the group appears to be a "natural descendent of a 14th century body of London scriveners known as the Writers of the Court Hand and Text Letters."[17] Their charter reserved printing privileges for members only. The company functioned as a self-policing body. Through licensing and registration, printing jobs were controlled and monopolized by the membership. Practicing "company manners," members agreed to avoid reprinting each other's works and to limit the size of their respective editions in order to spread printing jobs throughout the industry.[18] Many of the less affluent unlicensed printers suffered by the Stationers' Company monopoly, and attempted to overcome their problems by printing pirated works.

Under their protective umbrella, licensed publisher-printers were permitted to register selected titles in advance of publication to ward off the pirates. A publisher's submission of an "intent to produce" a title earned a "stay order" which helped to secure the title for him alone. Pollard cites the case of James Roberts, who on July 27, 1598, entered the play *The Merchant of Venice,* with a provision that the play "should not be printed until he had produced better authority . . . and that publication be postponed until it could not injure the run of the play . . . to make the task of the pirates more difficult."[19]

Literary and book piracy ran rampant as presses reprinted surreptitious copies of controlled works. The practice of reproducing copies of suppressed works "without leave" spread to the practice of reprinting, without permission, copies of popular works which had previously been printed under license. With charming understatement, Kaser writes that "things by 1700 were beginning to get out of hand, and the London booksellers repeatedly petitioned for relief by law, which finally came in 1710 with the passage of the so-called Statute of 8 Anne."[20] Literary piracy, a subject woven into the tangled mass of copyright history and law, is being investigated in a separate study by Brodowski, who defines a "literary pirate" as "one who appropriates or reproduces without leave for monetary gain, a composition, idea, or intention that he has no right to; especially one who fringes upon the copyright of another."[21]

By the seventeenth century the book trade had assumed truly international proportions, with traffic in books and other printed matter traveling through standard commercial arteries. Religious controversies stirred public interest. Nationalism intensified. Scholars, reassessing their cultural heritage, looked backward in history and literature for ways to counter current social ills. Older fields of scholarship, such as Anglo-Saxon studies, were newly researched.

Current interest in "area studies," evident in new curricula at colleges and universities, is to some extent an echo of these past scholarly practices. Contemporary research in African and Asian studies, for example, has created new markets for today's reprinters. Resurrecting old records, reprinters again serve a generation of scholars and readers who seek a better understanding of their cultural past.

LITERARY SOCIETIES AND THE PUBLISHNG WORLD

The formation and programs of literary societies and clubs are significant in the history of reprinting and should be mentioned briefly. Literary clubs frequently have engaged in reprint programs, sponsoring the production of type facsimiles for bibliographic scholarship and promoting reprints for the purpose of textual crticism. Club members interested in the bookmaking arts have encouraged facsimile reproductions of manuscripts and rare books in order to make copies available to more than the few scholars who have the privilege of access to the originals.

Many society works are currently in the public domain. These titles, unprotected by copyright, are freely available for modern reprinting. Just as new copies of valuable old texts were freed from a state of uniquity and made more widely available by society publication, so current reprinters send forth an unabating stream of reprints of these works.

The catalogs of some modern reprinters include lengthy lists of society publications. For example, Johnson Reprint Coproration's 1969 Catalog lists nearly eight pages of Camden Society publications. AMS Press catalogs over one hundred numbers of the publications of the Bannatyne Club, Edinburgh. Kraus Reprint Company's General Catalogue includes publications of the Augustan Reprint Society, a series Kraus says contains a collection of reprints (usually facsimile reproductions) of rare seventeenth- and eighteenth-century works, some of which are unavailable in any other form. These firms, and others, reprint many of these titles "by arrangement" with the various societies, which receive royalties or copying fees. Some firms reprint without requesting permission, which is well within their legal rights, but is a practice for which the industry is frequently criticized.

Further research into the relationship of literary societies and publishing is recommended, for even a cursory review of reprint editions of important society papers points to an intense need for improved bibliographic controls of these works.

REPRINTING IN AMERICA

The eighteenth century has been called by the noted rare-book librarian, Ellen Shaffer, "the century of svelte elegance in the book

world."[22] In Europe, there was great interest in new books of contemporary authorship. The century opened with a low level of typography, but
closed with a burst of magnificent inventiveness in the book arts. Reprinting of the classics continued to be the bread-and-butter business for
many Continental printers, but it assumed less importance to the trade
than the publishing of original works. Reprinting developed a new major
stronghold—in the American Colonies.

Crossing the Atlantic, many printers brought with them the practice
of printing without license or permission. As in England, although more
slowly in the Colonies, "a taste for secular literature was growing toward
the end of the eighteenth century."[23] Printer-publishers produced books
to satisfy a public hungry for popular literature authored by Englishmen.

Through the first 20 years of the nineteenth century Amrican publishing remained decentralized. Competition was keen among the early
printers, and cutthroat practices created such extensive competition that
the publishing channels were glutted and the market oversaturated with
periodical literature and with "cheap and nasty reprints."[24]

English and American authors were unprotected by reciprocal copyright agreements. A significant number of American-printed editions were
pirated copies of English fiction, printed without permission and rarely
accompanied by payment to authors or to the original publishers. The
fight was on, and ruthless it was, to snatch the first copies of English titles
that arrived on board the ships inbound from England. Publishers rushed
to their presses with pirated copy in hand and flooded the market with
reprints they made from newly set type. Book prices were shaved; the
quality of production continuously worsened; and reprinted books eventually were "unsalable on any terms which could be profitable for either
publisher or author."[25]

By the 1850s, which Boynton considers a turning point in modern
publishing, the publisher emerged as a capitalist responsible for financing
book production. He assumed the attendant publishing risks which today
are recognized as features of "real" publishing. Many firms that started
publishing during those hectic years are still active. The basic characteristics and methods of new trade book publishing have not changed much
since the early years, but reprinting has changed considerably.

A secondhand book trade grew, making its home principally along
New York City's Fourth Avenue. Some dealers began to specialize in the
sale of publisher's "remainders," those unfortunate reminders of a publisher's poor risks. Dealers in old and rare scholarly books became
"antiquarian" booksellers.

The low quality of many reprints merchandized during the frenzied
era of piratical publishing branded reprints with a stigma that has sur-
vived, to an extent, to date. To some persons in the book and library
community, the term "reprint" still conjures up a vision of a shoddy
production turned out by a mere book merchandiser seeking the fast
buck.

REPRINTING IN THE TWENTIETH CENTURY

Mass-market paperbound and hardcover "popular-priced reprints" are not included in this study, but brief mention must be made of the major thrust of this type of reprinting during the first half of the twentieth century.

In the 1930s, reprint editions were produced in uniform series by such famous houses as Grosset & Dunlap and J. & J. Harper. These inexpensive hardcover reprints were generally issued by arrangement with the original publishers, and were reprinted from existing plates. Authors generally were willing to accept a lower than usual royalty rate with the promise of large editions. These reprints, which satisfied the public's demand for inexpensive popular titles, differed in design, intent, and in edition size from the reprints of important out-of-print works offered today by specialist scholarly reprint publishers. There is, to be sure, some overlap between these two kinds of reprint publishing, but as Freeman Lewis, a pioneer in reprint and paperback publishing, once noted, "It is a peculiar characteristic of the book business that no single phase of it can be taken up without indulging for the most part in generalizations which will be immediately questioned by some particular publishing house or trade organization which is the successful exception."[26]

Madison has written a welcome one-volume review of the publishing industry's growth from the late eighteenth century through 1965.[27] In the chapter "Genteel Publishing in the Gilded Age," he relates many of the facts, fancies, and fiascos of piratical reprinting practices, recounting the agitation felt for reform beginning early in the nineteenth century, when the injustice of book piracy became very evident in this country.

Kaser reveals the problems of illicit reprinting and book trafficking that continue to antagonize publishers in the United States. Tracing the status of literary property from the time of King Diarmid's sixth-century dictum, "to every cow her calf; therefore to every book its copy," Kaser stops short of examining the current state of the reprinting art—and craft.[28]

There is ample evidence in the literature of the book trades that reprinting has been a pivotal, Janus-like publishing practice during the centuries since man first attempted to preserve, reproduce, and transmit ideas. Reprinting has been a significant factor in the growth and development of the publishing industries, providing scholars and readers with materials that might otherwise not have been readily available.

As the anguished world stood at the threshhold of World War II, however, and scholars, bookmen, and librarians became painfully aware that this country's library resources and publishing industry were not effectively organized or stocked to meet the research needs of a nation on the verge of a major war, reprinting was to take on a new, dynamic dimension.

Chapter 4

Republication Programs in World War II

The publishing industry reacted to wartime book and information exigencies in many imaginative ways. Most programs designed to bring original copies of foreign materials into the United States fall outside the scope of this study, but certain programs combined the acquisition of originals with reprinting efforts. For example, the Council of Books in Wartime supplied almost 125 million copies of 1,180 titles to members of the Armed Forces. Ninety-nine of these Armed Services Edition titles were reprints.[1] In addition to accomplishing its primary mission, the council was the predecessor of the American Book Publishers' Council, formed in 1946. By consolidation in 1970, the ABPC and the American Educational Publishers' Institute became the Association of American Publishers, which will be mentioned again later in this report.

Early in World War II, republication programs were initiated to make copies of war-urgent foreign publications available to United States and Allied scientists and researchers. The major republishing program was administered by the United States Office of the Alien Property Custodian (APC). The program was developed specifically to reprint European scientific and technical periodicals (and books) published in enemy and enemy-controlled countries during the war.

The philosophy and many operational details of the program are described in a 1945 memorandum by Eugene A. Tilleux, chief of the Copyright Administration Section, to Howland H. Sargeant, chief of the Division of Patent Administration. This informative document is cited hereafter as the Tilleux Report.[2]

Thomas P. Fleming, who generously provided information on this phase of the reprint story, was involved in the conception and operation

34

of the republication programs. It is his opinion, shared by the author, that "World War II republication programs were largely responsible for spinning reprint publishing off dead center and into a twentieth-century specialized publishing industry."[3]

Why the republication programs were needed, how they functioned, some results and implications for the future of the reprint industry are described in this chapter.

BACKGROUND

American research libraries contained many German and other foreign scientific periodicals prior to 1939 when World War II broke out in Europe. United States industrial and research organizations, scientific societies and libraries were spending about 1½ million dollars a year to acquire foreign books and periodicals.[4] Yet, some periodical series were incomplete. These lacunae created serious problems for scientists engaged in war preparations, particularly since German scientific and technical journals frequently made reference to earlier, unavailable reports. The matter of issues missing from American library collections was complicated by the fact that during some years, the more highly specialized journals had no subscribers in the United States.

European scientific journals were received in the United States after the outbreak of the war, but following the German occupation of the Low Countries in May 1940, little published information about enemy scientific and military activities entered this country through normal supply channels.

Shipments of European periodicals were often lost at sea or interned en route by British customs officials at Gibraltar, Trinidad, or Bermuda. In 1941, the British government agreed to let through $250,000 worth of European materials for nongovernmental American libraries. The U.S. Joint Committee on Importations, acting with State Department approval and assistance, and with the full cooperation of the Library of Congress, arranged to purchase these materials for distribution in this country.

Great Britain's willingness to allow these materials to enter the United States was the subject of a 1941 conference between Dr. Luther H. Evans, then Chief Assistant Librarian of Congress, and Dr. E. Wilder Spaulding of the State Department. For American libraries the policy was of great significance, as Dr. Evans reported to the Librarian of Congress in his "Report on Important Developments, No. 37 (December 16, 1941)." Dr. Evans, who retired in 1971 from his position as director, International and Legal Collections, Columbia University Libraries, discussed his long-standing concern with acquiring foreign materials for our libraries with this writer on August 24, 1970. Dr. Evans is a library statesman who, in the early 1940s, recognized a mutuality of interests that could and did grow into republication programs of benefit to the scholarly world. He also was instrumental in introducing Joseph William "Bill" Edwards, who was to play a major role in wartime reprinting, to Howland H. Sargeant.

THE PUBLISHING INDUSTRY IN WARTIME

The war economy of the United States in the early 1940s created critical manpower and materials shortages in the printing and publishing industries. By 1943, the paper shortage was so acute that the War Production Board began to allocate paper stock to publishers under a strict quota system. Scarcity of binding cloth led to price increases and made the purchase of small quantities increasingly difficult. Many elements formerly deemed essential to good book design and production had to be jettisoned. Publishers redesigned page layouts and produced smaller, thinner books. Metal shortages caused the government to put a three-year retention limit on publishers' metal plates, after which time the plates had to be melted down for salvage.[5] A similar situation prevailed in Europe, where the destruction of many publishers' stereotype plates eliminated reprint possibilities except by photographing original copies or resetting type.

Printers and binders were unable to meet normal delivery schedules. Work loads were heavy with war-incurred printing jobs. Publishers vied for position on book production lines. Most large houses allocated their scarce resources for the publication of current books. Trade publishers typically printed new titles in editions exceeding 5,000 copies, with potential bestsellers, of course, published in much larger initial printings. Many publishers were able to keep important backlist titles in print, but carefully considered whether they could afford to invest meager binding materials, paper, and labor in keeping more ephemeral titles alive. Since these titles had already passed their initial sale, slower-moving backlist titles, with an anticipated annual sale of fewer than 1,000 copies, were allowed to go out of print.

Against this backdrop of constraints in the publishing industry, it is little wonder that by the early 1940s the scientific and scholarly communities were increasingly aware of the need to inaugurate unusual plans to supply copies of foreign technical works selected as war-urgent. The anticipated market for these titles was typically 300 to 400 copies, far too small to be viable publishing ventures for most firms.[6] Regular publishers were unable to produce such small editions, and there was no organized reprint publishing industry in this country to systematically provide small editions of specialized titles on demand.

In Europe, reprints of scholarly works had been available for many years before the war. Many of these reprints were of poor quality, however, and American librarians and scholars resisted buying them unless they had no alternatives. In wartime Germany original works were frequently printed on poor quality "butcher" paper. These disintegrated too quickly to serve well as preservation copies for research libraries.[7] Periodicals were printed in a wide variety of sizes, often with practically no margins, so that even those originals that were available in the United States could not be rebound for library usage. Thomas P. Fleming had counted some 32 different-sized periodicals arriving from Germany in the early 1940s. Fleming recalled that he and Dr. Charles H. "Charley" Brown recommended standardizing on four sizes for the periodicals reprint programs then undertaken by Edwards Brothers of Ann Arbor, Michigan. Edwards was able to photographically enlarge or reduce the copy to meet reprint specifications, a farsighted idea that has since permitted libraries to handle and shelve those reprinted journals without undue formatting complications.

Photographic copying techniques had been utilized since the 1920s, providing libraries and scholars with important foreign scholarly works on film, but reading machines were not widely available. Securing photostatic copies for libraries was too slow a process to satisy ongoing scientific inquiries. Compounded, these conditions created serious problems for scientists and military personnel who needed to read foreign literature for current awareness of scientific advances abroad. How might duplication of effort in war preparations be avoided? How could American and Allied libraries be stocked with foreign publications to meet immediate and long-term research needs?

JOINT COMMITTEE ON IMPORTATIONS

In September 1939, several American national library associations cooperatively established a nongovernmental Joint Committee on Importations to expedite the acquisition of selected periodicals and books from warring countries. Special emphasis was placed on materials from Italy, Germany, and Spain. The joint committee, chaired by Harry M. Lydenberg (New York Public Library) from 1939 to 1941 and by Thomas P. Fleming (medical librarian, Columbia University) from 1941 to 1946, arranged to purchase from one to one hundred copies of desired journals and books for distribution in the United States.

INTERDEPARTMENTAL COMMITTEE FOR THE ACQUISITION OF FOREIGN PUBLICATIONS

The difficult task of locating and securing copies abroad for the government fell to the members of the Interdepartmental Committee for the Acquisiton of Foreign Publications, known generally as the IDC. With Frederick G. Kilgour as executive secretary, the IDC operated in strict secrecy under the general direction of the United States Office of Strategic Services. For security reasons, the IDC did not deal directly with any private concern in this country. All requests for material were filtered to it through other fedeal departments, particularly the Division of Patent Administration, Copyright Administration Section.

IDC also arranged for the deposit of positive microfilm prints of selected research material in 14 libraries. One, the Library of Congress, provided duplicate films or enlarged paper prints through its Photoduplication Service. The Library, which performed a service to the scholarly community by selling copies at prices close to preparation cost, could be entrusted with the sensitive screening task needed to prevent copies from readily falling into enemy hands.

In retrospect, one realizes the enormous difficulties those in charge of procurement and republication programs faced as they attempted to operate in secrecy. That the task was taken seriously is evident in the repeated notice in the "Confidential Announcements" distributed by the Alien Property Custodian to scientists, libraries, and industrial and research organizations:

> It is absolutely imperative that no publicity of any nature be given to the proposed program. If any publicity is given, it will mean the cessation of the supply of copy and total failure of the enterprise.[8]

Years later, recalling the chaos in the wartime book trades, Verner W. Clapp, then director of LC's Acquisitions Department, wrote about the library's satisfaction with the work of the Interdepartmental Committee for the Acquisition of Foreign Publications. In a February 14, 1945, letter to Lt. David H. Clift, acting as deputy to Lt. Frederick G. Kilgour, Clapp reflected that American libraries had previously had to depend upon sporadic, casual, and accidental sources for information about foreign books and for copies of the books. IDC's centralized procurement and distribution of foreign books, periodicals, and newspapers greatly enriched the War Agencies Collection in the Library, Clapp noted, with the result that "for many portions of the globe the available books are not only not inferior but actually superior to what was received in times of peace—superior in selectivity and coverage and superior in rapidity of transmission."[9]

EUROPEAN BOOKMEN IN THE UNITED STATES

Book and journal procurement became more difficult as the European war escalated. Bombing attacks destroyed much of the Belgian, Dutch, and French book industries. A number of European publishing centers fell into ruin. Nazi invasions forced many European bookmen to flee their homelands. Away from Axis control, some put their knowledge of European publishing and bookselling to work in this country and became integral parts of the reprint story. For example, Hans Peter Kraus, who left Vienna in 1939, organized a rare book business in New York City and subsequently developed the Kraus Reprint Company.

In 1939 Walter J. Johnson was allowed to leave Leipzig, where he had published important works under the Akademische Verlag GmbH imprint. After a difficult journey through Denmark, Sweden, Finland, Japan, and Cuba, Johnson, his wife, and two small children entered the United States. Tom Fleming, a long-time friend of the Johnson family, described their arrival in this country and noted the difficulties Johnson overcame as he organized his new publishing house, Academic Press, Inc., in New York City. In 1946, Walter Johnson formed the Johnson Reprint Corporation. His son, Herbert M. Johnson, is presently engaged in the reprint industry as vice-president and general manager of Walter J. Johnson, Inc., jobbers of reprinted backruns of periodicals and monographic reprints. This firm is a part of the Johnson "empire" not sold to Harcourt, Brace and World (now Harcourt Brace Jovanovich, Inc.) in 1969.

In 1940, Frederick Ungar came to the United States from Vienna, via Switzerland. In Vienna, according to Cazden, Ungar had founded the Phaidon Verlag in 1922, and directed the Saturn Verlag from 1926 to 1938. In the United States the Frederick Ungar Publishing Company has published original educational books and reprints of important foreign language materials since 1940. Robert E. Cazden, in his excellent book, *German Exile Literature in America, 1933–1950* (Chicago: American Library Association, 1970), captures the excitement and pathos of exiled bookmen. About the Frederick Ungar Publishing Company he writes, "The actual publishing record of the firm is very inaccessible; corroborative details have not been forthcoming from the present management." He adds, "Few of the literary reprints available for inspection carried a license from the U.S. Alien Property Custodian, although the large amount of paper utilized during a period of strict rationing suggests some kind of official sanction" (p. 102). See also Cazden's footnotes number 47 and 48 for further mention of Ungar.

The questionnaire sent to Mr. Ungar for the present study was not returned, and the records of the APC examined for this study do not mention his publishing house.

THE UNITED STATES ENTERS THE WAR

After the United States went to war in December 1941, the Joint Committee on Importations secured State Department permission to continue to purchase a limited quantity of enemy journals published in Europe in 1942. The valuable work of the IDC was acknowledged, yet some people criticized a program which might inadvertently aid the German economy. Although the United States paid for Axis-produced materials in dollars, and dealt only through neutral centers in Stockholm and Lisbon, according to Dr. Evans, some people feared the dollars might eventually be translated into German weapons. Since similar materials were being brought into the United States by the Office of the Coordinator of Information, State Department permission for IDC's program was not renewed.[10] Rather, a new program was proposed to secure single copies abroad and to arrange for commercial photo-offset reprinting in this country.

OFFICE OF THE ALIEN PROPERTY CUSTODIAN

On March 11, 1942, the Office of the Alien Property Custodian, which we shall call the APC, was established by Executive Order Number 9095, as amended. Under the energetic direction of Howland H. Sargeant, chief of the Division of Patent Administration, the republication program described below was operated as a Division of the Patents, Trademarks and Copyright Section. Sargeant's division was responsible for "the administration of vested patents, patent applications, copyrights, trademarks, and contracts and business relating to them."[11]

Empowered under the Trading with the Enemy Act of October 6, 1917, as amended, the APC was responsible for dealing with foreign-owned property problems arising from United States participation in World War II. Leo T. Crowley served as custodian until his resignation in February 1944, when he was succeeded by James A. Markham.

BOOK AND PERIODICAL REPUBLICATION PROGRAMS

A group of dedicated, visionary librarians and scientists, including members of the Joint Committee on Importations and of a Scientific Republicaton Advisory Council, urged the government into risking an initial investment of $1,500 to inauguarate a Periodical Republication Program, to be administered by the Alien Property Custodian.[12]

At the risk of oversimplifying what at best was an exceedingly complex problem, Tilleux conjectured that the custodian took over the job of periodical and book republication because no American publishing house was found which was willing to assume the considerable risk and the burdens inherent in the proposed republication program.

Nor, apparently, was any library association willing to accept full responsibility for administering such a program. Fleming's impression is that during the war years most librarians did little or nothing to encourage reprinting, although some librarians did express opinions about the desirability and selection of reprinted titles before publication; but when materials were reproduced, librarians did purchase copies for their collections. Fleming recalls that it was necessary for the advisory group to override the timidity of many librarians and to urge and cajole government officials into believing that the initial monetary outlay needed as seed money, although relatively small, would be secure.

Librarians may indeed have been timid about assuming responsibility for special reprint programs, but they were not disinterested.

During and after World War II, many librarians urged regular publishers to take more interest in resurrecting backlist titles. As Fleming recalls, their pleas mostly ran into stone walls, because publishers continued to utilize their resources to produce new titles.

Fortunately, members of the APC Advisory Group understood library purchasing and funding procedures. They reasoned that librarians might not gamble funds in advance of publication, but would be likely to purchase quality reprints once they were made available. Judging by the eventual success of the APC republication programs, the advisers were right.

The APC administered the republication program from early in 1943 until the functions of the Office of the Alien Property Custodian were transferred to the U.S. Department of Justice on October 14, 1946.

The vesting program involving German-owned property continued until April 16, 1953, although the vesting of Japanese-owned property in the United States had ended with the Treaty of Peace, which came into effect on April 28, 1952.[13]

HOW THE APC REPUBLICATION PROGRAMS OPERATED

After consultation with the Scientific Republication Advisory Committee, the APC put into operation a complete republication program, which included the "selection of materials to be reproduced, procurement of original copies of enemy-copyrighted materials, execution of reprinting and subscription contracts, granting release from paper quotas, announcements of available materials, and arrangements to assure the widest dissemination of the more important war-urgent foreign scientific materials on a regular and continuous basis."[14]

In 1943, a basic list of 125 current and back volumes of journals to be considered for reprinting was selected. Notices were mailed to 8,000 firms and individual potential subscribers, indicating that the works most in demand would be republished by photo-offset, and offering future lists if demand for the titles on the first list justified the continuance of the reprinting plan. The custodian planned to handle reprints as a matter of public service, at cost, based on the number of pages per issue, with subscription prices for the periodicals based on the known number of subscribers. Promptness in entering subscriptions was urged, for it might be feasible to reduce prices if the number of copies reprinted at one time could be realistically enlarged.

The APC was willing and anxious to do what was necessary to get Axis publications to the greatest number of people in the shortest time possible. In "Report on Important Developments, No. 268 (October 15, 1942)" Evans noted that Rice, of the Office of the APC, asked Fleming for an estimate of the joint committee's demand for multiple copies. Fleming replied that with $250,000 available, the joint committee was unable to meet the demand for original copies. Orders for 1942 materials placed with foreign agents were slow to be filled due to transportation difficulties. The orders totaled 10,300 subscriptions comprising 2,250 individual titles with many duplicates. Fleming estimated that there were two or three times as many requests for journals as the joint committee was able to order, and that the demand would be even greater if the periodicals were reproduced in this country, as the moral issue of buying from the enemy would not be a factor.

VESTING COPYRIGHTS

One form of control used by the custodian to deal with property under his jurisdiction was the outright transfer of title of foreign-owned property to himself. Seizure was accomplished through a vesting order. Vesting enabled the custodian to collect royalties on copyrighted materials and to grant licenses for the commercial republication of selected materials "to insure the availability of desired publications to those engaged in the war efforts."[15]

In its first year of operation, copyright interests in about 72,000 works were vested in the APC. It should be noted that 70,000 of these were titles in the field of music, originally issued by Italian and French publishers. Remaining copyrights were for 504 books, 783 periodicals, 7 plays, and 480 motion pictures, charts, and maps. When the program of vesting began, the APC vested copyrights only if the material was in demand, or if royalties were payable. Through changes in vesting orders, German copyright interests in the majority of books published abroad during the war years were later vested, according to the APC "Terminal Report," "to prevent restrictions upon American access to technical and scientific information of German origin." By October 1946, the APC held at least a half million copyrights. The custodian had vested property with an estimated value of $247,000,000.[16]

PRINTING CONTRACTS

Specifications to bid for commercial photo-offset reproductions were mailed to 38 firms in January 1943. Eleven bids were returned to the APC, including one from Edwards Brothers, Inc., a Michigan printing and book manufacturing firm. After adjustments were made to the original specifications, Edwards Brothers quoted an average cost of $1.72 per page to republish editions of up to 400 copies.[17] The contract for republishing periodicals for the APC was awarded to Edwards Brothers. The APC agreed to the firm's request for permission to produce an overrun, or surplus printing, of 25 percent, on all periodical orders received. Extra copies presumably were to be stored against possible later orders from the APC, and the expectation of a domestic or foreign market for the unsold copies after the war.

Tilleux states that a thousand or more letters were exchanged between the APC and Edwards Brothers. The gist of many of these letters is made clear in the Tilleux Report, but the original correspondence was not sought for this investigation. Tilleux indicates that copies of many of the documents he cites rest in the Copyright Office files, a rich mine for future researchers on this topic.

Under the Trading with the Enemy Act, the APC could only undertake the reproduction of a periodical if assured that income from subscriptions would be sufficient to retire all printing costs. Edwards offered to waive payments owed them for copies in excess of subscription income if all printing charges were not met by subscription. Thus, the APC was assured that there would be no further charge than $1.72 per page, and that a large edition of each journal would be published to cover at least those orders received by the subscription agencies. The reprinted periodicals were distributed by regular subscription agents: F. W. Faxon Company, Boston; Moore-Cottrell Subscription Agencies, Inc., North Cohocton, New York; and G. E. Stechert & Company, New York City. It was agreed that the balance of stock would be sent to the New York City APC Unit, under Fleming's charge until the summer of 1944, when he assumed a consultative role because of a change in his professional employment at Columbia University Libraries. The Republication Program Unit was given space in Columbia's South Hall (now Butler Library) and handled by the administrative assistant, Phyllis Mary Frame, presently librarian at the National Agricultural Library, Washington, D.C. The New York Unit was to supply the distribution agencies from stock until the cessation of hostilities with Germany, when the remaining stock of journals would be returned to Edwards. Obviously, disposition of stock was a matter not treated lightly by the APC or Edwards. Later, reviewing these plans, Tilleux commiserated, "Now that the days of struggle are over and the program is a financial success, it may 'hurt' a little to live up to our agreement to surrender all unsold volumes and separate issues, but the contractual offering is in writing."[18]

Edwards printed some periodicals below cost, and in other ways helped to assure the success of the APC's program. For the important bibliographical and abstracting work, *Chemisches Zentralblatt*, the firm agreed to "whatever cost subscriptions to date will warrant . . . in this case, between $1.10 to $1.20 per page cost."[19] *Chemiker Zeitung* was reprinted for $1.30 per page, a low cost quoted by Edwards primarily to enable the APC to republish this significant title.

ROYALTY PAYMENTS

Royalty arrangements were designed to promote republication at a "minimum cost without granting windfall profits to publishers."[20] Since the market for most of the technical works was small, the APC granted a six-month grace period to publishers to give them the opportunity to complete and to market their editions. This practice offered protection of the right to publish, even though the APC policy was to issue licenses on a nonexclusive basis. Licenses provided for a number of royalty-free copies to cover reproduction costs, after which time royalties of 40 percent accrued to the custodian.

Funds collected by the custodian for copyrighted properties were held in escrow and later used to pay off claims of U.S. citizens against the German government. The money did not actually return to the German war economy. Funds could also be used to brace up the republication programs and carry them to new production and performance levels. By November 1945, printing costs to the APC were substantially less than gross subscription income, estimated at $311,292.92.[21]

Although Edwards Brothers was the primary printing contractor for the periodical republication programs, APC also received requests for periodical and book republication licenses from Johnson's Academic Press in New York, and from other firms. Academic Press was already reprinting, under licenses, a number of books originally printed by its predecessor company in Germany. In June 1944, Academic expressed interest in reproducing the entire run of the *Monatshefte für Chemie,* to run 74 volumes in 300,000 pages. Licenses to reproduce the back volumes of *Kunstoffe* and Hoppe Seyler's *Zeitschrift für Physiologische Chemie* were also requested by Academic. In a June 2, 1944, letter from Academic Press to Sargeant, it was suggested that "no license has yet been granted because Academic reports that it is exploring the demand before submitting formal applications."[22] The firm apparently considers its June 1945 reprint of the 31-volume German technical journal in the field of plastics, *Kunstoffe,* its first reprint title.[23]

Stechert-Hafner was another firm bidding for license, primarily to reprint the Polish mathematical journals the firm had handled before the war. The reprint program helped the company to maintain its product line, and provided it with paper to do so. Subsequent reprint programs of Academic Press–Johnson Reprint Corporation and Hafner Publishing Company are noted in a later chapter.

Many foreign journals were not protected by copyright in the United States, such as the Dutch *Physica* (published by Martinus Nijhoff, The Hague) and most French titles. Lacking protection, these periodicals were in the public domain in the United States, and, theoretically, could be reproduced by any printer. The custodian's program helped to conserve the interests of European publishers against freelance reprinting by unauthorized persons. Government control of paper, the short supply of publishing materials, the general unavailability of equipment and labor, and the small market for reprint editions were factors that inhibited the unlicensed reprinting of journals and shortrun books.

Paper shortages continued to plague publishers throughout the war years. Edwards' appeal to the War Production Board for paper, in May 1945, is but one example. In addition to APC work, Edwards used paper allotments for offset-printing the Library of Congress Depository Catalog. Edwards feared that his firm would have to stop printing either the APC titles or the LC Depository Catalog if paper was not forthcoming. Paper was allotted for both projects.

The LC program, outside the scope of the APC projects, was very distinctly a forerunner of the Edwards' later reprinting efforts. Early in 1942 there had been discussion within the Association of Research Libraries (ARL) and the Library of Congress to decide if Edwards would reproduce the LC Depository Catalog cards by photo-offset or if the project would be assigned to Albert Boni's Readex Microprint Corporation for reproduction. According to Luther H. Evans' "Report on Important Developments, No. 53 (January 7, 1942)," the Library of Congress was then anxiously awaiting word from Paul North Rice (New York Public Library) and his Committee of the ARL to determine this matter. Earlier Evans had been in personal contact with Boni to discuss the possibility of microreprinting the Catalog. Edwards had also talked with Evans about this project. On January 14, 1942, Evans noted that "Edwards intends to approach various libraries in an effort to ascertain what the demand will be, and promised to have a definite decision by the time of the ALA meeting in June."[24] Photo-offset was the method preferred by the ARL and members of the Library of Congress, but if reprinting by this method seemed infeasible, then it was proposed to proceed with Boni's plan to microprint the cards.

The reproduction of the Library of Congress Catalog and the APC republication programs afforded Edwards Brothers opportunities to improve upon existing photo-offset techniques, and to secure a reputation for high-quality work. Fleming remembers J. W. "Bill" Edwards as a "mild man, who wanted to stay in the printing and book manufacturing business. He had no desire to become a publisher and go into competition with his own customers."[25] Encouraged to produce works of enduring quality by Fleming, Edward A. Chapman then chief, Copyright Administration Section, since 1946, librarian, Rensselaer Polytechnic Institute, Troy, New York, and Edwards' own senior editor, Dr. B. A. Uhlendorf (formerly on the library staff, University of Michigan), the firm expanded its capabilities for reprinting, continued contract shortrun edition manufacturing after the war, and is so engaged at the present time.[26]

KINDS OF MATERIALS REPRINTED

To fulfill its primary purpose, the APC republication program concentrated on scientific periodical reprinting. The reprinted journals covered many subjects vital to the interest of a nation at war. Leading journals in the following fields were reprinted:

acoustics	mechanical engineering
aluminum	metallurgy
aviation	microscopy
biochemistry	mineralogy
ceramics	mycology
chemistry	nutrition
crystallography	oils and fats
electronics	paper chemistry
engineering	parasitology
enzymology	pathology
explosives	petroleum
fermentation	pharmacology
geology	physics
geophysics	plastics
infectious diseases	rubber
immunology	spectrochemistry
instruments	steel and iron
magnesium	textiles
mathematics	virus research

Of the journal subscribers 48 percent were industrial concerns; 33 percent scientific institutions, universities, and research organizations; 8 percent U.S. and British government agencies. The remaining subscriptions went to Canada, Australia, Great Britain, the Union of South Africa, and New Zealand.[27]

During the program's operation the APC offered 138 periodical titles. Demand was sufficient to reprint 116 periodical titles, or about 3,200 issues, comprising all or part of 282 volumes.

BOOK REPUBLICATION PROGRAM

Reprinting of books ran a course parallel to the periodical republication programs, with some distinctions due to physical format and to distribution methods. Single copies of foreign scientific books published from 1941 through 1944 were surreptitiously obtained by the IDC. Books were reprinted under license by commercial printers and publishers on a basis calculated to encourage the most extensive dissemination at least cost to APC and to the purchasers. Prices charged for the reprint editions were generally far less than prewar prices.

Nearly 700 book titles were licensed for republication. The books covered a wide range of subjects, primarily of war interest, such as gas, metals, and food analysis, magnesium, optics, organic chemistry, and sound measurement.

One of the first titles to be reprinted, by Edwards Brothers, was the major reference work, Beilstein's *Handbuch der Organischen Chemie*.

Before the war Beilstein was available in the United States from the German publisher at a cost of from $1,800 to $2,000. Edwards' photo-offset reprint edition sold for $400, one fifth of the prewar price. By 1951, according to APC records, this title had earned about $135,000 in royalties for the APC.

Books reprinted in the APC program were generally well-photographed, printed on good-quality paper, and sturdily bound. Fleming recalls that Edwards, Hafner, and Johnson were greatly concerned with quality productions. They consulted with the American Library Association on paper standards and with the National Bureau of Standards for assurance that their reprints were manufactured to meet quality specifications. Finally, influenced by Howland H. Sargeant and members of the library world, the War Production Board agreed to allot a higher grade of paper than they originally had tried to assign to the reprint programs. Knowing that to reprint scholarly works on poor-quality paper would be to add yet another class of ephemera to library collections, those in charge of the reprint programs have earned the gratitude of generations of researchers who can utilize wartime reprints that are not disintegrating, as are copies of many extant originals. Hardcopy reprints of Justus Liebig's *Annalen der Chemie*, for example, are now reported to be less brittle and easier to read than copies of the original edition.

REPRINTS OF NONSCIENTIFIC MATERIAL

As the republication program for scientific materials progressed, European cities suffered more intense raids and destruction. Reports arriving from Switzerland and Sweden grimly described the destruction of old-line European publishing houses, creating a sense of increasing anxiety in the library world. In December 1943, 90 percent of Leipzig's "Book City" was destroyed. To a contemporary German scholar, the destruction of Leipzig "could only be compared with the burning of the Library at Alexandria."[28]

Foreign works of cultural significance would be lost to the scholarly world forever if some means were not found to reproduce books and journals in nonscientific fields. How could scholars be provided with foreign works in the social sciences and the humanities?

ASSOCIATION OF COLLEGE AND RESEARCH LIBRARIES

On May 7, 1944, the Association of College and Research Libraries' Committee on Wartime Activities met to determine what methods were available for making non-war-urgent material available to American libraries.[29] Ways were explored to encourage the reprinting of pre-1939 journals, works not protected by copyright, and other nonscientific scholarly works with a predictably limited market. These materials were outside the scope of the APC programs.

J. W. Edwards, who by this time had considerable experience in reprinting scientific materials for the APC, suggested that his firm would take over the bulk of the task of reprinting non-war-urgent materials if members of the ALA and the Association of Research Libraries would give this program their unqualified support and publicize their endorsement. This idea was not a new departure for Edwards, who had previously announced his intention to republish complete back files of some major German periodicals that were outside the scope of the APC programs if paper was allotted for his firm. In August 1944, Edwards requested licenses to reprint files of the *Berichte der Deutschen Chemischen Gesellschaft* (244,000 pages), Justus Liebig's *Annalen der Chemie* (for 1924–1939 in 96 volumes), the philological journal *Anglie* (for 1939–1944, in 6 volumes) and others.

By November 1944, the APC was asked, and agreed to consider vesting and licensing the republication of humanistic and social science works, but only works of enemy origin. The material would be vested and licensed if the requesting firm could secure "specific and unequivocal representation of need and public interest by individuals and organizations qualified to judge such matters."[30]

MICROREPUBLISHING

Extensive microfilming projects were also considered a way to help meet the need to preserve, store, and make available selected nonscientific materials.

Eugene B. Power, then president of University Microfilms, Inc., and a former employee of Edwards Brothers, Inc., was the microphotographer most keenly interested in securing licenses to microfilm European materials. In December 1942, Power had been granted an APC license to reproduce 254 enemy scientific and technical periodicals on film. Power was licensed to charge 1½¢ per page, and, on order, to provide paper prints (usually on two pages) at $.22 each, with a minimum order of $1.00 required. The license was to terminate in one year, but was renewed at Power's request, first for one year, then for five. In October 1944, Power asked to revise the charges upward to $.30 for each paper print, with a minimum fee of $2.00.[31]

As early as November 1941, arrangements were being made for Power to go to London to film materials in the British Museum collection. This program, under the jurisdiction of the American Council of Learned Societies (Dr. Waldo Leland, director) was subsidized in part by the Rockefeller Foundation and had the full cooperation of the Library of Congress, which agreed to serve as the American depository for the filmed works.[32] The Library of Congress also helped to arrange for Power to travel to England, a difficult task in wartime.

Power set up a camera in the British Museum and eventually microfilmed many pre-1640 English books that he selected from Pollard and Redgrave's *Short-Title Catalogue* (STC) and other important works in the museum's collections. From his master negatives, Power later produced microfilm copies on demand for libraries that were trying to build retrospective collections. This publishing project and the experience Power gained from wartime activities formed the nucleus for the development of the giant enterprise that today is University Microfilms, subsidiary of the Xerox Education Group, Xerox Corporation.

THE APC WANTS OUT

By October 1943, librarians were encouraging programs to republish a broad range of scholarly materials. The custodian was already offering subscriptions to 68 reprinted journals; private firms showed increasing interest in reprint publishing. The custodian, anxious to get his office out of the publishing business, was exploring ways to transfer the republication programs to those persons (librarians) presumably most interested in having the materials made available by reprinting.

Sargeant, by letter (October 23, 1943) to Carl H. Milam, executive secretary of the ALA, proposed the transfer of the Republication Programs to the ALA, suggesting that the association . . .

> consider a project to take over from the APC the complete Periodical Republication Program as it was currently operating, and to expand that program to include additional scientific periodicals and the more significant titles in the social sciences and humanities fields for which the Custodian has been receiving requests, from libraries, universities and learned societies.

> As an inducement to the ALA to undertake the project, the Custodian offered to: (1) assist in initiating the work under American Library Association auspices, (2) solicit for the Association the complete cooperation of the Interdepartmental Committee (to secure copy abroad), and (3) vest, and to license to the Association, all copyrighted titles which they thought worthy of inclusion under the expanded Program.[33]

Milam considered the proposal so important that a meeting to consider the possible ALA takeover was arranged for November 6, 1943.[34]

Reaction to the proposal was extremely favorable. The ALA indicated a desire to investigate the potential take-over and to seek a grant from the Carnegie Corporation sufficient to get the program underway. The ALA asked Princeton University to make available the services of its associate librarian, Lawrence Heyl, to investigate the matter and prepare a proposal to submit to the Carnegie Corporation.

Edward A. Chapman prepared a statement of the custodian's willingness to liberalize the vesting policy so that materials in any research field could be made available for reproduction; to adjust licensing procedures if necessary; and to cooperate fully with the association to assure the successful operation of the project.

Heyl surveyed 35 libraries (a 10 percent sample of libraries participating in the work of the Joint Committee on Importation). He listed 128 titles for reproduction, and solicited expressions of interest from librarians. The 14-page Heyl report, entitled "Proposed Project for the Reprinting of Foreign Research Material: Report on the Problem of Selection of Materials to be Reprinted," was considered by seven leading librarians at a December 2, 1943, meeting at the New York Public Library.[35] In summary, it was agreed that the program should not be undertaken by the ALA because it would not pay its own way, and would burden the association with extensive publishing programs. The committee recommended that the custodian continue to operate the republication program. This was done.

Reflecting on the negative ALA decision, Chapman wrote to his friend William Warner Bishop at the University of Michigan, "The proposal was gently surveyed out of existence."[36]

APC continued to operate the republication program until October 1946, when the functions of the Office of Alien Property Custodian were turned over to the U.S. Department of Justice. Although the APC programs terminated, the ultimate disposition of copyrights remained a major problem, "intensified by the long life of copyright protection."[37]

SUMMARY

The book and periodical republication programs administered by the Alien Property Custodian were financially and socially successful. Reprint programs earned more than $60,000 in profits for the U.S. government. More important, scholars were provided with current and back issues of some 116 periodical titles and about 700 books which might not have been available for immediate wartime and long-range research use.

Many public acknowledgments were made attesting to the program's inestimable aid to scientific research. Perhaps the most thought-provoking is that attributed to Dr. E. J. Crane, then editor of *Chemical Abstracts:* "There is not the least doubt in my mind," he said, "that your republication program was one of the factors which made the atomic bomb possible."[38] Reprint publishers have sometimes been accused of piracy and other unethical practices, but so far as is known, this is the only account that suggests responsibility of such magnitude! Less dramatically, the program served to secure and preserve important scholarly materials, and provided scientists with a working knowledge of what the enemy was doing during the war years.

We have seen that some publishing and printing firms remained in business during wartime because the reprint programs provided them with paper and with jobs to perform. Since World War II, reprint publishing has become a large-scale sector of the publishing industry. Major producers of wartime reprints are actively engaged in the current reprint industry, and it is reasonable to assume that their earlier successes have helped to lure other publishers into the reprint business.

Various aspects of wartime republication programs relate directly to postwar reprinting, and are of interest in light of the chapters to follow.

1. Printers and publishers found better and more economical ways to reprint scarce, scholarly materials for small markets.

2. The physical quality of reprinted editions improved greatly over prewar production, particularly in photographic reproduction of halftone illustrations. The quality of the paper and binding materials was generally superior to prewar reprints. These improvements were largely motivated by librarians and other advisers who guided wartime reprinting programs and encouraged high standards of performance from printing contractors.

3. Book-trade awareness of the library market for scholarly reprints of shortrun titles increased, encouraging booksellers and publishers to enter this field after the war.

4. Certain marketing practices that were apparently acceptable to reprint purchasers under wartime exigencies were later adapted by publishers to postwar reprint publishing programs. Such practices include prepublication market testing (i.e., seeking subscriptions and advance orders for titles before publication), and the advertising of anticipated publication dates rather than actual dates for reprints.

5. Microphotography, simmering on the side burners of the publishing industry since the 1920s, assumed a more central position during the war, as a means to preserve, store, and make materials available to specialized markets.

Chapter 5

A Wide-Angle View of Current Reprint Publishing

Regular publishers were generally inattentive to the activities of small-edition reprint publishers in the years following the war and into the late 1950s. Trade and textbook publishers were busy publishing the *new* titles needed to satisfy the reading publics here and abroad, and books for the school and library markets. In most trade houses it was considered more important to keep up the fast publishing pace than to catch up on backlist titles.

By 1959 the number of books in print in this country was estimated by Kingery to be about ten times the annual U.S. title output, with the expectation that approximately 10 percent of the titles then available would be out of print the next year.[1] In addition, a very large number of older trade and university press titles dropped into the public domain each year because copyrights were abandoned or could not be renewed.

At that time, in the late fifties, the specialized reprint sector of the publishing industry began to attract a new and prolific generation of publishers. Their entrance rate quickened and continued to expand throughout the sixties. To a large extent, the growth and changes in the reprint industry in the sixties were a reaction to and a result of a great deal of hectic activity within the general publishing and printing industries and in university press circles.

As the new reprinters scurried to put large numbers of older titles into production, so established firms such as Johnson, Stechert-Hafner, and University Microfilms accelerated their reprint production. The older firms responded to the same expanding markets that lured the newcomers.

GROWTH OF THE REPRINT MARKETS

It is axiomatic that prosperity in scholarly publishing is closely linked to educational expenditures and to changing academic trends. It would have been a languid publisher indeed who was not challenged by the exponential increases in educational enrollments (which from 1958 to 1968 equaled the growth of the previous three centuries),[2] the construction of new schools and libraries, and the greatly rising budgets for the purchase of library materials. Programs to effect these changes were implemented in the fifties and became the hallmark of the sixties.

In order to provide a backdrop for a closeup view of the current reprint scene, it might be useful to specify some of the economic facts that were instruments of change in the publishing industry.

W. Vance Grant, specialist in the U.S. Office of Education's National Center for Educational Statistics, summarized the salient trends in American education from 1960 to 1970. Among other facts, he offers these:

> The number of students in the Nation's educational institutions (all levels) increased by approximately one-third in that ten year period.

> Degree-credit enrollment in institutions of higher learning more than doubled during the decade, rising from 3.4 million to about 7.1 million students.

> Federal contributions to higher education followed a steadily rising pattern. By the end of 1969, Federal funds accounted for more than one-fifth of the total budget of the Nation's colleges, universities and professional schools.[3]

The vast growth in the size of library collections at most colleges and universities in recent years is largely a result of funding provided by federal, state and local legislation, including the Higher Education Act of 1965, the Library Services and Construction Act, the Medical Library Assistance Act of 1965, the National Defense Education Act, and others.

That reprint publishers soon learned the provisions of these laws, and understood their implications in terms of support for reprint programs, is evident in the ways the firms selected and reproduced titles of particular appeal to the library market. Many publishers were quick to get a foot in the door of this obvious growth area, some firms with faster reaction times than others.

The preparation of large blocs of special subject materials (e.g., American literature, English history, exploration and travel accounts); lengthy (and continuing) publishers' series (e.g., OP titles selected from the *Essay and General Literature Index* and various short-story series); OP titles culled from standard bibliographies and recommended booklists (e.g., *Books for College Libraries* (*BCL*) and Howes' *U.S.-iana*); long runs of special forms of materials (e.g., newspapers on microfilm, government publications, antislavery pamphlets, periodicals of centuries past); "packages" of materials of contemporary interest (e.g., black history and culture, civil rights, women's rights, Asian and Slavic studies, criminology, law, war and peace) were obvious attempts to satisfy a voracious library appetite for scholarly materials. During the affluent sixties, libraries needed to buy many titles quickly.

Librarians and scholars traditionally have cooperated in the preparation of special-purpose booklists and selective bibliographies. The better lists frequently are useful to other people as selection aids and buying guides. In the late 1920s, for example, the Carnegie Corporation channeled several million dollars to college libraries for book purchases. According to Radford, these funds were expended through a centralized purchasing office at the University of Michigan.[4] To help librarians identify and select titles, an advisory group on college libraries was established. From 1928 to 1932 it helped with the preparation of Charles B. Shaw's *List of Books for College Libraries* (published by the ALA). Similarly, from 1934 to 1937 another group supervised the compilation of the *List of Books for Junior College Libraries*, by Foster E. Mohrhardt (published by the ALA). In both of these classic works, an effort was made to include mostly titles in print and thus available for purchase. Librarians generally were able to find copies of the small number of the listed OP titles they needed in the used book market.

A list of 60 reference works and recommended booklists was compiled for the present study (see Appendix B) from citations appearing in reprint publishers' catalogs and promotion literature. Voigt and Treyz' *Books for College Libraries* is the source cited most frequently. The original purpose of *BCL*, stated clearly in its preface, has been adapted to serve the interests of at least 20 reprint firms, the majority of whom describe their use of *BCL* fairly and accurately. But one publisher's 1969 catalog went so far as to imply to the unwary (in a way that makes one suspicious of intent) that faculty members and librarians who were consultants to *BCL* might have had something to do with the firm's selection of titles for reprinting! This particular catalog lists, in boldface type, the names and affiliations of the original *BCL* advisers, a practice that may be legally unassailable, but one that seems of questionable ethics.

Whether or not one is critical of the practice of title selection from standard booklists, the fact is that these lists are a keystone in the structure of the reprint industry. The reasons for this are clear. Reprinters soon realized that librarians review lists when they consider titles to add to collections, and both they and the librarians identify many important titles as OP. As recounted in a later chapter, during the frenzied period of buying in the 1960s there were not enough used copies of the OP titles available to satisfy demand, or for some titles librarians did not search the OP market for available originals.

The identification and resupply of OP titles from recommended booklists has obvious appeal to alert reprinters. If a reprinter finds a title OP, checks its copyright status, and determines that the title is in the public domain, he can freely publish new copies. If a title is OP but still under copyright, the reprinter can, of course, try to negotiate reprint rights with the copyright owner. These titles are generally listed in reprint catalogs as reprinted "by arrangement" with the publisher.

THE LIBRARY MARKET

From 1960 to the end of the decade, the number of libraries in this country increased almost 90 percent, from 15,860 to 29,163 libraries.[5] These figures do not include school libraries, which, with the possible exception of high schools, have not been very significant markets for most reprint publishers.[6] Libraries need and continue to buy books, despite librarians' heightened interest in acquiring all the other forms of media.[7]

In the 1960s, 515 new college and university libraries were born; they increased in numbers from 1,379 in 1960 to 1,896 by the end of the decade. More than 400 new junior colleges (i.e., two-year and community colleges) were established, their number growing from 645 in 1960 to 1,072 at the end of 1969. It is little wonder that junior colleges have been called the fastest-growing segment of the college market for the publishing industry.[8]

Although junior colleges first appeared on the American education scene only 70 years ago, the challenge they now offer publishers is great.[9] By 1975, 30 percent of all first-time enrollees in higher education are expected to attend junior colleges,[10] a projected 69 percent increase in total enrollment.[11] The traditionally competitive spirit among publishers is highly aroused, for many firms would like a piece of this blossoming market.[12]

Public libraries, a significant market for publishers, albeit one that reprint publishers believe they have not yet fully tapped, increased in numbers by 1,424 in the past decade. There were 10,621 public libraries in 1960 and 12,045 toward the end of 1969.[13]

REPRINT PUBLISHERS: WHO THEY ARE

By the late 1960s, the reprint industry most resembled a big, three-ring circus, with no ringmaster to direct the action and no program to identify all the players or the acts. Star performances by some firms were spotlighted on center stage; others, not necessarily less skilled, played off to the shadowed sides.

Without belaboring the analogy, the point may be made that the industry has appeared to many spectators, and to some performers, as an amorphous mass of faceless "they's" who are reprint publishers. Perhaps this is a realistic picture of an industry comprised of some 300 independent publishers who do business as loners, without a sense of their collective attributes.

One can be ruthless and say that a reprint publisher is anyone so motivated, who owns, borrows, or buys printed materials with the intention of copying them, and who has the money needed to get the works reproduced and sold. This is true, but saying it this way is grossly unfair to responsible publishers who have or hire the expertise to select titles that merit reprinting, who reprint the best or most useful edition, who produce materials of acceptable physical quality, and as Sol Lewis once said, "take a dedicated bookman's chance on its publication."[14]

If an industry may be said to have a personality, the dominant trait of the reprint industry is defensiveness, most noticeable in an uneasy, almost adolescent self-consciousness revealed by the lack of trust and edgy communications among reprinters.

Before the industry grew large, most publishers knew each other well. They understood each other's seeming arrogance and self-interest. They worked hard; they were ambitious. Some were successful, but very few made their fortunes by reprinting. Publishers argued personally about competitive editions and titles they "intended" to produce, and then frequently entered into business agreements as copublishers, exchanged title pages, affixed their own imprints, or distributed their competitor's title. This was especially true if a particular title had already been included on their own list, in advance of publication. But, and this is one of the big changes in the industry, the early publishers were in the habit of keeping their business affairs private. Not many outsiders knew, or seemed particularly interested in knowing, how the industry functioned. Customers generally were delighted to have titles resuscitated. Most titles were selected because these men knew there was a demand for them. They knew because they were bookmen, experts in their fields. They also knew their suppliers, and could arrange to schedule their titles at slack times at the printing presses. They learned how to buy paper and cloth economically in small quantities. They knew or they learned these aspects of bookmaking over a period of years. Meanwhile, if customers had to wait for titles, they waited. If one looks back in literature, "waiting" for delayed deliveries of reprints or promised titles that never did come to life again is a recurrent complaint.

As the industry has grown it has become more complex. There is a degree of resentment toward the "new fellows." Oldtimers no longer know all their competitors well; some do not even acknowledge the existence of new firms. Now more publishers have more difficulty in scheduling small editions with printers and binders. Competition for titles and for sales is keen. Reprinters very seldom share the old-fashioned publishing industry "loving cup."

At least one highly respected reprint publisher, Peter Smith, of Magnolia, Massachusetts, has become so disenchanted with the goings-on within the current reprint industry that he indicated, during a personal telephone conversation, that he might prefer to think of himself once again as a "secondhand bookseller."[15] The fact that a person of Smith's caliber and reputation harbors these thoughts about an industry that he helped pioneer in 1929 is indicative of the disparate nature of the modern reprint industry.

REPRINT PUBLISHERS: HOW YOU FIND THEM

The fragmented and competitive nature of the reprint industry makes identification of reprint houses a time-consuming task. The search is hampered by the lack of a comprehensive directory or central clearing-house of up-to-date industry information. By checking and correlating existing lists of publishers, the names of more than 100 reprint firms were collected. These publishers were contacted for current information, much of which is reported in the Directory in Appendix E. Other companies were (and continue to be) found by chance, from advertisements and notices in professional and trade journals, or because somebody mentioned the firm's existence. Directory-type sources of reprint publisher information checked for this research are reviewed below.

NCR Microcard Editions, Inc. (Washington, D.C.), publishes the most useful specialized reprint reference guides. The annual, cumulative *Guide to Reprints*, issued since 1966, includes a list of publishers. Parent companies, imprints, and divisions are, however, listed separately. This practice, which is not unique to NCR, creates some confusion for reprint customers and a great deal of difficulty for anyone trying to determine the size of the reprint industry. For example, in the 1970 *Guide,* Greenwood Press, Greenwood Reprint Corporation, and Negro Universities Press are counted as three firms, though they are parts of one parent company. Gale Research Company is listed separately from its divisions. Plenum Publishing and DaCapo are listed as two firms, as are Kennikat and Friedman, Rothman Reprints and Fred B. Rothman, and more.

It will be helpful in interpreting the findings reported in this book if the reader understands that for the present study, the number of reprint firms has been determined by counting a firm only once, *not* by its imprints or divisions.

Publishers do not pay for listings in NCR services. This fact, according to Albert J. Diaz, executive director, necessarily affects the amount and kinds of editorial work which can economically be invested in searching out new publishers, and in verifying, correcting and restyling publisher-supplied information.[16] Some important reprint houses are not included in the *Guide*. A major house like Books for Libraries, for example, is absent. To summarize, the list of publishers in the *Guide* is the most useful available, but is not a comprehensive listing of American reprint firms.

Table 1 shows the growth of the *Guide to Reprints* since its inception.

TABLE 1
GUIDE TO REPRINTS

Edition	U.S. Publishers	Total Publishers	Titles
1967 (c. 1966)	69	69	12,000
1968 (c. 1967)	86	101	17,000
1969 (c. 1968)	107	183	25,000
1970 (c. 1970)	126	253	38,000

AB Bookman's Yearbook is a rich source of systematically arranged reprint information, particularly since its publisher has gathered scattered advertisements into a consolidated specialist-reprint section. The reader is left, however, to distinguish reprint publishers from reprint sellers. *AB Bookman's Weekly* is useful for discovering small new reprint houses that are essentially booksellers, for notification of changes of ownership and address, and for succinct, timely reviews of selected titles.

Bowker's *Literary Market Place 1968–1969* (*LMP*), which was examined for this study, lists 20 publishers under the heading "hardbound" reprints. The majority of these firms are trade publishers. Under "scholarly" reprints, 24 firms are entered. These are not all scholarly reprint publishers, according to the definitions used herein. Reprint information in *LMP* is misleading in that major reprint houses such as Gale Research Company and Books for Libraries are entered in *LMP* but are omitted from the classified section listing reprinters. The 1971–1972 edition lists 33 "hardcover" and 34 "scholarly" reprint firms, but still does not classify Gale and Books for Libraries as reprinters. This evidence is sufficient to suggest that *LMP* does not serve well as a current source of reprint publisher information.

Bowker's *Publishers Trade List Annual* (*PTLA*), on the other hand, is a good source in which to identify reprint publishers, if one patiently reads each firm's list, especially those in the Supplement. The searcher again has the problem of distinguishing firms that publish from those that only sell reprints. The 1969 edition of *PTLA* yielded the names of some 30 firms that were contacted for this study.

All 1968 issues of the *Publishers' Weekly* (*PW*) "Weekly Record" section were examined, item by item. This unsystematic method of identifying publishers was perhaps the most productive of all in terms of picking up some of the lesser-known or new reprint firms. Reading each entry, one also learns a great deal about the kinds of titles being reprinted and becomes acutely aware of the perplexing variety of descriptive cataloging and other bibliographic problems that attend reprints.

In 24 issues of the 1968 *PW* (i.e., two issues per each month), the number of scholarly reprints was compared with the total number of titles entered. The spectacular result was that 10 percent of all the titles included in the Weekly Record sections were reprints. Specifically, of 13,593 titles listed, 1,348 were the kinds of reprint editions under consideration in the present study (i.e., mass-market paperbacks, translations, juveniles and book catalogs were not counted).

S. A. Belzer's "An Informal Directory of Reprint Publishers" included 37 specialist reprint firms.[17] Belzer's directory has been updated by Sam P. Williams' "Directory of Reprint Publishers" in a *Three-Year Index to The Reprint Bulletin: Years 1965-1967, Volumes X-XII*.[18] The Williams directory (no date, but assumed current to July 5, 1968, the preface date) includes 98 publishers. Eight are general trade publishers and 29 are university presses. Four of the latter, Indiana, Oxford, Florida, and Cornell, do not consider themselves reprint publishers according to the results of this survey. Williams gives cross-references, but the connection between Kennikat and Ira Friedman is not noted. Brief but informative annotations are provided for 25 American firms. Unexplained omissions from the list include Octagon, Greenwood, and Patterson Smith, three very active firms.

Several foreign guides to reprints were also reviewed for their possible inclusion of American reprint organizations which might have escaped the search net. Ostwald, which lists about 275 reprint publishers, including 37 American firms, and *Bibliographia Anastatica* (see Bibliography) proved interesting for other bibliographic checking, but neither guide provided the names of additional firms to contact.

Another approach to finding reprint firms is by subject specialities or by forms of materials. Only a few examples are cited here, but those who persevere in this approach are apt to be rewarded.

The *African Studies Bulletin* yielded a few firm names not readily available elsewhere. A list of 50 firms (16 foreign) is included in an excellent article by Joan Ells.[19] A list of publishers (American and foreign) is also included in the *Newsletter* of the Association for African Studies.[20] Reprint publishers listed in *Periodicals and Serials Concerning the Social Sciences and Humanities* include many foreign firms, but not many unfamiliar American ones.[21] This is a useful bibliography for checking comparative prices, but the list of publishers is no longer current.

NCR Microcard Editions also issues the annual, cumulative *Guide to Microforms in Print* and its biennial companion, *Subject Guide to Microforms in Print*. These reference aids, which report information about books, journals, and other materials available in microform, are admittedly not comprehensive, but they are the most useful systematic lists of microforms currently published.

The 1968 Guide, which lists 51 firms (all American), was compared with the 46 "Micro-Publishers" included in the 1968–1969 *LMP*. Thirty-one *LMP* firms are also listed in the NCR Guide. Fifteen entries in *LMP* are not in the NCR Guide. Collation of the entries from both lists identifies a total of 66 micropublishers, a large number of which are university presses, libraries, and historical and professional associations.

The uncertainty that accompanies the search for all active reprint publishers is expressed in Patrick Wilson's statement: "There is a distinction between not finding what we are looking for, and finding that what we are looking for is not there; the former is a failure, the latter a negative success."[22]

TYPES OF REPRINT FIRMS

It is seldom possible to draw clear lines distinguishing one type of reprint business from another. Companies venture into related fields; printers issue titles under their own imprints; booksellers take a publishing gamble; libraries and associations publish. In this survey, an effort was made to determine whether there are significant differences between firms that have recently entered the industry and firms established for longer periods of time. The former are called "new," the latter, "established" firms.

Since the beginning of 1960 at least 120 firms have entered the reprint industry or have begun to publish scholarly reprints. Founding dates and/or the year reprint programs were initiated are included in the Directory for 213 publishers. Of the 274 firms surveyed, 98 have pre-1960 founding dates; 89 firms were founded in 1960 or after; and 24 were founded before 1960 but began reprint publishing in or after 1960.

Of the organizations that began reprint publishing within the past 10 or 20 years, 21 were founded in the nineteenth century. Harper appears to be the oldest trade house currently engaged in the reprint industry. Although its rather modest J & J Harper Editions reprint program does not seem to reflect this long publishing heritage, it is interesting that the firm's 1817 origin can be traced to the printing expertise of two of the Harper brothers. Barnes & Noble, founded in 1873, probably is the largest of the old-line bookseller-publishers of significant reprints. The company has published about 600 reprint titles since its Facsmile Library program began in 1938–1939. This firm, which changed ownership and characteristics since late in 1969, has primarily been engaged in wholesaling used textbooks. The great majority of the firm's reprints (124 of the 140 published in 1968) are copublished imports, most from Great Britain.

British publishers in particular seem aware of the fact that they have many backlist titles which might find a new college and university market in this country. American firms that copublish with foreign firms usually provide a substantial part of the capital for the books to be manufactured abroad and contract to buy part of the edition (perhaps 750–1,000 copies) for sale here. This guarantee permits the foreign publisher to go into print with an edition. Without the involvement of the American firms, many titles might not be reborn.[23]

Table 2 offers evidence that people with a wide variety of business backgrounds and primary interests are engaged in reprint publishing.

TABLE 2

NUMBER OF REPRINT PUBLISHERS, BY TYPE OF PRIMARY BUSINESS

Type of Business	Number (N = 234) (86.6% of Firms Surveyed)
Commercial Publisher (COMM)[a]	122
COMM/BKSL[b]	7
Bookseller (BKLS)	42
BKLS/PRTR	2
University Press (UNIV)	17
Micropublisher (MICR)	16
MICR/COMM	2
Association or Society (ASSN)	9
ASSN/BKSL	1
Printer (PRTR)	7
PRTR/COMM	3
Library (LIBY)	2
LIBY/MICR	1
Foundation (FNDT)	2
FNDT/MICR	1

Source: Responses to Question 2.
a Specialist reprint houses and trade publishers with nonbacklist reprint programs are in this category.
b Dual listings are assigned to organizations that specified that their business is divided into two "primary" parts.

This fact underlies the industry's problems as well as its attributes. Eight different types of organizations that publish reprints have been identified. The eight catagories and the frequency of their occurrence (for 235 firms, or 86.6 percent of the firms surveyed) are shown in Table 2. Since all firms are included in the present survey *because* they publish reprints, the first group, called "commercial," may need clarification by example. The 134 firms in the commercial publisher group account for 56 percent of all the publishers surveyed. These 134 firms include 12 firms that are "multiple-type" businesses. That is, the firms are equally engaged in printing and publishing (PRTR:COMM) or other combinations shown in Table 2. Humanities Press, Citadel Press, and World Publishing are regular trade publishers, but engage more than occasionally in non-backlist reprint programs. Other trade houses have reprint divisions or subsidiaries, such as Farrar, Straus & Giroux's Octagon Books, Atheneum's Russell & Russell, and Harcourt Brace Jovanovich's Johnson Reprint Corporation. Several firms in the commercial group also engage in nonpublishing ventures, such as Macoy Publishing and Masonic Supply House, and Argonaut, Inc., a Chicago coin dealer.

Scholarly bookmen, as we know, contribute to scholarship in their fields of interest by selling new or used original copies of scarce works. This tradition is changing somewhat as many antiquarian booksellers now sell or produce reprints. Of the 42 booksellers identified who publish reprints, most are antiquarian bookmen. Examples include Biblo & Tannen, Dawson's Book Shop, Cooper Square, and William Salloch. "Antiquarian booksellers can no longer ignore the rapid, indeed phenomenal, growth of reprints. Reprints are here to stay," said Bernard M. Rosenthal, discussing the influence of reprints on the antiquarian book market.[24] The firm of Bernard M. Rosenthal, Inc., Booksellers, is an example of reprint knowledge put to work. Rosenthal does not reprint, but is a specialist bookseller who serves his customers by handling reprints of scholarly works in selected humanistic subjects. He maintains an extraordinary up-to-date file of publishers' announcements, price changes, publication due dates, and subject information about reprints. Rosenthal's catalogs, which include annotated descriptions of the titles, are valuable contributions to the bibliographic control of reprint titles. From his experience in selling reprints, Rosenthal "protects" his customers by automatically advancing a reprint publisher's promised delivery date so that his customers will not be discouraged by seemingly late deliveries of reprint titles.[25]

It seems ironic that university presses, long the pirate's prey, have increasingly joined the ranks of their "adversaries," albeit with small reprint programs in relation to their primary publishing goal—to provide new books for their specialist scholarly communities.

The 17 university presses known to issue scholarly reprints of non-backlist titles are recorded separately from commercial houses in Table 2, although this may be an artificial distinction. While many aspects of university press publishing and regular trade publishing are different (profit versus nonprofit programs, publishing subsidies), in other ways university presses closely resemble scholarly reprint publishers. They all produce small editions, primarily use direct-mail sales techniques, depend upon specialized bibliographical aids and review media, and anticipate small markets.

University presses are also beginning to resemble trade publishers as more of their titles appeal to a general market, and more trade titles are being used as supplementary texts in educational institutions. Although this survey could not delve into the changing nature of university press publishing, this is a fascinating topic for anyone interested in the publishing industry, and extremely important to the future of the reprint industry.[26]

The availability of public domain titles and the apparent success of some of their customers has given some printers and binders the idea of going into the reprint business themselves rather than devoting their efforts solely to job printing and binding. Some firms have also acquired publishing properties as a result of unpaid bills. Haskell House is a printing firm that has so become a publisher of reprints.[27] Printer-turned-publisher is a pattern traceable also to the vast growth of the offset printing industry, a result of technological breakthroughs. Shortrun reprinting is now economically feasible.

During interviews with several publishers is was revealed that one printer was believed to be reprinting some of his customer's public domain titles and selling copies to other competitive publishers to be marketed under this own imprints. At this writing at least one publisher is thought to be investigating this serious charge.

Seven printers are included in the present survey; three are equally engaged in commercial publishing. A small number of firms (Crane, Donnelly, and Edwards, for example) are primarily printers or book manufacturers who produce most titles to other publisher's specifications, but these firms might occasionally issue titles under their own imprints.

Libraries, associations, historical societies, and foundations have for many years arranged for the publication of unique or rare materials from their collections. Within the past several years institutional publishing programs have become more common. Institutional publishers sometimes reprint under "copublishing" contractual arrangements with commercial firms. Such an agreement was made by the New York Public Library with 3M/IM Press, for example.

In other cases, an association might serve as exclusive distributor or representative in the United States for reprints published abroad. The ALA, for instance, is the exclusive representative in the United States and Canada for the Italian publisher Stabilimento Tipografico Julia's "Antiqua" Series of facsimiles of "rare, hand-printed Italian works of the period between 1450 and 1850."[28] Traditional "library photoduplication service" departments are outside the scope of this study.

The micropublisher group in the present study is comprised of 16 firms, and 2 more that are equally involved in hardcopy publishing. Some firms also produce microreprints on hire, much as a traditional printer serves the book publishing industry.

About 95 (including 35 firms interviewed and 60 questionnaire respondents), firms may be considered reprint specialists; that is, reprint titles comprise 75 percent or more of their total list. Kelley, McGrath, and

Scholars' Facsimiles & Reprints are examples. The percentage of a firm's list that is devoted to reprints (i.e., as opposed to original publications) is known for 124 firms, as shown in Table 3.

TABLE 3
PERCENTAGE OF REPRINTS ON PUBLISHERS' LISTS

Reprint Titles	No. of Respondents	"Established" Firms	"New" Firms
Entire list	33	12	21
("95–99% of list")	5	1	4
Approx. 75% of list	22	9	13
Approx. 50% of list	13	10	3
Approx. 25% of list	16	8	8
Very small part of list	35	25	10
TOTAL	124	65	59

Source: Responses to Question 5, cross-tabulated with each firm's response to questions 3 and 4.

The number of identified reprint specialists, 95, is about double the usual "guesstimate."[29] As might be expected, a considerable number of the new firms (at least 60, and more likely 100) intended from the start to be reprint publishers, in contrast to a majority of older firms that got involved in scholarly reprinting somewhat "accidentally," as an adjunct to another primary business.

REPRINT PUBLISHERS: WHERE THEY ARE LOCATED

The reprint industry, like other types of publishing, is concentrated in New York, home for 92 firms. The second most hospitable state for reprinters is California, with 34 firms. Reprint activity is, however, spread over a total of 39 states, as shown in the Directory entries.[30]

The high degree of urban concentration is somewhat surprising since reprint houses do not generally have as much need as general publishers to be near megalopolitan clusters of authors, authors' agents, and publishing personnel.

The firm in a state that has only one reprint publisher is generally engaged in reprinting regional materials, or is part of a university press or of a bookselling or printing firm. Scarce Western Americana titles are reprinted by Ye Galleon Press, described on the owner's letterhead as "The private press of Glen C. Adams, postmaster of the pleasant country village of Fairfield, Washington, and avocationally a printer of thin books from hand set type."

Adams selects titles such as *The Munger Journal: Two Years in the Pacific and Arctic Oceans and China. . . . A Whaling Voyage*, by James

F. Munger (reprinted in 1967 in an edition of 401 copies) and *Melyer Casler's Journal Giving the Incidents of a Journey to California. . . . 1859* (reprinted in 1969 in an edition of 488 copies) because, as a scholarly bookman-printer, he knows these are scarce and historically significant. His books are well-researched, priced reasonably (the titles above sell for $5.00 and $9.00 respectively) and put together with tender loving care. One of Adams' comments is worthy of quotation here, for it exemplifies a kind of reprint publishing philosophy that is not generally known. In discussing one of his recent titles, Mr. Adams wrote, "It is a book of zero popular appeal but rare material . . . some researcher may bless me some day but for the moment the book is no highway to Heaven."[31]

Reprints of regional history come from Dr. Parker's Paisano Press in Balboa Island, California, and from Fred Rosenstock's Old-West Publishing Company in Denver. Southwestern titles are issued by Calvin Horn in Albuquerque, and Bible studies by the Newby Book Room in Noblesville, Indiana. Bison Books, including works of regional and historical significance are sent forth by the University of Nebraska Presss, while Davis and Jasek's Texian Press provides titles of Texas history.

Some firms, of course, go farther afield. Beautiful, inexpensive reprints of Japanese, Hawaiian, and Canadian works, for example, are published by Charles E. Tuttle, of Rutland, Vermont, and Japan. In Michigan and Arizona, in Kentucky and the nation's capital, in Massachusetts, Maryland and Maine—all across the country—reprint publishers are giving new vitality to old books. *American Book Collector,* the journal published by W. B. Thorsen in Chicago, pays excellent attention to reprints and provides fine scholarly reviews.

What do these facts and figures about the structure of the industry reveal? Aside from underscoring the industry's diversification, the significant point is that reprint publishing has attracted people from many backgrounds. Reprint publishers have particular talents and some peculiar traits. When Hayward Cirker, Dover's innovative president, discussed some reprinters-who-would-be-publishers, he aptly likened some to vanity press operators, with librarians rather than authors supplying the funds.[32]

The reprint industry has no formalized structure. It is a mosaic without grout, an industry fragmented in terms of the publishers and their products. There is a richness of product that comes from this diversity. On the other hand, some reprinters lack "real" publishing experience and the "gentleman" approach that some people apparently still consider to be the telltale of the publishing industry.

Chapter 6

A Close-Up View of Reprinters' Programs

As a consequence of technological, economic, and social changes that took place in the 1960s, we have seen that the present generation of reprinters entered the business more massively and energetically than their predecessors.

But anyone who has searched for reliable information about the members and programs of the current industry knows that finding it systematically recorded is as chancy as unearthing ruins in the jungles of the Yucatan. Just as an archeologist is responsible for interpreting his "dig," so the findings of the present exploration of the reprint field need to be set forth. Only in this way can the reprint scene be defined a little more sharply. The picture that emerges is largely a reflection of publishers' own views about distinctive aspects of the industry, specifically formats, forms of original materials copied, title selection practices, subject specialties, and long-range outlooks for their programs.

To provide a framework, an estimate of the total number of titles published by the reprint industry is offered. While numbers alone obviously provide no measure of quality—no real depth of focus on the industry—they help to suggest the extent of reprint activity.

THE NUMBER OF REPRINT TITLES

It is difficult to determine precisely how many titles have been published by scholarly reprinters since their programs began. First one must surmount the recurring dilemma of title-counting (titles versus volumes, titles in series, and the like). Then one must realize that the 201 hardcopy publishers who responded to Question 9, which asked the number of titles reprinted within given ranges, may have checked a higher rather than a lower number for reasons of prestige, business pride, comparative status, or whatever. It must be stressed that the estimate of the numbers of reprinted titles is subject to cautious interpretation. Using the UNESCO and *PW* system of counting each volume in a set only if it has a different title and is sold separately, it is estimated that these 201 firms have reprinted at least 85,000 titles. The total number of publishers identified within each title range is shown in Table 4. These data for individual firms are included in the Directory.

TABLE 4
ESTIMATED NUMBER OF TITLES REPRINTED

Range	No. of Titles	No. of Companies (N = 201)	Possible No. of Titles in Each Range
A	Under 10	45	45– 450
B	10– 49	58	580– 2,842
C	50– 99	19	950– 1,881
D	100– 299	35	3,500–10,415
E	300– 499	6	1,000– 2,994
F	500– 999	12	6,000–11,988
G	1,000–1,499	10	10,000–14,990
H	1,500–2,999	3	4,500– 8,997
I	3,000–5,000	4	12,000–20,000
J	Over 5,000	9	45,000–45,000[a]
Maximum Total Titles			119,557[a]
Minimum Total Titles			84,375

Source: Responses to Question 9.
[a] Because the J range is open-ended there is no upper limit. Therefore, only the lower limit (45,000 titles) was added to the sum of ranges A–I (74,557 titles) to arrive at an estimated lower limit for the maximum range: 119,557 titles.

If the total number of microrepublished titles were known and added, the figure could jump well into the millions, as evidenced by even a few examples. Readex Microprint Corporation, for instance, had already issued about 1 million titles by 1970, and, according to its president, Albert Boni, the firm plans to add about 100,000 titles each year.[1] A reader-printer now makes it possible to produce electrostatic prints of Readex Microprints at a cost of less than three cents per page. Readex has also produced some titles in a "Compact Edition," where the type size is photoreduced so that a single page may carry four or more original pages. An excellent example is the Readex Edition of Diderot & D'Alembert's *Encyclopedie,* 35 volumes in five, bound in buckram. The famous *Pictorial Encyclopedia,* originally published in 12 volumes, is available in a single volume, bound in half-leather and priced at less than $100.00. In 1971, Oxford University Press offered the invaluable *Oxford English Dictionary (OED)* in the same useful format.

University Microfilm's 1971 OP Catalog includes over 45,000 titles offered as xerographic copies on a custom-print basis.[2] The company also produces hardcopy reprints in series such as its "March of America" titles. The paper prints made from film are usually perfect bound in a paper cover and cost about four cents per page. Cloth bindings are also available.

The Micro Photo Division of Bell & Howell has reproduced well over 23,000 out-of-print titles by their Duopage process, a reprinting method combining microfilm, xerography, and a proprietary process which results in a two-sided printed sheet. Books are produced with generous margins for rebinding, and no reduction in original page size is necessary up to a maximum of an 11 inch page width. Library bindings are used rather than perfect bindings, with hardcovers available at $2.50 and up, depending upon size.[3]

Micropublishers tend to issue vast quantities of titles, although the number of copies of each title may be relatively small. Sometimes, as noted above, only a single paper copy of each title is produced from the master film negative, usually by the copyflo process, on demand. This kind of instant publishing is a trend which has tremendous implications for reprinters and for other publishers of scholarly materials, with publishing costs increasing and readership remaining predictably low.

The estimate of 85,000-plus titles shown in Table 4 is derived by multiplying the number of titles in each range by the number of firms selecting that range. For this reason, and because only 201 (of 274 identified firms) supplied this information, the estimate is believed to be very conservative. The figures are suggestive rather than conclusive.

The largest cluster of firms (58) published between 1,500 and 2,999 titles. About 78 percent (157) of the 201 firms have each published fewer than 300 titles (ranges A–D). It might be helpful to note that in the present report the "size" of each firm has been determined by the number of titles published. That is, for purpose of discussion, an "A" firm is considered a very small firm: a "J" firm, very large.

The most significant point of the "numbers game" is that, without any doubt, the reprint industry is responsible for returning a great many more titles to market than is generally acknowledged. Since reprint publishers compete not only with each other, but with other types of publishing companies for book-buying dollars and for readership, the reprint industry is a significant segment of the total publishing industry in the United States.

REPRINT FORMATS

A publisher's choice of format for his titles is dependent upon many variable factors, such as the nature and quality of the original material, production facilities and capabilities, prospective markets, projected costs and selling prices, and competition.

Format information is known for 228 firms, or 83 percent of the 274 firms surveyed. Well over half the firms (66 percent) publish reprints in hardcovers, as shown in Table 5.

TABLE 5
FORMAT INFORMATION

Format	No. of Firms
Hardcover books (HC)	183
Paperbound books (PB)	103
Microfilm reels (MF)	31
Microfiche (MI)	15
Electrostatic prints (EL)	12
Micro-opaques (MC)	8
Microprints (MP)	3
Ultrafiche (UM)	3

Fifty percent of the firms (114) produce reprints in only one format. The remaining firms publish in a variety of formats. A single title may be reprinted in more than one format, as Greenwood Press does for its "Radical Periodicals in the United States," available in hardcopy and in microform. Or, as is frequently the case, a firm may produce different titles in different formats.

A small number of firms now reproduce parts of series or titles in microform, with supporting finding aids (e.g., eye-legible indexes) in hardcopy. The United States Historical Documents Institute's Dual-Media reproduction of the *Proceedings* of the United States Congress is an example. It should be noted that some back-issue periodicals dealers also combine formats occasionally. They reprint scarce or unavailable issues and round off their "packages" with original copies from their stock. This kind of mixed format is not under consideration here.

There appears to be a ground swell of interest in publishing more titles in mixed media and mixed formats. Where this trend will lead can only be surmised, but it is reasonable to expect many more different kinds of books and multimedia "systems" in the future than we have known in the past.

To determine if there is any significant correlation between a publisher's choice of format and the size of his firm, the responses describing format or percentage of titles in each format (Question 7, Appendix D) were cross-tabulated with data about the number of titles published (Question 9). The only significant findings are that micropublishers are among the firms publishing the largest numbers of titles (i.e., more than 5,000 titles) and firms that produce very small numbers of titles (i.e., fewer than 10 titles) generally publish hardcover books. These data are shown in Table 6.

Table 6
Single vs. Multiple Formats, by Company Size

Format	Number of Titles											Total
	A	B	C	D	E	F	G	H	I	J	NA	
HC only	21	25	9	12	2	7	4	1	1	0	2	84
HC + any other	34	51	16	31	5	11	9	2	3	3	0	165
PB only	7	3	0	3	0	0	0	0	1	0	1	15
PB + any other	19	28	6	21	3	4	5	1	3	2	2	94
HC + PB	12	25	6	18	3	4	5	1	2	2	0	78
HC or PB	41	54	16	34	5	11	9	2	4	3	4	183
Microform only	0	2	1	0	2	1	1	1	0	6	1	15
Microform + any other	2	6	2	3	2	3	2	1	1	9	2	33
HC or PB + Microform	2	4	1	3	0	2	1	0	1	3	1	18

Source: Response to Questions 9 and 5.
Note: Column totals exceed the number of publishers in some categories because the "only" class is subsumed. To illustrate: The 84 "HC only" firms are included in the 165 "HC + any other" format. Single and multiple format information is provided because each group helps to describe the variety and combinations of products published by the reprint industry.

FORM OF ORIGINAL MATERIALS REPRINTED

Reprint publishers' lists are rich with titles that have lived before as books (monographs and books in series), periodicals, newspapers, government documents, pamphlets, manuscripts, music scores, travel accounts and diaries, art works, library and trade catalogs, genealogical records, and others. At least one firm, Chelsea House Publishers, copies archival films; another, Theosophical Publishing House, "palm leaf manuscripts, scrolls, etc."

Original works are reprinted as "exact" or "near" facsimiles, or the contents of the original may be anthologized, excerpted, extracted, added to or subtracted from. Some publishers reproduce copies with a fidelity to the sense and style of the original; others merely make the textual contents reavailable.

Librarians and scholars acknowledge the benefits of increased access to scarce original materials. But, how does a potential customer know which firm is likely to have a particular form of material on its list?

It is increasingly difficult to second-guess publishers' lists since many of them produce a great variety of original materials. Before the reprint boom, prospective customers knew which firms specialized in specific forms. If one sought reprints of scientific journals, a Johnson, Hafner, or Kraus catalog was a reasonable place to search. Reprints of classic economic monographs were apt to appear on Kelley's list. One might turn to Readex or to Central Book for reprints of government documents, and to Micro Photo or University Microfilms for newspaper runs. One sought microforms from microrepublishers and hardcopies from "traditional" photo-offset republishers.

The need for a "form" approach to reprints was less urgent than it is now that microforms are available from firms that are not micropublishing specialists, and hardcopies are produced by microform publishers. For example, in addition to the hardcopies one might expect to be available from AMS, Greenwood, Johnson, and Maxwell, these firms now issue microforms; and, as was noted above, University Microfilms, Micro Photo, and Readex also produce hardcopies.

An effort was made to find out what kinds of original materials are being reprinted; what forms each firm reprints; and which form, if any, is the specialty of the house. Form data collected from about 205 firms (74.8 percent) appear in the Directory. These were gathered largely by personal interviews and by reading publishers' catalogs. Only the questionnaire recipients were asked to estimate the percentage of their list devoted to each form of material.

The vast majority of reprinters (195, or 95 percent of all identified firms) republish works that originally appeared in book form, as shown in Table 7. Periodicals clearly rank second (51 firms, or 25 percent), and

TABLE 7
FORM OF ORIGINAL MATERIAL REPRINTED, BY NUMBER AND
PERCENTAGE OF FIRMS

	No. of firms (N = 205)	Percentage of firms (100%)
a. Books (monographs and books in series)	195	95
b. Periodicals	51	25
f.[a] Reports (annual reports, travel accounts, dissertation, patents)	29	14
d. Government documents	23	11
c. Newspapers	19	9
f.[a] Anthologies (short stories, essays, plays)	18	9
f.[a] Manuscripts	17	8
e. Separates (maps, sheet music, art works)	14	7

Source: Responses to Question 8.
[a] The three "f" groups are delineated into separate classifications from "other" responses.

"reports" third (29 firms, or 14 percent). This latter class of materials, "reports," was not offered to respondents on the questionnaire form, but subsequently became a sufficiently large group of "other" material to warrant attention. The same is true of anthologies, republished (in some cases "reconstructed") by 18 firms (9 percent), and separate items such as maps, arts prints, and sheet music.

It was found that 86 of the 125 questionnaire respondents specialize in reprinting a single form, with books the original for 81 of the firms, or 64.8 percent. Three firms reprint only periodicals. One firm specializes in government documents, and another in "collected music editions, so-called 'Gesamtausgaben,' or complete composer editions reprinted from bound copies." This latter firm, University Music Editions, Inc., is the publisher of a Microfiche Reprint Series, organized into bound books, with indexes to the works included. Here we have a good example of the mixed-format publisher.

An additional 30 firms publish book originals and other forms, but only 2 publish a higher percentage of other forms than book. Works that appeared originally as books are the most frequently reproduced materials for at least 111 firms. Reprints of books account, in fact, for more than 50 percent of the titles published by all but 2 of the publishers who supplied these data. These 2 firms assigned a 20 percent figure to books and 80 percent to periodicals.

To summarize, a large majority of firms reprint a single form of original, yet a wide variety of other forms are also reprinted. Very few companies (sometimes one) select the same combinations of forms. The multiplicity of the responses precludes clear presentation of these findings. We may conclude that there is great diversity in the programs of the reprint industry.

The reasons why publishers specialize in particular forms of material may be surmised. Probably a major influence is relative ease of access to personal or library collections of special materials. Technological capabilities and a publisher's experience in handling particular forms of material is another. Newspapers, for instance, need special care and handling quite different from books. Individual publishers have knowledge and enthusiasm for certain kinds of works, such as government documents; and, importantly, there are more standard bibliographies and recommended lists of books than of other materials. It is interesting to speculate about whether or not there will be a new flurry of reprint activity stirred by the *Core Collection for College Libraries,* edited by Richard D. Tettrau (ALA, 1972).[4] It seems unlikely that library buying based upon this list will match the enormous wave of buying activity created by *BCL,* because there is less library money available for retrospective purchasing in the early seventies. Should funding pick up, the Core Collection will probably be a highly useful guide for library reprint purchasing.

TITLE SELECTION

Publishers were asked whether they selected titles primarily on the basis of personal knowledge of subject fields, their awareness of unmet demands for copies on the used-book market, appearance of titles on booklists, advice from paid consultants, or advice from faculty members, librarians, or other scholars (Question 13, Appendix D). The question was based on the hunch that "established" firms select titles mostly from personal knowledge of their subjects or from bookselling experience. It was guessed that "new" publishers, by contrast, depend more upon outside advisers or on the kinds of lists we have been discussing. The publishers' responses proved the guesses wrong, although there could have been some skewing of responses due to the inclusion of the word "primary" in the question. Many firms checked more than one category. A majority of all the respondents say they depend primarily upon in-house knowledge of subject fields. Unexpectedly, only 3 questionnaire respondents say they pay for advice; and only 8 firms admit to a dependence upon faculty, librarians, or other scholars for title selection, while 34 firms consider themselves primarily self-reliant for titles selection, and 95 include this choice as one "primary" basis for selecting titles to reprint. Interestingly, no questionnaire respondent, either new or established firm, admits to sole reliance on recommended booklists, although 13 checked this category as one selection criterion. There was no significant difference in the responses from new and established firms.

Title selection criteria were discussed by 31 of the publishers interviewed. These firms indicated primary dependence as follows: 23 depend on personal knowledge; 5 base their selection on an awareness of unmet market demands; 2 "buy" advice from consultants, and 1 publisher frankly admits that his business was begun because he knew that librarians would depend heavily on selection of titles from *BCL*, and so, very soon after publication of this list, he researched every title to determine its current status. Titles found to be in the public domain were further researched, and many became the central core of a now large and diversified publishing business. During interviews, only a half dozen or so publishers said they buy their selection advice from consultants. This seems a small number, considering the number of librarians and bookmen who say they "work with" reprint houses.

There would seem to be no valid reasons for furtiveness on the part of those who serve the industry as consultants, nor on the part of those firms who seek such help. Indeed, the names of many well-known scholars appear in reprint advertisements. Some firms and their consultants appear reluctant to make this information known. This can be interpreted as another symptom of the industry's uneasiness, or an expression of an individual reluctance to admit these involvements. This kind of undercurrent adds to the previously noted defensive trait of the reprint industry.

The subject of title selection provoked divergent opinions from publishers. Seven noted that, while they are mostly self-reliant, they also check bibliographies to see which OP titles have been recommended. Three publishers do not feel that list-checking alone is sufficient to motivate them to reprint, but if they are "on the fence," they will veer toward listed titles. A large number of publishers believe that librarians regard recommended booklists as authoritative; yet seven publishers strongly criticized some librarians for being what several called "stupidly" dependent upon these lists. According to these bookmen, librarians do not exercise professional judgment when they buy a title in reprint just because it happens to be available again. In fact, one bookseller noted ironically that some of the same titles that were selling well in reprint had been sitting for years in their original state, gathering dust on his shelves. This point will be discussed more fully in a later chapter.

Hafner's respected vice-president, Harry Lubrecht, observed that his firm's reprint title selection policy has always been predicated on the philosophy that subject fields would be sought where there is a real scholarly need for rare and OP materials.[5] The firm takes the position that it will not be influenced by the titles' public domain status, but rather will "seek quality of content and makeup, and pay for the privilege of reprinting if necessary." Titles are selected mostly on the advice of recognized scholars in the chosen fields, particularly botany and medicine. Working closely with leading scholars, Lubrecht feels that he and his firm have "captured the friendship and continuing advice of eminent scholars," some of whom serve as series editors.

As an important byproduct, the firm finds that other scholars voluntarily submit new manuscripts for publication. Reprint editions have thus attracted important new works in the firm's special subject disciplines. A specific example might be of interest. Joseph Ewan, professor of Biology at Tulane University, serves as editor of the Hafner Reprint Series Classica Botanica Americana. In 1967, Hafner issued a catalog entitled "Early American Botanical Works: With a Miscellany of other Botanical Rarities." (Catalog number 353). In the catalog is an article by Ewan on "Reference Tools for the Botanist." The importance of this catalog as a contribution to scholarship is evident. The catalog was the basis of an exhibit in the Mullen Library at Catholic University in 1969. When Lubrecht learned of this use of the catalog, his comment was, "Fine. Our work is being used and the knowledge shared."[6]

Perhaps this kind of maturity in publishing is part of a heritage, for it was in 1905, when reprinting nonfiction was most unusual in this country, that Alfred Hafner began issuing anastatic reprints, a reproduction process using an acid-etching technique. The firm, then known as G. E. Stechert & Company, reprinted *Schools, School-Books and School-Masters* (1887) by William Carew Hazlitt. More titles followed, and were appreciated by contemporary students and some of the then living original authors. But, according to Lubrecht, the quality of the titles was good but the anastatic prints were not (the paper had a grayness that was unattractive). Hafner had to wait many years for reprint technology to catch up with good reprinting ideas.

Howard Fertig, who entered the reprint field with a background in trade publishing (editor at Knopf, member of the *Commentary* staff, and head of Grosset & Dunlap's paperback division, Universal Library), offered another interesting view of selection practices. His publishing philosophy is one of selecting titles "in context." That is, his list is shaped by his personal scholarly interests and knowledge of the subjects he reprints. Interested in the "history of ideas," Fertig feels a commitment to trace a set of ideas backward through history, selecting works central to his themes (fascism, for example) and making these available to a later generation of scholars. By seeking a coherent presentation of ideas on particular subjects, his books attempt to show "how earlier contributions to a subject have influenced or impressed current thinking."[7]

The energetic president of Arno Press, Arnold Zohn, entered the publishing industry with years of experience as a printing broker. In his comments about selection policy, Zohn noted that Arno's aim is to publish "programs" of books and supporting materials such as teacher's guides, to form a package to be directed specifically to schools and to the library market. Arno published more than 400 titles in its first two years of existence, with most titles focused on topics of current interest (e.g., black studies, social history, public affairs). As he put it, "Arno tries to find works that anticipate interests in advance of a felt need in high schools and in libraries."[8]

Some of the industry's harshest critics of poor title selection are participants in the industry. Octagon's Henry G. Schlanger, for one, has suggested that some firms that have been reprinting out-of-print titles on lists, "such as *BCL*, from A to Z," have had little regard for the value and real scholarly need for some of the titles. These publishers soon found that reprinting was vastly different from "real" publishing, but, Schlanger wisely added, many of these firms are "now rediscovering the basic economic problems of real publishing."[9]

John Mladinich, a gentleman of quick perception of librarians' needs, knows the problems they have in acquiring older scholarly works. He is critical of publishers and librarians who select titles for reprint programs when less expensive, good original copies are readily available. Mladinich closely follows dealer and library "want lists." He visits bookstores here and abroad to see old books and buy some. Bookstore visits produce new ideas for titles to reprint, he says, "because booksellers are the real experts on marketing. They are the men who feel the pulse of the market. They handle the orders and know which titles librarians and scholars seek."[10]

Some years ago Sol Lewis (now president of Library Editions, Ltd.) discussed the complexity of the problem publishers face when selecting titles for reprinting. He called this the "key factor which separates the potential 'sellout' from the eventual 'remainder.' "[11] Lewis noted four variable factors which publishers generally consider: importance, availability, demand, and cost of production and resale price. Thoughtful publishers continue to consider these selection criteria of major importance.

To summarize, some publishers are highly critical of certain titles selected for reprinting by others. Several publishers suspect that the buying public may be "bilked," and the entire industry made to suffer from the bad taste exhibited by reprinters who do not select titles based upon informed professional judgment.

There appears, however, to be a greater degree of similarity between the established and new firms regarding their title selection practices than any significant degree of difference.

SUBJECT SPECIALIZATION

Specializing in particular subjects has been a characteristic trait of the reprint industry. Many reprint firms are known for their titles in special subject fields, such as music (DaCapo), theater arts (Blom), criminology (Patterson Smith), or economics (Kelley). The reasons are implicit in the background and interests of the publishers themselves, and in the fact that the reprint industry is essentially market-oriented.

No publishing firm, of course, has exclusive rights to any subject field. Every publisher is free to succeed or fail in any field. Because the market for reprints in all fields is relatively small, however, competition to publish many similar titles in a subject discipline is generally overruled by the natural laws of the marketplace. Too many titles republished in a subject tends to overcrowd the field and increases the financial risks for each publisher.

Publishing titles in the same field is quite different from publishing the same titles. An occasional title may be duplicated inadvertently, but some rival programs appear to be intentional. The practices and malpractices involved when the same title is reprinted by more than one firm raise ethical problems of great concern to some people in the industry. In his address to the ALA in 1970, Daniel G. Garrett, president of Garrett Press, Inc., spoke about "deceptive marketing tactics" and needless duplications of titles, and raised a serious charge: that some very large firms with "financial muscle" were intentionally duplicating titles in order to force smaller firms out of the reprint business.[12] Several firms are believed to specialize in other firms' specialties, regardless of what or how many titles may already be available.

One firm has on its list many titles that duplicate or closely approximate titles on several other lists. This firm keeps careful records of other publishers' advertised prices and appears to adjust its prices accordingly. Customers may be able to buy a few reprints at less cost while these internal industry battles are being fought, but price certainly should not be the sole influence on a decision to purchase.

Subject specialization is a changing feature of the industry. In the early 1970s, a considerable number of houses built lists that extended into many diverse subject areas. The reasons may be found in the changing structure and increased size of the industry and the expanded market for reprints. Some firms diversified because they inherited new subject fields through company acquisition and merger.

Small businesses in need of more capital have been taken over by large companies. Along with access to more funds, some of those acquired apparently are being encouraged to get large numbers of titles into production simultaneously, in order to reap the advantages that accrue in buying printing and supplies in larger quantities, and to reduce unit selling costs. It is less expensive to sell and distribute a list of titles than a single title.

Under these circumstances, there is less leisure for a publisher to choose a "pet" title and nurture it into prominence. In earlier days, publishers generally were involved in producing only a few titles at one time. They waited until their costs were recouped and their bills paid, or until credit was extended. They used these funds to launch new titles. The need to operate close to the belt—taking funds from one program, pocketing some profits, and putting funds back into another program—shaped the ways of the early reprint publisher.

The current belief that it is less expensive to publish and to purchase "packages" of titles is evident in the creation of the ubiquitous publishers' series. The current practice is to group single titles in a subject field into a newly named series. In such subjects as black studies, the names of the series, perhaps unavoidably, are so similar as to create confusion for prospective customers and for competitive publishers.

Another reason for the subject approach to reprinting is that book-lists from which titles are selected are frequently arranged by subject. All a reprinter has to do is select his subject target area, scout for originals to copy from who knows where, and issue a "new" series of selected titles on, say, "History of the Arts from XYZ," or "Background and Development of the Mexican-American."

In the present survey, 215 subjects have been identified from responses to Question 12, which asked publishers to list up to six subject areas in which they specialize. Subject specialities are included in the Directory. A 253-term subject index appears in Appendix F, the Directory of Subject Specialties. This index is a first effort to offer a subject-specialty approach to reprint houses. It is a start which perhaps can be improved cooperatively.

The social sciences and the humanities far outweigh the sciences as subjects for reprint programs. Probably this fact relates to the nature of scientific research and its modest call for older printed materials. In addition, probably most publishers are less familiar with scientific literature and its reference sources than they are with the humanities and social sciences.

There are 21 different subjects in which 10 or more publishers are known to specialize. The subjects and the number of firms active in them are as follows: African studies (10), Americana (24), Americana-Western (12), anthropology (12), art (14), Asian studies (11), bibliography and reference (24), black studies (24), education (14), history (46), history—Europe (12), history—U.S. (22), history—U.S.—regional (11), law (10), literary history and criticism (19), literature (15), literature—U.S. (14), music (19), political science (11), religion and theology (18), social sciences (11), and sociology (16). The term "general" is assigned to 26 firms that publish in too many subject fields to permit itemization.

Four "forms" of materials have been included with the subject terms in Appendix E: government documents (13 firms), newspapers (10), periodicals (19), and rare books and manuscripts (11). This unorthodox inclusion was made so that users of the Directory can know which firms publish these kinds of materials, which are frequently sought.

THE OLD BACKLIST IS THE NEW BLACK LIST

Reprint publishers (and, one might add, reprint purchasers) tend to climb on subject bandwagons. Let one firm announce or publish a series on nineteenth-century writers, for example, and soon, this idea surfaces on other lists. It should be noted parenthetically that no attempt has been made to compile a list of all reprint series titles. The plethora of publishers' series made the contest too great to enter.[13] Competitive reprint editions of the Sears Roebuck and Montgomery Ward mail-order catalogs is perhaps a most amusing example. The point is that this follow-the-leader practice is an underlying cause for secretiveness in the industry. Publishers are reticent to announce their subject programs for fear that their ideas will be taken up by competitors. Three publishers privately stated that for this reason, they would not submit their lists of titles for inclusion in the NCR Guides. Several publishers have said they are, in fact, concerned that some publishers of reprint reference tools might themselves draw publishing inspiration from the lists submitted.

Topical programs that may appear to be duplicated efforts are not always intentional. Some similar programs are planned quite independently. Publishers who are sensitive to subjects of contemporary interest are apt to recognize the same unmet needs for titles, particularly if the subjects interest college and university faculty members and librarians. Black studies and foreign area studies are two recent examples. Reprint publishers have seen the same need, they know the market, and react as quickly as they can to satisfy demand. Reprint publishing is very much a hurry-up business.

IS THE TITLE WELL RUNNING DRY?

Either by direct statement or by implication, people both within and outside the reprint industry are asking to what extent the industry may be approaching saturation. With the tremendous numbers of new reprinters in the field, and the vast numbers of titles being reprinted, people ask, "Is the market glutted? In another few years, will there be titles of merit left to reprint?"

Question 27 asked publishers to react to this question in terms of their own long-range outlook. This was an attempt to stir the coals, to elicit publisher opinion about the quality and quantity of titles available for their future programs.

Responses to this question were correlated with information about reprint and founding date and subject specialties. The purpose was to determine to what extent certain emerging industry trends might be related to publisher concern about a drying up of the title well. Specifically, is there evidence of a relationship between the continuing availability of really important titles and (1) a growing interest among reprinters in moving into general, current publishing, and (2) the increasing numbers of firms publishing titles in more than one format (i.e., hardcopies and microforms)?

Although the number of responses that could be correlated was small (93 firms, or about 30 percent of the total), the results are interesting nonetheless. The data indicate that the large majority of respondents (about 75 percent) are confident in the future of their programs. Their confidence ranges from quiet expectation to great enthusiasm.

Some of the following representative responses express confidence:

Hell no. There is no end in sight. What is in print today will be OP tomorrow. There will be a market for an unlimited period.

Six confident firms agree that there is a long way to go before the well dries, but there could be a problem regarding the availability of purchase funds and selectivity among an increasing number of reprint publishers. One highly successful paperback publisher does not see the well drying. On the contrary, he states:

The real possibilities of photographic republishing are only now being realized. Areas of study are expanding and thousands of valuable books go out of print every year which scholars and libraries will continue to need.

One more vote of confidence is of interest. A firm that offers hardcover and paperback books sees the well far from dry, noting that "programs are only limited by lack of capital and personnel."

The highest proportion of firms that express confidence are micropublishers or publishers of paperbacks. These firms apparently have carefully planned their programs with a long-range view, in contrast to some publishers who came dashing into the industry willy-nilly while reprint activities were mounting a crest in the successful sixties. Also, the problems of information storage would seem to spell at least temporary success for microforms, and paperbacks are becoming increasingly popular.

As might be expected, firms that specialize in reprinting in well-defined subject fields are among the most enthusiastic. These firms include publishers in the areas of archeology, entomology, Chinese studies, regional history, criminology, medicine, and selected ethnic studies, and firms with especially tailored programs within more general subject areas, such as European history, business, and economics. These subject specialists have good titles in mind. They know who needs which titles and when. They are familiar with the supply of originals in the used- or rare-book markets.

Fifteen firms are unsure of their program's future. Eleven of these less confident firms have been in the reprint business for ten or fewer years; several for only one or two years. Representative comments from this group are:

To a certain extent the well is drying.
Close to the truth.
May be so already.
Popular titles are well exploited.

There is a need for many other titles of value but low sales potential. The boom is draining the well rapidly.

Nine firms that express least confidence about their future programs published in the following subject fields: Western Americana, history, political science, black studies, and sports. Their comments:

The well is about dry.
We plan to continue a modest program of only a few titles a year.
Most important titles have already been done.
Our field (Western Americana) is running dry.
Yes. The well is dry.

In the opinion of about ten publishers, primarily hardcover re-printers, the well may be drying, but only in the sense that "the over-priced, overballyhoo'd book" might not sell as well as before. One firm noted that such titles had been chosen "only to make a profit for the publishers. The titles were not necessary to aid scholarship, as evidenced by the extensive remainder market." Several firms do not expect to en-large their programs, but rather will, as one put it, "rewrite and expand upon old titles, issuing reprints that are substantially improved over the originals."

Reading their comments and listening to the publishers, one is struck by the fact that there seems to be a great deal of soul-searching going on within the industry. Members of some older firms are disheartened by current reprint practices. Four publishers agree that those who will have problems in the future are the "quick-buck reprinters who lack an appreciation or real insight in the contents of the books they reprint." For such publishers, one firm noted, "after the Voigt-Treyz book, there is nothing left to do."

Yet, during the interviews several publishers mentioned that they felt reassured because they select titles that have already been through the publishing mill at an earlier date. They check contemporary reviews and feel certain that they can continue to find a new market for an old title if they choose their subjects and their titles intelligently.

As others have said before, reprint publishing is a "curious" business.

Chapter 7

Reprinters' Editorial and Production Practices

After a publisher selects his proposed reprint titles, he still faces many important business decisions. How he makes these not only determines the physical and intellectual quality of his products, but gives style to his house, helps to establish his reputation in and outside the industry, and influences his chances for success, perhaps even his survival as a publisher in the highly volatile reprint industry.

As one successful reprint publisher said about some of these troublesome areas where policies and practice must be determined, "Here is where the men get separated from the boys, for there is a great deal more to publishing reprints responsibly than simply the making and peddling of copies."

It is characteristic of the publishing industry generally that a host of editorial and production decisions need to be made for each unique title. These are difficult decisions, for what seems right for one title might spell disaster for another. This is the kind of ambiguity the director of the Princeton University Press, Herbert S. Bailey, Jr., writes about incisively as the "irrationality of publishing."[1]

High on any list of challenges to reprint publishers are the decisions each must make about the addition of new matter to reprints, and about manufacturing and production procedures, including the size of initial print orders. Reprinters must also be concerned with the public domain versus copyright status of the originals they copy. This is the arena in which the specter of industry ethics is often raised, and equated with a publisher's willingness to pay royalties or other reprinting fees. Publishers who participated in this study addressed themselves to these points in interesting, diverse ways. What they said and what they do are reported below. In addition, this chapter is concerned with rival reprint programs, reprint pricing, and publishers' viewpoints in discussing the need for an association of reprint publishers.

NEW MATTER

The term "new matter" generally defines any textual or illustrative material added to an original work being reprinted. New matter may be newly created, or may be "old" materials newly gathered from existing scattered sources and printed as part of the reprint edition.

Publishers were asked whether they usually, sometimes, or never add new matter to their reprints, what kinds they add, and why. One publisher pinpointed the ambivalence of the issue by stating, "In scholarly publishing, sometimes it is justified, and sometimes not. Simple!" The question was answered more specifically by 92 publishers whose statements were interpreted into an attitude scale (see Table 8), with the result that about 70 percent of them feel that reprints are enhanced by new matter. As shown in Table 9, publishers seem to favor new introductions and indexes, but also add updated bibliographies, updated biographies (to place the original writer into his scholarly milieu), and critical

TABLE 8
PUBLISHERS' OPINIONS ABOUT ADDING NEW
MATTER

Publisher's Opinion N = 92	Total
Essential to add new matter	11
Generally in favor	54
Generally opposed	27

Source: Publishers' response to Question 11.

TABLE 9
FREQUENCY AND KINDS OF MATTER ADDED TO REPRINTS

New Matter Added	Number of Firms (N = 123)		
	Usually Add	Sometimes Add	Never Add
a. Introduction	51	45	5
b. Index	26	34	13
c. Updated bibliography	15	28	15
d. Updated biography	16	20	12
e. Critical notes	18	29	15
f. Other	0	25	0

Source: Publishers' response to Question 10.

notes (to alert the modern reader to research that has amended or expanded upon original scholarship).

The 25 publishers who sometimes add "other" kinds of new matter specified major critical or bibliographic essays; extra illustrations, including maps and plates not in the original edition; errata or addenda; letters; supplementary new information; and tables of contents.

The 27 publishers who oppose adding new matter do so because it is too costly; creates unwarranted publication delays; is intentional "gimmickry," or "padding," or does not satisfy any real scholarly need. Several publishers seem to agree with the one who wrote, "New matter must be more than a sort of testimonial"; or with another, who commented, "Putting new matter into a reprint is usually nothing more than a 'sales push' intimidating to librarians who feel obligated to buy the title for fear of overlooking a new piece of significant scholarship."

An index added to a reprint may be newly constructed or could have existed before, but not as part of the edition being reprinted. During an interview Jules Chodak, late president of Genealogical Publishing Company, offered insights gained from years of selling old books to collectors and reprinting in his subject specialty.[2] After selecting titles, his firm searches for the "best" edition to reprint and for extant printed or handwritten additions or corrections. If it is determined that an index is required or that a new introduction would bring the contents more sharply into current perspective, scholars are asked to prepare these, "sometimes for a fee." Unpublished, corrected author's copies of the titles are also sought, for these occasionally contain handwritten marginal notes which can be photographed as inserts in the reprint, as Genealogical did in their 1968 reprint edition of Stella Pickett Hardy's *Colonial Families of the Southern States of America* (2nd ed., with revisions and additions by the author, originally published in 1911). Some new indexes are prepared by the publisher's staff (e.g., for *Passenger Arrivals: 1819–1920*, a U.S. Senate document reprinted in 1967 with an added 54-page index and a new title); or a separately published index may be located in the periodical literature and incorporated. In an interesting aside, Chodak noted that scholars criticize reprinters "if they do or if they don't" add new matter, but he felt it "far better to have a 'poor' book made available immediately than to wait a lifetime for a so-called corrected copy to appear—with every chance that this alleged corrected copy would itself contain errors."

Another view was given by Gabriel Hornstein, president of one of the largest reprint houses, AMS Press, who stoutly criticized certain kinds of new matter as being "scholarly indulgences," new introductions which are added mostly to give some scholar an opportunity to command $200–$500 and, at the same time, satisfy his need to "publish or perish."[3] Rather than add such "unnecessary" introductions, Hornstein prefers an occasional tightly written bibliographic essay, perhaps only a few paragraphs or several pages in length, intended to relate the reprint to later works and save the user's time by gathering pertinent information about the title in one place. In Hornstein's opinion, students of a subject are usually qualified to judge the work on its own merits, or knowledgeable enough to seek published sources of information.

Taking yet another tack, Garrett Press decided to rely mostly upon an editorial board of advisers for title selection and for suggestions and recommendations about new matter. According to the firm's president, Daniel G. Garrett, new matter is added only when scholars deem it really necessary, generally not to biographies and anthologies. Since it is "substantive" new matter that is needed, Garrett pays to attract notable authors to prepare these materials. Their editorial board in American literature, for example, includes such well-known authorities as Oscar Cargill (New York University, emeritus), Lewis Leary (University of North Carolina), and Clarence Gohdes (Duke University).[4]

Hafner's Harry Lubrecht staunchly advocates adding new matter "to orient the significance of the work and to help the modern user understand unfamiliar procedures in presentation and composition."[5] The firm makes interesting use of newly constructed tables of contents and its Machol Edge Index (U.S. Patent No. 2680630) which indicates variously paged sections and provides access to the contents. For instance, *The Theophoraceas of North America,* by E. A. Bent, has 15 differently paginated sections, excerpts from the *Annals* of the Missouri Botanical Gardens, bound together. Because old references cite original page numbers, it was not feasible for the reprint to be continually paginated, so the edge-marking device was conceived. A full description of the contents is printed on the contents page as well, an example of creative reprinting considerate of today's readers.

This topic has been treated in some detail because it surfaces again and again in discussion in reprint houses and among librarians. We have seen that publishers hold varying views about adding new matter to reprints. Some feel that books with a sufficiently long afterlife to warrant reprinting should be offered as straight copies and left to stand on their own merits. Others feel duty-bound to add new matter to place older scholarship into modern perspective. Several publishers came right out and said they do not have the funds needed to commission good introductions, but would if they could. The addition of new matter has sales value for some firms and yet is a point of contention to others. As in other aspects of the reprint industry, there is apparently no single best pattern to follow. Each publisher must treat his titles in ways that seem wise to him, knowing that, as a reprinter, his wisdom will usually be measured in the marketplace.

REPRODUCTION PROCEDURES AND PROBLEMS

While this study has made no attempt to report details about how reprints are manufactured, it is essential to recognize certain basic production patterns and problems and to learn how these affect other publishing decisions. The information in this section focuses on hardcopy reprinting, whether casebound or paperbound. Microform technology is discussed briefly. Film is increasingly serving as an intermediary vehicle carrying information for duplication, onto other film, or for printing onto paper.

It is not unusual to hear a chagrined reprint publisher blame his manufacturer or suppliers for problems he, the publisher, has in fulfilling commitments to customers. These problems typically relate to the publisher's inability to meet a promised publication date, or to the fact that the quality of his product is inferior to what he says he paid for and expected to receive from his suppliers. The frequency with which publishers speak of these "disappointments" is lessening; but some complaints persist, and keep alive the "guarded" stance of the reprint industry.

Publishers were asked two questions, one about their reproduction methods and the other about production problems, in an attempt to find out how many firms might be subject to problems they say stem from doing business with outside suppliers, and to learn specifically what these often-generalized problems are.

To the question, "Do you manufacture your own reprints or deal with an outside service company?" 94 of the 128 respondents replied that they buy their manufacturing from service companies. And 80 percent (117 of 193) of the firms who described their hardcopy reprinting process utilize photo-offset techniques. The fact that a majority of reprint houses do not own or operate printing or binding facilities is somewhat surprising, for the printer-publisher was thought to be a more prevalent figure on the reprint scene. A considerable number of the 80 percent are new firms, which points to an important trend in the industry. That is, reprint publishing is beginning to follow the production pattern of general trade publishing, where almost all book manufacturing is now done on hire by service companies. Reprint publishing still has a larger proportion of "manufacturing publishers" (i.e., 20 percent) than regular publishing, but the gap is narrowing.

Certain production problems which reprinters face are the result of pressures felt in the printing and binding trades over the past decade or so. Logjams along book production lines were created by an increasing number of titles published and a lack of sufficient printing and binding facilities to meet all publishers' needs on a timely, first-come, first-served basis. At least this is what many reprinters said during this survey.

Faced with a rapidly changing typesetting technology, soaring labor costs, and major explorations into new printing and binding processes and equipment, many printers are still uncertain about new directions for their industry. Will they turn to printing by COM (computer-output microfilm), CRT (cathode-ray-tube imagery), photographic composition linked to electronic-scanning input devices, or other techniques yet to be developed? Instead of changing from conventional printing methods to an uncharted course, many printers continue to operate with outmoded equipment and without enough staff. (It is generally agreed that there are fewer printers' apprentices now than there were even several decades ago, although the trend toward career education in the seventies might reverse this course.)

Arthur E. Gardner viewed these difficulties during the important COMPRINT 90 Conference held in New York City in 1970. Among other significant conclusions reached about the future of the printing trades, Gardner stated that, "While most of the printing industry basks unbeknowingly in the self-satisfied splendor of five hundred years of hoary history, its technology is embroiled in a tremendous upheaval."[6] And, he admonished, "It is high time that printing's apathetic, hermit-like practitioners accept the fact that the industry is changing dramatically." Until the visions become realities, however, present-day reprinters face many significant problems in getting their books produced.

There are, to be sure, some commercial printers who have taken the plunge and invested large amounts of money in modern equipment. These firms generally favor customers who can place very large print orders so efficient use can be made of their fast, high-powered printing machinery. Edwards Brothers, Halliday, and some other firms have modernized and do specialize in shortrun printing, but these are exceptions, not the rule.

Binderies too have been reluctant to change. Many small binderies employ hand operators, a slow and expensive way to put books together. Most binderies that have installed automated, production-line systems also favor large-edition binding jobs.

Thus all shortrun publishers, not only reprinters, have been caught in the book production crunch. Reprinters possibly have felt it most keenly, since scholarly reprinting does not generally place a publisher in a favorable competitive position for scheduling small photo-offset runs.

REPRODUCTION METHODS AND PRODUCTION PROBLEMS

A large number of firms that did not specify their reproduction process are also known to reprint by offset lithography, taking advantage of recent improvements in photographic equipment and printing methods, new plastic plates, fast-drying inks and other printing industry advances that now make small printings practical.

Twenty-five firms use photo-offset except for newly prepared introductions or other new matter, which are printed by letterpress. One printer specified the use of "Itek plates and Dick offset." Unexpectedly, 4 firms produce scholarly reprints only by letterpress; another uses various combinations of photo-offset, letterpress and gravure processes; 2 use photo-offset, letterpress or collotype, whichever printing process they deem preferable for a particular title; 3 of the 117 produce only microfilm editions; and 2 others use diazo duplicate microfiche.

The 18 firms that reprint by photo-offset and/or letterpress mentioned certain qualifications. The most significant remarks follow.

The choice depends upon the condition of the original.
Ninety percent of our printing is by letterpress from all new type, ten percent if offset facsimile.
Sometimes we combine the two, using letterpress when the edition is bought abroad.
We do our own letterpress, which the company prefers, but we buy offset printing and all binding.

To determine to what extent, if any, problems differ for established and new firms, and to identify significant relationships between production problems, reprint format, and other variables, cross-tabulations were made of responses to Questions 3, 7, 9, and 15. This was possible to do for only 57 firms. The findings, statistically inconclusive, are believed representative of the industry generally, and some are worth noting.

New firms have more production problems than established firms, or at least they are more vocal about them. Only 14 of the latter mentioned production problems compared with 47 new firms. Publishers who have produced fewer than 300 titles acknowledge more production problems than firms that publish a large number of titles.

Interestingly, 8 firms that *do* operate their own printing and/or binding facilities each singled out the same major production problem: increased costs of labor and materials. The 4 publishers who mentioned having problems when they were new in the reprint business noted that after three to five years they now, as one firm put it, "Have a grip on production problems and they are few." Several major houses agree that their reprint production problems are the same ones normal to other kinds of printing and binding projects. At least 6 firms with no particular problems at the time of their response noted that their outlook would change if more firms begin to issue reprints while the number of printers and binders specializing in shortruns remains the same.

Another point made by several publishers is that variations in the levels of federal funding programs affect the numbers of titles reprinted and sold so substantially that crystal-ball gazing is nonsensical.

The problems that emerged from publishers' responses fall into four clusters:

1. Problems of securing originals to copy.

Difficulty in locating reprintable originals was expressed by 12 firms (1 established, 11 new). Often, they say, there is need to locate multiple copies because none is clean or complete enough to serve as a master copy for reproduction. The high costs of searching for and securing originals, either to purchase or to borrow, was noted by 6 firms (1 established,

5 new). Several publishers linked this problem to their publication delays. Two firms mentioned problems in dealing with libraries, particularly with regard to obtaining permission to film rare editions that are in poor physical condition.

2. Problems in dealing with printers and binders.

The 32 firms (6 established, 26 new) that have trouble meeting promised delivery dates place the blame for this upon their suppliers. The most frequently noted problems are:

> Bindery holdups and machinery breakdowns.
> Binding problems because they produce small quantities.
> Postponements of their runs by printers or binders, which generates doubts about the firm's reliability among its customers.
> Delivery dates delayed by as long as sixty to ninety days, a problem that seems to be getting worse.

Of the 8 firms (all new) that have difficulties in scheduling short runs with printers and binders, 4 complained that:

> We have trouble in competing with larger establishments or older customers for time on production lines.
> If a "better customer" orders work done, our runs seem to get pushed way back in the production schedule.
> It is difficult to estimate the size of our initial printing order, so we sometimes have to go back to press with small orders.

Promises, promises.

3. Problems of product control.

Of the 39 firms (15 established, 24 new) that mentioned problems concerning quality control, 2 remarked that these stemmed from their geographic removal from the place of production. As one firm commented, "Our printers and binders are frequently far removed from our headquarters. With our small staff, it is difficult to properly oversee those operations." As an aside, it should be noted that several firms interviewed have recently mentioned changing printers, some for this reason, and some because they feel they should get better work for their money.

The other comments about quality control are encompassed in the following remarks:

> Books are shipped to us and arrive with crushed corners, with covers not squared, with inked tops blurring text on pages. It is expensive and time-consuming to try to improve the edition once we have received the shipment.
> We use skin-packaging (i.e., plastic wrap), but even this does not guarantee clean copies.
> We are especially troubled by photo-reproduction quality, for we often deal with poor original copies.

Quality of the products we get from some of our suppliers is awful, even though we pay high prices.

Quality control is very troublesome, even more so than delayed delivery dates.

Cost of printing high quality books in small editions is very high.

How can we explain poor quality to our customers? They cannot be expected to understand, yet we contract in good faith, and pay through the nose.

4. More money problems.

Cost problems were noted by 33 firms (9 established, 24 new). The problems included those caused by rising production costs, including labor and materials; high costs inherent in producing small editions versus setting realistic retail prices; high finance charges and problems of getting good terms from printers and binders for paper and cloth necessarily bought in small quantities.

In the reprint industry, firms that operate their own production plants might have certain advantages. They can schedule their own small editions advantageously. Their titles can be fitted in between contract jobs. At least one firm that manufactures its own reprints is known to wait for an order before printing (the original volumes the firm advertises are part of a vast personal library collection). When an order is received, a copy of the book is printed and bound. For some titles for which the publisher anticipates (or has received) multiple orders, a small run of perhaps 25 copies is produced. This firm publishes and advertises reprints under a variety of imprints. For some reason, probably having to do with speed in fulfilling orders, the firm prints a different title page for each imprint and binds all of them together into each book. When an order is received, the title page with the appropriate imprint is left intact; the others are cut away, and the book is ready for shipment to the customer.

Shortrun production methods and attendant high costs greatly affect the physical quality and appearance of reprinted volumes. Reprints have been criticized for a generally lackluster appearance. A publisher of small editions can do one of two things. He can buy high-quality materials and dress up his books with nicely designed covers, or he can settle for a simple format that remains fairly uniform. The latter choice is the more customary for it allows shortrun printers to make gang runs. Thus many reprint volumes look much alike. There are exceptions. Gale Research Company, for example, has produced period covers, with designs that simulate or reflect the era or the topic of the book's contents.

If one visits Edwards Brothers, in its clean and spacious quarters, with production lines sending forth thousands of books, one is struck by the fact that competitive reprint products push each other down the lines. It is kind of fun to watch arch rivals' products marching through the bindery in close proximity.

None of the 12 firms that produce hardcopies by a xerographic or other electrostatic printing process singled out particular production problems. Their copies are mostly produced by a copyflo process on demand, from master negatives already in their vaults or from originals located and filmed by special request. The lack of clear halftone reproductions is not considered a production *problem,* but rather a technological factor of increased cost and increased time to produce these versus customer demand and willingness to pay.

The microform publishers surveyed are generally concerned with product standards (size and quality) and seem well-aware that the lack of standardized hardware (readers and reader-printers) creates confusion and added expense for customers. A few firms are experimenting with or are already publishing "ultrafiche," a transparency as small as 2 × 2 inches that can contain more than 9,000 pages of printed matter. NCR's PCMI (Photo-Chromic Micro Image) is one of the earliest examples. In this system, each 4 × 6-inch transparency stores up to 3,200 pages of information, or more than 30 times the capacity of conventional microfiche. "Of no comfort to publishers of reprints of OP books," an industry newsletter wrote, "NCR says its material will be available at about one-tenth the estimated book costs and stores in one-sixtieth the normally required shelf space."[7] Micro Photo Division of Bell & Howell is investigating ultrafiche publishing, and Library Resources, Inc. (a division of Encyclopaedia Britannica) has begun to publish its vast series of Microbook Libraries® on high reduction microfiche.

Photographic quality control, humidity and temperature as storage factors, fire and dust retardant vaults, standardized sizes of reels, spools, cartridges, packaging, and hardware—these are the kinds of production matters of concern to micropublishers.

To summarize these findings, experience obviously alleviates some production problems and knowledge of suppliers helps to diminish others. Certain production problems apparently will continue to burden shortrun reprinters so long as they publish small editions for highly specialized markets, or at least until new printing and communications technology becomes realistically applicable to their needs.

SIZE OF REPRINT EDITIONS

In the printing industry, the size of an edition generally refers to the number of copies of a title printed at one time. There is a direct relation between the number of copies of a title printed and the unit manufacturing cost. Obviously each publisher must consider his unit costs when he sets the retail sales price per copy and when he determines what, if any, discounts he will offer.

Shortrun and *small-edition* publishing are terms used synonymously to describe the reprint industry, but neither term refers to any standard number. To try to get a better idea of what these terms mean to the industry's participants (reprinters generally describe themselves as short-run publishers), reprinters were asked the average size of their initial pressrun for reprint editions. As Table 10 indicates, the largest cluster of respondents (41) selected range "f," or 1,000–2,000 copies. The second-ranked edition size is "d," or a run of 500–749 copies.

Of the 16 firms that print fewer than 100 copies, the majority are micropublishers who issue most titles on demand.

These data, provided by about half of all identified firms, were interpreted in the light of conversations with printers and others in the publishing industry with the result that the "d" range (editions of 500–749 copies) appears to be a realistic estimate of an average shortrun edition for scholarly reprints.

Many important publishing decisions relate to the size of the print order. Some firms print, but do not bind, all copies. A publisher might hold unbound sheets as inventory until firm orders for the titles are received. This practice saves binding costs on copies that may not be sold, and provides tax advantages for some publishers. Since warehousing costs are high, particularly in urban areas, publishers also save on storage and handling charges. As an example, in 1969 in the Ann Arbor, Michigan, area, it cost 1.8 cents per book per month for dead storage in a public warehouse. Publishers generally have to figure on costs ranging from $.21 to $.60 per copy per year just to house and move books in and out of the warehouse. Shortrun publishers, including university presses, usually keep unsold copies as inventory for longer periods of time than trade houses. The quick pace and volume of trade publishing generally forces publishers to let their books go OP or onto remainder tables faster, in part due to the very high costs of storage and handling. Within the past several years, storage costs have risen considerably nationally. In the New York metropolitan area such costs may be as much as 45 percent higher than in other parts of the country.[8] On the other hand, because all copies are not bound and ready for immediate shipment, some publishers are late in delivering books to customers when orders come in. Small

TABLE 10
EDITION SIZES

Initial Pressrun		No. of Firms
a.	Under 100	16
b.	100– 249	6
c.	250– 499	19
d.	500– 749	36
e.	750– 999	13
f.	1,000–2,000	41
g.	Over 2,000	18
Total firms		149

orders are frequently held for a slow time at a bindery; and the cost per volume to bind a small number of copies is generally higher than for binding large orders. It is reasonable to assume that a publisher will try to pass along at least some of these costs to the customer by incorporating actual and projected binding costs into the retail price of each copy sold.

Is the size of the printing a variable related more significantly to format or to the number of titles a firm publishes? The search for answers proved too statistically scattered to be meaningful. It was found, as one might expect, that paperbound publishers generally issue larger editions than hardcover reprinters, and a firm that publishes in both formats adjusts the print orders accordingly. A few typical examples: a firm that prints 200–300 copies of hardcover reprints orders 5,000 copies for paperbounds. Another orders an edition of 1,000–2,000 hardcover copies for "scholarly" titles and over 3,000 copies for his "more popular titles, in paper covers."

Each publisher tries to discover the right quantity to print initially in order to satisfy immediate and short-term demand. Ideally, he avoids going back to press for small, expensive additional printings; but his overrun must not be so large that stocking unsold copies wipes out his profits. With experience, some publishers have learned to estimate demand for particular kinds of books they can publish in series, thus taking advantage of better terms when buying paper and cloth, and printing in larger quantities. This undoubtedly is one factor underlying the increasing number of offerings in newly contrived publishers' series.

TESTING THE MARKET TO DETERMINE PRINTRUNS

Reprint publishers frequently base their initial print orders on market reactions to feelers they put forth in advance of printing. If the demand for a title appears to be great, the printing is larger. If the demand is low, the title may not be published at all, or only in very small numbers and then usually at higher unit prices. There is no mystery about the relationship between the size of a printing and the size of the anticipated market. The practice of pretesting the market has, however, generated a great deal of animosity toward some reprint publishers— those who promise but do not produce.

Trade publishers also pretest markets. Generally they solicit expressions of interest from names on selected mailing lists. Their reasons for market research are similar to those of the reprinter, to determine whether or not a book is a viable publishing venture. The difference is that most trade publishers will either tell the person being solicited that the title may be published if there is sufficient demand, or a notice will be sent saying that the project will be dropped, if that is the decision. Most reprint publishers do not do this. They announce, they advertise, and they solicit information from prospective customers. If the project dies, the customer generally is not informed; nor, one should add, are other publishers. There are known instances when another firm might have published a particular title but decided not to go into production because the first reprint had been announced. Since certain titles not feasible for one firm might do well on another list, this practice of usurping titles and not publishing them is a contentious point in the industry. It is also a great irritant to prospective customers. At its best, the practice might be well-intended; at worst, fraudulent.

In contrast to regular publishing, a reprinter can plot his production course and make editorial decisions well in advance of actually locating an original to copy. Most regular publishers make final estimates about production methods and costs, size of printruns, pricing, and basic editorial decisions only after a manuscript is in the house. A reprinter has recourse to earlier reviews and descriptions of the contents and physical characteristics of the work he proposes to reprint. This kind of information is usually available to him even if he has never seen a copy of the original.

Thus, once a reprinter has a title in mind to reprint, he can describe the title in promotional literature and list it in his catalogs. He can, and some reprinters do, accept orders and payments for titles in advance of production.

The problems that rise from such practices are legion; they have in fact been told so often that they need not be repeated here. It is a fact that a considerable number of reprinters list and promote titles which have not been produced.

Aside from what probably is a small number of hucksters who add many titles to their lists without honestly intending to publish them (generally to stake a claim in order to dissuade other publishers from these properties), there are other reasons that a firm might announce and not publish, according to some publishers. A firm might advertise and really plan to publish a long backrun of an old periodical, for instance. Certain volumes might be printed and sold when the publisher runs aground, unable to locate reprintable copies (or any copy) of certain issues.

Asked why they did not locate and get permission to reprint a full set before advertising and selling parts of it, some publishers remarked that (a) it takes so long to locate all the parts to copy that some volumes would be available a very long time before they could be sold, (b) the money earned from the early sales helps to pay for publishing the later volumes, and (c) another publisher might get wind of the project and bring out the same titles more quickly, probably diluting the sale for both publishers, or cutting off the first publisher's sale completely.

It would seem that some publishers have not done their homework before they advertise, for titles have been listed as reprints which never have existed as originals. In such cases, the publisher obviously has done shoddy research or has taken as gospel the information in some library union list of holdings. One publisher was heard to complain vehemently about such "dishonest" library reference tools. It did not seem to occur to him that he might be sticking pins into the wrong effigy.

REPRINT PRICES

In book production and editorial decision-making the differences between reprinting and regular publishing become quite apparent. Trade publishers usually describe their manufacturing costs in terms of plant and production costs. Plant costs include the fixed costs of typesetting or other composition, plate costs, and all other manufacturing costs incurred before going to press. Production costs include makeready and printing, paper and binding. In addition, publishers allocate funds for what the industry calls "G&A" or general and administrative costs, including salaries; editorial and design costs; the production department operations; the costs of selling, advertising, and promoting; and shipping and warehousing costs. For an adult trade book, G&A might typically consume 15–20 percent of the publisher's net receipts.

Typical G&A costs (if there *are* typical figures) for scholarly reprint publishing have not been discerned. It may be presumed that the expenditures for G&A will generally be less than for trade publishing, for usually there are lower composition, editorial and production department costs, and perhaps lower promotion and advertising expenditures.

Regular publishing's rule-of-thumb ratio of manufacturing costs to retail price per book is five to one. That is, if it costs $2.00 to manufacture a book, the retail price might be set at about $10.00. Publishers who were queried about a comparable figure for the reprint industry generally stated that their manufacturing/cost ratio is about the same as the trade publishers', for the money the reprinter saves by eliminating some costs (especially expensive composition) is consumed, they say, by the higher costs to produce, sell, and deliver very small editions for specialized markets. In what hopefully is an extreme case one printer-publisher is known to price his books at about ten times manufacturing cost. He prints in very small editions and has apparently been successful because he does have good difficult-to-find titles on his list.

When a conventionally published book is in an early planning stage, its publisher does not usually know how many copies will sell. He estimates, he gambles, and he hopes. He prints at least the number of copies which, if sold, will return his investment. This number, the so-called break-even, or get-out, point, might typically be about 7,000–8,000 copies for an adult trade book and perhaps 4,000–6,000 copies for a university press title. Break-even points for scholarly reprinters generally range far below traditional publishing, but vary so extensively that to be specific is difficult. The edition size varies from house to house, and within each house, perhaps from title to title. A few examples might clarify the muddle. One reprinter who prints 500–600 copies breaks even at 150–175 copies. Another prints an edition of several hundred copies and breaks even at between 80 and 90 copies. It should be emphasized that sets of paired characteristics are involved: the smaller the printing, the higher the unit cost; the higher the unit cost, the higher the retail price; the higher the retail price, the earlier the break-even point is reached. For a relatively good-selling title, scholarly reprinters break even when they have sold a much lower number than regular publishers.

One pricing practice that appears to be widespread is that of basing the retail price for a reprint on the publisher's anticipated initial sale, which generally is spread over the first and second years (sometimes longer) after publication. These initial copies bear the price burden for all subsequent copies that may eventually be sold. This means that after the initial sale, a publisher probably has reached or surpassed his break-even point and other copies sold bring in the gravy. This practice has been criticized by some industry observers who feel that reprinters in general do not take "normal" publishing risks.

Reprint publishing usually is considered a lower-risk industry than regular publishing. In general terms, it costs less to reproduce copies of older books than to create totally new ones.

Until recently reprint publishing was considered a shoestring operation. Before the industry grew large and as highly competitive as it is now, and when printing and binding costs were lower and financing less burdensome, a reprinter could go into business with, say, four or five thousand dollars. He could get several thousand books printed and bind several hundred copies of each title, i.e., those which he knew would sell initially. When the first 80 or 90 copies were sold, the publisher began to make a profit.

With present labor and materials costs for printing and binding high and steadily increasing, reprint publishing can no longer be considered in the same light. It now costs more to search for and secure titles to reprint; it costs more to have copies made; it certainly costs more to sell books. Rising publishing costs that affect regular publishers also affect reprint publishers.

The pricing of reprints is a topic that generally churns a considerable wake. People ask why reprints cost so much, but rarely does anyone say what it is that reprints cost. The complaints are generalized. Yet it is unsafe to generalize any discussion of reprint pricing, for too often the comparisons mix "peaches and pears." Daniel C. Garrett, Fred Rappaport, vice-president of Johnson Reprint Company, and Robert F. Asleson have discussed pricing practices for hardcopies and microforms publicly.[9] According to Garrett, a reprint in an edition of 500 copies that sold out in its first year would be considered a runaway bestseller. Garrett makes a strong point that one cannot compare reprints with trade books on the basis of price. Sigfried Feller, chief bibliographer, University of Massachusetts, attempted a price sampling comparing hardcopy and microform reprints of titles from *BCL*. He found an extremely wide range of prices, but his findings were tentative and have not been published.

The industry has been criticized for pricing reprints according to what the market will bear. Undoubtedly some publishers do charge what they have found customers will pay. Others consistently price their books low. Dover, Peter Smith, and Tuttle are good examples. The price of reprints will eventually find acceptable levels, but this will naturally be determined in the marketplace. If prices seem too high, no customer is forced to buy. This seems the most realistic way to serve notice to those publishers who are "scalping," and to give support to responsible publishers. However, it is necessary for customers to be aware of pricing factors. For example, in 1969 one printer remarked that an advertisement listed a five-volume reprint of the journal, *The Colophon* for $875. In the printer's opinion, this was $375 more than the price at which his firm could successfully reproduce the five volumes, the originals of which he owned. This argument is of interest for several reasons. First, in cirticizing the higher-priced set, the printer did not allow for the costs to locate and secure copyable originals, nor the costs of advertising and marketing the reprint edition. These costs must be included in the retail price. The manufacturing cost is far less than the cost of publishing a reprint.

Before presenting the results of this study's effort to gain insight into pricing practices and to seek an "average" price for current hardcopy reprints, the inherent and recognized pitfalls must be underscored. Even in reprint publishing, where so many books look alike, it is rare that any two titles are absolutely comparable. Every publisher has many reasons and the right to price one book differently than another. He might, for example, own an original, in which case he will not bear the "front end" cost of searching and securing an original to copy. He might or might not pay royalties. He might print the work himself, saving in labor and other manufacturing costs. He might publish a poor-quality product on cheap paper or print on special acid-free paper to assure long shelf life. In sum, he might meet exacting standards, or none.

Adding new matter costs money. A book may be promoted (at professional exhibits, through distribution of review copies, and the like) or may only be listed in a sales brochure. Without further emphasis, it should be clear that any attempt to generalize about pricing policies and practices within the reprint industry, or to compare reprint and trade-book prices, or prices of used books and reprints, is very likely to be distorted. Yet, the industry needs to begin to gather some basic facts, if only to prove incomparability.

Four different pricing exercises were undertaken for the present survey. First, in order to determine the average retail price of hardcover reprints, all hardcover separately priced reprints (621 titles) listed in 12 1968 issues of *PW* were selected. Periodical sets and multivolume sets were excluded.

It was found (see Table 11) that these reprints sold at from $2.00 per copy to $326 per copy, which demonstrates some of the futility of comparing prices of books. In this sample, the average price (rounded) per title is $12; the median (74 titles offered), $10. The second most "popular" retail price for hardcover reprints is $7.50 (for 75 titles). Second,

TABLE 11

RETAIL PRICE OF HARDCOVER REPRINTS, BY FREQUENCY OF OCCURENCE

Price	No. of Titles	Price	No. of Titles
$ 2.00	1	$ 16.50	18
3.00	2	17.50	14
3.50	1	18.00	3
4.00	9	18.50	3
4.50	4	19.00	3
5.00	20	19.50	3
5.50	4	20.00	12
6.00	22	21.00	1
6.50	20	21.50	1
7.00	25	22.00	3
7.50	57	22.50	6
8.00	23	23.00	1
8.50	32	25.00	5
9.00	42	27.50	2
9.50	17	28.50	1
10.00	74	29.00	4
10.50	4	30.00	1
11.00	14	32.50	3
11.50	10	33.50	1
12.00	20	37.50	3
12.50	53	38.50	1
13.00	4	45.00	2
13.50	12	50.00	1
14.00	9	60.00	1
14.50	9	80.00	1
15.00	28	110.00	1
15.50	2	125.00	1
16.00	5	326.00	1
Total price		$7,593.15	
Total titles			621
Average (mean) price per title		$12.21	
Median price per title		$10.00	

Source: "Weekly Record" section of *Publishers' Weekly*, 1968.
Note: Selected titles include all hardcover reprints listed in 12 *PW* issues, i.e., one issue per month. Price for paperbounds and titles offered as sets without separate volume price is rounded to the nearest half dollar. The number of titles included (621) is slightly less than half the number of reprints entered in the 24 *PW* issues searched to determine total title output.

from the same sample, every twentieth item which reported preliminary and/or total pagination (75 titles) was selected, in order to estimate the price per page based on the retail price per copy. The average retail price for these 75 books was slightly less than $12; the average price per page (at retail) about 3¢. (See Table 12.)

TABLE 12
ESTIMATED RETAIL PRICE PER PAGE OF HARDCOVER REPRINTS
PUBLISHED BY 32 FIRMS

Firm	PW Issue (1968)	No. of Prelim. Pages	Total Pages	New Matter Added	Orig. Pubn. Date	List Price	Average Price per Page
A	9/30	—	109	—	1879	$ 5.00	$.046
B	4/8	—	243	Ill., Maps	1905	5.95	.025
	12/2	16	387	—	1868	9.00	.023
	12/16	4	166	—	1907	6.00	.036
	11/19	—	216	—	1836	7.00	.032
C	6/3	25	389	Ill., Maps	1887	14.50	.037
	6/3	32	432	Ill., Maps	1939	10.00	.023
	8/19	16	506	Ill., Port.	1911	12.50	.025
D	4/8	8	451	Ill., Maps	1930	15.00	.033
	12/16	9	332	—	1944	10.00	.030
E	7/29	10	104	Ill., Plans	1790	25.00	.240
	10/14	—	136	405 Ill.	1930	32.50	.239
F	2/12	—	227	—	—	7.75	.034
	2/12	—	252	—	—	9.50	.038
	3/18	—	305	—	—	8.50	.028
G	3/18	(ltd. ed.)	200	Ill., Plans	—	15.00	.075
H	11/18	—	786	Ill.	1897	14.95	.019
I	7/29	12	311	Crit. Essay	1906	6.95	.022
	12/16	10	531	—	1909	12.50	.024
J	6/3	20	355	Preface	1940	15.00	.042
	10/28	11	292	Intro.	1921	12.50	.043
K	5/27	14	400	—	1930	9.50	.024
	11/18	17	414	Maps	1910	11.00	.027
L	7/29	—	125	Ill.	1811	10.00	.080
	8/26	12	264	Ill., Facs.	1928	25.00	.095
	9/30	11	95	Ill.	1926	16.50	.174
M	8/19	44	439	Fwd., Music	1933	10.00	.023
	10/28	10	225	—	1882	7.80	.035
	12/16	—	306	—	1882	7.80	.025
N	3/18	—	698	Addenda	—	15.00	.021
	12/16	—	292	—	1890	7.50	.026
O	11/18	16	233	—	1895	7.50	.032
P	7/15	7	396	—	1894	10.00	.025
	7/15	—	431	—	1900	10.00	.023
	7/15	—	518	—	1852	10.00	.019

continued

TABLE 12 (Continued)

Firm	PW Issue (1968)	No. of Prelim. Pages	Total Pages	New Matter Added	Orig. Pubn. Date	List Price	Average Price per Page
Q	7/29	—	411	—	1911	$14.75	$.036
	8/19	5	217	Intro.	1955	9.25	.043
	10/14	17	529	Ill., Maps	1936	21.00	.040
	12/16	11	456	—	1924	18.50	.041
R	12/16	4	104	Ill.	1900	17.50	.168
S	7/30	9	542	Ill., Maps	1947	12.50	.023
	5/27	13	204	—	1939	7.50	.037
	9/30	9	118	Ill.	1949	5.50	.047
T	4/8	9	382	Intro.	1924	12.95	.034
	6/3	12	645	—	1929	15.95	.025
U	1/29	—	232	—	1847	8.50	.037
	2/19	—	189	Maps	1955	15.00	.079
	6/3	4	233	—	1938	28.35	.122
V	9/9	41	567	—	1777	25.00	.044
	6/3	8	509	—	1881	5.00	.010
	11/18	8	171	—	1877	7.50	.044
W	1/29	21	371	Intro.	1911	12.50	.034
	6/3	—	194	—	1921	6.50	.034
	9/30	—	256	—	1922	7.50	.029
X	8/19	17	212	Ill., Plans	1959	19.50	.092
	8/19	22	443	Plates	1947	30.00	.068
	10/28	—	342	—	1951	12.00	.035
Y	8/26	10	152	—	1939	8.00	.053
Z	5/20	14	498	Addenda	1936	10.00	.020
	6/3	10	185	—	1954	7.50	.041
aa	9/30	18	240	Ill.	1936	8.00	.033
bb	2/12	14	454	Ill.	1952	13.00	.029
	2/19	8	351	Maps	1927	9.00	.026
	3/18	—	61	—	1936	5.00	.082
cc	9/9	—	506	—	1955	12.50	.025
	12/2	12	255	Ill.	1894	4.50	.018
dd	4/29	—	88	—	1903	4.00	.046
	10/14	—	536	—	1847	13.50	.025
ee[a]	5/20	—	1511	Ill., Maps	1951	30.00	.020
	6/3	16	702	Ill., Port.	1950	10.00	.014
ff	8/26	9	653	Plates	—	10.00	.015
	12/16	41	249	Ill.	1897	2.95	.012
gg	3/18	22	121	Edited	1587	10.00	.083
		Total	25,222			$875.90	(.035)

Source: *Publishers' Weekly*, 1968 "Weekly Record" Section.
a Each of these titles issued in two volumes, but can be purchased separately at half the total price shown.

To offset any inadvertent bias in the selection of titles from *PW*, a third study was made. Catalogs from ten well-known reprint publishers were searched. The first three titles that qualified (same criteria as for the *PW* sample above) from each subject section of each catalog made up the sample. The average retail price per book (162 books) was found to be about $13; the average retail price per page (69,584 pages) again about 3¢. The per page price varies among the ten publishers from a low of about 2¢ per page (retail) to slightly more than 6¢ per page, supporting the theory of pricing variance noted earlier.

One might conclude from this evidence that reprints are not as unreasonably high-priced as has been suggested. Yet, the omission of periodical sets and series or other multivolume works undoubtedly skews these figures to the low end of the price curve. One might speculate that it is *these* forms that are the expensive reprints causing outrage. Pricing practices for reprints other than hardcover monographs need further study. Because pagination for such reprints generally is not advertised, the works would need to be examined item by item.[10]

Perhaps the most interesting and significant pricing study undertaken in the present survey (obvious pitfalls notwithstanding) was one which compared prices for the same reprint titles published by more than one reprint firm. Titles that were duplicated (or triplicated) in the author entries in the letters A, B, and C in NCR's *Guide to Reprints, 1969* comprised this structured sample. (See Table 13.) Ninety-five titles were found to be issued by more than one publisher (and this only from the first three letters of the alphabet!) with the unexpected discovery that, if any buyer selected only the least expensive edition of each of these 95 titles, he would spend almost $665 *less* than if all the more expensive editions were purchased.

If the same pattern held true for the entries in the remaining 23 letters of the alphabet an additional $5,320 could possibly be saved. This amount of money is so considerable that the findings suggest that reprint buyers need to be alert to the possibilities of saving a large sum of money if they select carefully. In the long run, of course, some titles might be more of a bargain bought in the most expensive editions, but this should be carefully ascertained by comparing products, not titles.

PUBLIC DOMAIN, COPYRIGHT, AND THE PAYMENT OF ROYALTIES

As background for interpreting publishers' responses to Question 25 (proportion of titles on list in public domain, i.e., unprotected by copyright in this country) and Question 26 (opinion about royalty payments on noncopyrighted works), it should be noted that some reprint publishers and critics of the industry have reacted heatedly, in published and in private statements, to the question of whether an author, heirs, or the

TABLE 13
RETAIL PRICE COMPARISONS OF TITLES ISSUED BY
TWO OR MORE U.S. PUBLISHERS

Author (N = 95)	List Prices		Price Differential[a]
Adair	$ 20.00	$ 22.50	$ 2.50
Adams, E. D.	11.00	10.00	1.00
Adams, J. T.	8.95	12.00	3.05
Aitken	24.95	31.25	6.10
Alcott	4.95	5.95	1.00
Allen, C. D.	17.50(1894)	10.00(1895)	7.50
Allen, F. H.	21.50	8.50	13.00
Allen, W.	45.00	40.00	5.00
Ambler, C. H.	15.00	8.50	6.50
Amer. Dict. of Printing	19.00	27.50	8.50
Amer. J. of Psychology	1,450.00	1,518.00	68.00
Amer. Philological Assn. Trans.	560.00	560.00	—
Andrews, A.	21.95	24.00	2.05
Andrews, W. (& William)[b]	4.75	4.75	—
Ashton, J.	12.50	12.75	.25
Ashton, J. (& John)	10.00	10.00	—
Ashton, J.	12.50	9.50	3.00
Atkings, J. W. H.	8.50	4.00	4.50
Atkinson, G.	10.00	15.00	5.00
Baker, G. P.	35.00	7.50	27.50
Baker, S. W. (& Sir S. W.)	30.00	18.50	11.50
Bateson, F. W.	5.00	6.00	1.00
Bax, E. B.	12.50	9.50	3.00
Beard, C. A.	8.00	6.00	2.00
Beecham, J.	20.00	15.00	5.00
Bekker, W. G.	6.50	7.00	1.50
Bishop, C. F.	13.50	7.50	6.00
Bishop, J. L.	50.00	60.00	10.00
Bisschop, W. R.	10.00	16.50	6.50
Bjorkman, Erik	12.95	12.95	—
Black, W. G. (& Wm. G.)	10.00	12.50	2.50
Blackwell, A. S.	12.50	19.50	7.00
Bohn, H. G. (& Henry G.)	12.50	14.50	2.00
Bonner, R. J.	18.50	25.00	7.50
Boswell, E.	12.50	8.50	4.00
Boucher, C. S.	14.25	10.00	4.25
Bougainville, L.	26.50	25.00	1.50
Boulenger, J. (& J. R.)[c]	3.85	25.00	21.15
Bourgeois, M.	10.00	9.00	1.00
Bowden, W.	12.50	15.00	2.50
Box, P. H.	8.50	14.00	4.00

TABLE 13 (Continued)

Author (N = 95)	List Prices		Price Differential[a]
Bozon, N.	$ 17.50	$ 18.00	$ .50
Brackett, A. G.	12.00	15.00	3.00
Brennecke, E. (& Ernest)	6.50	15.00	8.50
Brooke, S. A.	7.00	8.00	1.00
Brown, A. (Alexander)	16.00	13.95	3.95
Brownson's Quarterly	600.00	580.00	20.00
Bryant, W. C.	20.00	17.50	2.50
Bucher, C.	10.00	9.00	1.00
Buckingham	17.00	19.95	2.95
Budd	6.00[d]	17.50	11.50
Budge, E. A. W.	12.50	6.50	6.00
Burroughs, E. R.	10.50[e]	4.00[e]	6.50
Buxton, C. R. (& Charles)	6.00	4.95	2.95
Buxton, T. C.	18.00	14.50	4.50
Caird, E.	32.00	32.00	—
Calhoun, J. (& John C.)	85.00	69.95	15.05
Campbell, O. W. (& Olwen)	8.50	8.25	.25
Carey, H. C.	6.50	8.50	2.00
Carpenter, F. I.	4.50	14.00	9.50
Case, S. J.	11.50	14.50	3.00
Catch Club of Merry Companions	9.50[f]	7.00[f]	2.50
Catterall, H. H. (& H. T.)	123.50	200.00	76.50
Chalmers, A.	650.00	650.00	—
Chamberlain, C. J.	20.00	5.00	15.00
Chartist Circular	110.00	75.00	35.00
Charvat, W.	3.75	8.50	4.75
Chekhov, A.	8.50	4.00	4.50
Cherniss, H.	12.50	9.00	3.50
Chesnutt, C. W. (& Chestnett, C. W.)	10.00	12.50	2.50
Chesnutt, C. W. (& Chestnett, C. W.)	10.00	15.00	5.00
Chevalier, M. (& Michael)	12.50	5.00	7.50
Child, L. M.	9.75 (1833)	7.00 (1836)	2.75
Cibber	27.50	14.50	13.00
Clark, T. D.	2.45	5.00	2.55
Clarke, P. N.	7.50	7.50	—
Clawsing, R.	25.00	12.50	12.50
Clymer, Wm. B. S. (& Wm. Branford S.)	7.95	7.95	—
Cobb, S. H.	16.50	12.50	4.00

continued

TABLE 13 (Continued)

Author (N = 95)	List Prices		Price Differential[a]
Cobbett, W.	$1,250.00	$1,250.00	$ —
Coffin, L.	18.00	15.00	3.00
Conway, M. D. (& Moncure Daniel)	9.95	9.95	—
Cook, Albert S.	14.95	14.95	—
Cook, Sir Edw. T. (& Sir Edward Tyas)	35.00	35.00	—
Cooke, G. W.	15.00	15.00	—
Corns, A. R.	16.50	14.50	2.00
Courtney, W. P. (& William P.)	14.50	12.50	2.00
Cowper, W. (& Wm. & William)	82.50	49.00 49.00	33.50
Crane, T. F.	18.50	15.00	3.50
Crawford, C.	70.00	97.50	27.50
Creizenach, W.	12.50	15.00	3.50
Cressey, P. G.	8.50	12.00 15.50	7.00
Croly, H. D.	13.00	11.00	2.00
Crosby, S. (& Sylvester S.)	25.00	18.50	6.50
Cuthbertson, J. (& John)	17.50	25.00	7.50
Total Price Differential			$663.05

Source: *Guide to Reprints: 1969* (Washington, D.C.: NCR Microcard Editions, 1969), pp. 1–40.
a Price differential is calculated to be the difference in retail price between the least expensive and the most expensive edition listed.
b Items in parenthesis in Author column indicate that the titles are not consecutively listed in the alphabetical author list in the Guide, due to different style of author entry.
c Title varies.
d Title is offered as part of a microfilm series.
e One firm offers three titles at $3.50 each; the other firm's title is three volumes in one at $4.00.
f One firm issues two volumes at $5.00 each, or $9.50 the set; the other is an edited edition.

original publishers should be offered payments for reprints that are in the public domain in the United States. Publishers have diametrically opposed viewpoints, and some are middle-of-the-roaders.

Complex matters pertaining to the status of the copyright law and its potentially imminent revision, and the very considerable differences between United States and international copyright laws fall beyond this present study's scope, but the fact is that "there is no such thing as an 'international copyright' that will automatically protect an author's writings throughout the world."[11]

British works published before 1956, when the United States joined the Universal Copyright Convention (UCC), are unprotected in this country, even though a British publisher may hold copyright abroad. The U.S. Copyright Office provides a special five-year "ad interim" copyright, obtainable upon request, for English-language books and periodicals manufactured and first published outside the United States. The works must be registered here within six months after first publication abroad. Importation of up to 1,500 copies of the foreign edition is permitted.

Under the copyright law, once a work falls into the public domain it may never again be copyrighted. Only new matter added to reprints is copyrightable. A public domain title may therefore be copied freely by one publisher, or by as many as select the title for republishing. This fact accounts for rival reprint programs and leads to criticism from some quarters of the "outrageously high" prices charged for "mere" reprints.

Whether or not a title is in the public domain in this country is generally assumed to be a matter of great significance to reprint publishers. Public domain status eliminates any legal need to secure publishing rights and permissions. Some persons apparently feel that public domain (versus copyright) status strongly influences a publisher's selection of titles. It has also been noted that if a title is in the public domain, reprinters save time and money that would be incurred if the firm had to seek and to pay for copyrights and legal permissions.

Though data for a reprint manufacturing cost analysis were not obtained for this survey, as noted earlier, there are reasons to believe that the price-public domain relationship is one of the myths surrounding the reprint industry. Public domain status does not appear to be at the nub of the pricing problems. Yet the public domain feature is an aspect that is largely responsible for many so-called unethical traits of reprinters. There are skeptics who view the reprint scene as the place where "book-aneers" become "buck-aneers," stealthily procuring free titles and turning them into gold.

For these reasons at least, the evidence provided by publishers' responses to Questions 25 and 26 is highly significant. Only 67 firms, or slightly more than half of the respondents (i.e., 56 percent), have a majority of public domain titles on their lists. Fewer than half of the titles that comprise the lists of 50 firms are public domain titles. An unanticipated finding is that 8 reprint publishers report no public domain titles on their lists. One firm that reported more than half of its titles in the public domain anticipates that proportion will decrease radically in the seventies, a statement echoed by several of the interviewed publishers. (See Table 14.)

Because the interviewees had more opportunity to discuss this changing trend, i.e., from reprinting public domain to reprinting copyrighted works, it may be worthwhile to interject some of these publishers' opinions here.

The major reason for reissuing works still under copyright involved securing titles that publishers feel are needed to round out reprint series or programs on related subjects. If a publisher deems a title essential to a

TABLE 14

PROPORTION OF PUBLIC-DOMAIN TITLES ON LIST, AND PUBLISHER'S
ATTITUDE TOWARD PAYING ROYALTIES

Titles in Public Domain	No. of Firms	Attitude Toward Paying Royalties					
		Highly Favor	Generally Favor	Indif-ferent	Generally Opposed	Highly Opposed	Don't Know
All or most	31	1ᵃ	8	3	12	7	1
More than half	18	4	8	2	2	2	0
Less than half	10	0	6	1	2	0	0
Few	21	3	6	4	5	2	1
None	3	1	1	0	1	0	0
TOTAL	83ᵇ	9	29	10	22	11	2

Source: Response to Questions 25 and 26.
a One firm that did not dig out information in response to Question 25 "always pays royalties to someone, even where in the public domain," and is included in column "a" by presumption of the writer.
b Questionnaire forms were returned by 87 respondents. Four were not usable. These publishers provided either question marks or exclamation points as responses.

program, and if the title is in copyright, the publisher must negotiate for reprinting rights in order to stay within the law. If, on the other hand, that same publisher had been one who had previously engaged in "piracy" (particularly of titles published abroad), chances are good that the copyright holder will not be prone to deal on friendly terms; indeed he may prefer not to do business with that firm at all. It is therefore as *a safeguard for long-range planning* and to protect their future relations within the worldwide publishing community that some publishers pay for copyrighted material that they reprint. Among reprinters there are also a large number of men and women who believe that authors and/or the original publishers are entitled to payments for their original creations.

Altruism aside, there is a further, perhaps obvious, point to make. Copyright status prevents one reprinter from republishing the works of another. The results of this question should be considered in relation to the responses made by publishers to Question 26, which asked about payment of royalties on titles not under copyright.

It should be emphasized that firms that choose not to pay for reprinting public domain materials are within their legal rights as the laws now stand. Those who pay royalties or fees for public domain materials do so out of a sense of responsibility to the owner or creator of the original works, or to protect their relationships with firms with whom they might wish to continue doing business concerning copyrighted materials in their possession.

Several of the interviewed publishers noted that they make a practice of checking the records of the Copyright Office. If they find that a British publisher has made the effort to secure short-term protection, they pay royalties or ask for rights to reprint even if his five-year copyright has lapsed.

Problems occur within the reprint industry and in its relationship with other types of publishers because some publishers do not follow what others believe is the spirit of the copyright laws.[12] It is not for this survey to judge the merits or the ethics of each point of view, but rather to report the reprint publisher's expressed opinions. The findings from this query (Question 26) follow.

To seek emerging patterns from the variety of responses to Question 26, each answer was interpreted into one of five opinion ranges. These responses were also correlated with responses to Question 25 to determine to what extent the proportion of public domain titles on a firm's list is related to the publisher's decision regarding royalty payments. (See Table 14.)

Taking into account here only the stronger expressions (highly or generally opposed to, or in favor of, royalties), as might be expected, 19 publishers who have all or most public domain titles are firmly or generally opposed to royalty payments, as compared with 9 who favor payments. In an interesting switch, as the number of public domain titles on publishers' lists decreases, the attitude toward paying royalty payments becomes more favorable. The total number of questionnaire respondents who favor royalty payments (38 firms) is slightly higher that the number opposed (33 firms.)

Interviewee responses to the query about royalty payments tend to raise the favorable response even higher. Royalty payments were discussed with 20 firms. Only 3 publishers pay no royalties for titles that are not copyrighted, while 17 always pay royalties or negotiate for permission to reprint.

To summarize these findings, the total number of reprint publishers known to favor royalty payments is 55 firms (38 questionnaire respondents and 17 interviewed publishers). This number is significantly higher than the number opposed to payments—36 firms.

Actual responses to Question 26 reveal a variety of positions, and give some insight into the varied personalities of the people in the industry. Many publishers say they spend a lot of time and effort to search for heirs and "old authors." To conclude this review on a light note, one might presume that an enterprising businessman could establish a new and vital service for the reprint industry: a Bureau of Potential Royalty Recipients (BPRR).

ASSOCIATION OF REPRINT PUBLISHERS

The concept of a reprinters' association is not a new one, but has recently surfaced again as an area of heightened interest among some reprint firms. No reprinters' association now exists. Publishers were asked whether or not they favored meeting with their colleagues to discuss the possibility of forming some kind of an association of reprint publishers. Fifty-five percent of the publishers (152) responded to the question.

About 66 percent of the respondents (101 firms) expressed a degree of willingness to meet for further discussion. Of this group, 75 publishers appeared more or less enthusiastic about the idea of discussing an association, while 19 indicated that they would probably meet for discussion but stated very clearly their insistence upon knowing the purposes and procedures of such a group meeting. Specifically they point to federal antitrust laws and note the need to avoid any possible accusation of collusion in restrain of trade. Many publishers are reluctant to discuss such an organization for fear of future suspicion on the part of the federal government or other publishers that attempts were made to control public domain materials. The author has a list of publishers' positions at the time they answered the question. This listing could be provided to those concerned in constructive efforts to call future meetings.

Qualified interest in meeting was shown by 11 firms with comments such as "If convenient," "We may be too small to be involved," and "It may be too time-consuming."

Among the publishers who expressed enthusiasm about holding further discussions about an association are Garrett Press, Inc.; Patterson Smith Publishing Corporation; Kennikat Press; Arno Press, Inc.; Research Reprints, Inc.; Library Editions, Inc.; and Lawrence Verry, Inc. It should be noted that since these findings were analyzed, several of the respondents have become members of the Association of American Publishers (AAP), an indication of their willingness and desire to join the publishing industry mainstream rather than establish a separate special-interest group.

Another cluster of publishers thought that the idea of a reprint association is good in principle but might be unrealistic in practice, because of the competitive nature of the reprint business. They are Shoestring Press, Genealogical Publishing Company, Barnes & Noble, Hafner Publishing Company, and Russell & Russell. Barnes & Noble and Russell & Russell (Atheneum) are members of the AAP.

Some pros and cons of group involvement were raised in open discussion at the April 23, 1970, meeting called by the ALA Reprinting Committee and the then American Book Publishers Council (now the AAP). More than 70 reprint publishers attended. The idea of an association surfaced as a primary topic. On the matter of forming an association, Sanford Cobb, AAP's president, offered the advice of the AAP's legal counsel to interested reprint publishers, and also suggested the possibility of divisional status for reprint publishers within the AAP, if the members of the association found such a division necessary.

Some people can see strong points in favor of a group effort. An association of reprint publishers with staff and facilities to develop programs might offer help in encouraging standards of reprint quality; a central source of information and guidance for new entrants into the industry; a public relations effort to enhance the overall reputation of the industry; plans to exhibit reprint products cooperatively at professional meetings; a clearinghouse to collect and disseminate public information to publishers and to prospective customers; a focal point for liaison between reprinters and other publishers, library, and other professional associations that relate to reprinting; ways of informing publishers about developments in allied fields, such as graphic arts, micropublishing, and librarianship; and most important, a collective voice of responsible publishers to help gain funding support for educational and library programs. These purposes would also be served if reprint publishers joined the existing trade associations.

On the other hand, the competitive nature of the reprint industry does indeed make it clear why some publishers feel they have little need, and less desire, to share their "trade secrets," or to set themselves up as advisers to their competitors. These are complex matters which cannot be solved here.

What the collected evidence does make clear is that a large number of publishers apparently are ready and willing to talk further about a reprint association. The ball is in the hands of the reprinters; it is up to them to decide whether or not formal cooperation would benefit them and their customers at this time.

Chapter 8

The Marketing and Distribution of Reprints

It is generally believed, as Lacy has stated, that libraries have a strong determinative effect on the reprint industry.[1] This assumption is supported firmly by the way publishers defined their reprint markets in the present survey. If for none other than pragmatic reasons, therefore, publishers need to understand the problems librarians have as buyers of reprints, as lenders of material for copying, and as the professional group probably most concerned with the content and quality of reprints.

Up to now, the industry has been described mostly from the trade's view. In this and subsequent chapters, as we look at reprinting from the librarian's perspective as well, the communality of interests between publishers—including reprinters—and librarians, so well described by Castagna, becomes increasingly clear.[2] So do some of the sources of discontent. It is hoped that this tandem presentation will stimulate creative problem-solving efforts to mutual advantage, for publishers and librarians should be working together to meet the real requirements of the situation.

A large number of publishers who contributed to these findings did, in fact, express a serious desire to learn more about library processes and needs. Many of their questions dovetail, like jigsaw puzzle pieces, with problems identified by librarians. For instance, publishers have questions about borrowing materials to copy; librarians are perplexed about lending them. Publishers ask about cataloging and bibliographic techniques; librarians wonder why all publishers do not consistently provide basic, accurate information about each title published. While publishers devise standing order plans with new wrinkles, librarians reexamine the value of existing purchasing systems for reprints. Publishers question why librarians want or need original place and date of publication information printed in the book and in promotional literature; librarians ask how any thoughtful publisher could omit such essential bibliographic information.

The Library of Congress is not a reprint publisher, but the Library is necessarily concerned with reprints for a variety of reasons. Some publishers question what their own role should be in providing customers with LC cards and card numbers, and what LC's responsibility is with regard to the consistent cataloging of reprints, particularly microforms. It should be noted that since July 1971, when the Cataloging in Publication (CIP) Program was funded (by matching grants from the Council of Library Resources, Inc. and the National Endowment for the Humanities) and implemented by LC, the relationship between reprinters and the Library has improved dramatically. In very simplistic terms, CIP is a program designed to permit the Library to catalog books before publication. In cooperation with publishers the Library sends catalog data to those who submit galleys or data sheets and agree to print this information in their books, usually on the copyright page. The purpose of CIP is to help librarians diminish serious cataloging backlog problems and avoid duplication of cataloging efforts locally. CIP is not an altruistic program. Realistic advantages are anticipated for librarians and publishers alike. CIP extends the active life of books by getting them to readers quickly. Publishers hope that "freed" library funds (i.e., those saved in technical processing) will be invested in buying more books. It is the mutuality of interest that makes CIP more than an empty goodwill promise.

Four reprinters were among the first 27 active CIP publishers. When LC designed the data-gathering forms for CIP, it made extensive efforts to identify cataloging problems which might be unique to reprinters, and provided a special data-collection tool for reprints that would compensate for the lack of galley proofs in the reprinting process. Republished monographs in microform are included in the CIP. In numerous other ways (e.g., preassigning LC card numbers, putting CIP onto MARC tapes, etc.) the Library provides help to participating CIP publishers. Those reprinters who have wisely decided to cooperate will continue to benefit from working closely with LC on CIP, which is an important breakthrough in publisher-library relations and is one tangible step many reprinters have taken to enter the bibliographic mainstream and thus improve their relations with their customers and with the library world generally. Reprint publishers participating in the CIP Program as of March 1972 are identified in the Directory.

MARKETS FOR REPRINTS

Publishers were asked to identify their markets. As shown in Tables 15 and 16, 150 publishers provided usable responses, selecting relevant options from seven categories offered, or providing new insights about reprint markets. Before discussing these responses, a few remarks about

TABLE 15
MARKETS FOR REPRINTS RANKED BY 116 PUBLISHERS

Markets	Markets, Ranked[a]							
	1	2	3	4	5	6	7	0
	No. of Publishers							
College & university libraries	78	16	9	7	2	0	1	10
Wholesalers (jobbers)	16	27	11	9	7	4	0	32
Secondary schools & libraries	14	5	13	12	15	13	1	31
Public libraries	24	28	22	16	9	6	0	10
Bookstores	22	9	14	18	17	4	0	26
Individual customers	35	10	18	8	9	15	6	18
Other[b]	2	3	2	0	1	3	2	0

Source: Responses to Question 19. The 78 firms that ranked college and university libraries as primary are 61 percent of the 116 respondents.
Note: The number of firms in the primary categories (b–g) is more than the total number of respondents because some publishers indicated that more than one type of market is of primary or of equal importance.
[a] The rankings 1–7 identify the primary through least important market. Ranking 0 indicates the publisher does not sell to this market.
[b] Other markets specified are special libraries (law, theological, historical society, genealogical, hospital and nursing homes, seminary and bible institutes); graduate students; religious congregations, "outdoor stores," teachers, authors, and own staff.

the design, wording, and tabulation of these data are in order. First, two university press publishers returned questionnaire forms with comments about the market categories listed in Table 15. James W. Torrence, Jr., sales manager of Stanford University Press, stated that "wholesalers and bookstores sell to other categories listed; they are not a market." Thompson Webb, Jr., director of the University of Wisconsin Press, noted that "wholesalers sell to libraries, so it is all one market."

Possibly there is ambiguity between the terms "market" and "distribution channel." It is not known whether any other publishers were troubled by the categories, although none said they were. Because the question was so interpreted by two knowledgeable publishers, however, the findings should be cautiously considered.

Second, 19 publishers who returned questionnaire forms did not rank their responses, but checked more than one kind of market. Although they assigned no priorities, these responses do define the markets a publisher considers his targets, and therefore are significant. For this reason, the number of responses in the tabulations exceeds the total number of respondents.

Third, the unexpectedly large number of permutations (92) in the multiple markets publishers selected suggests a larger degree of difference in marketing practices than was anticipated. Such a wide variety of reprints and types of publishers are clustered into the findings, however, that the seeming disparity may be more a function of unmatched publisher characteristics than is evident. Future research should be directed towards clarifying this question.

Last, this study's effort to secure marketing and distribution information can be considered only a preliminary attempt to seek factual information about major reprint markets and to begin to understand what other markets publishers consider important. This topic needs to be explored in greater depth to learn how reprints are sold, to whom and with what problems. What new markets might reprinters anticipate? How could more customers (students, perhaps) be served better by the industry? Indeed, when it comes to marketing and distribution of all kinds of books, not only reprints, a great deal more systematic research is needed and should be undertaken.

Almost 75 percent (78 firms) of the 116 publishers who responded to the question asking them to define their markets indicated that they sell most of their reprints to college and university libraries. The second-ranking "primary" market is, unexpectedly, individual buyers, the most important customers for 35 firms. In contrast, however, 18 firms do not generally sell to individual customers. A few more unanticipated responses are worth noting. Specifically, the data reveal that:

1. At least 10 firms do not sell reprints to college and university libraries.

2. Public libraries are the most important market for 24 firms and the second most important for 28 firms.

3. Bookstores, ranked as primary market by 22 firms, are not considered an important market by 26 firms.

4. Wholesalers are a primary market (distribution channel?) for 16 firms, but 32 reprinters do not sell at all through wholesalers.

Six publishers mentioned the difficulty they have in knowing how to sell reprints to public libraries. They questioned library selection and acquisition policies, and which public library office or kinds of personnel are generally responsible for the selection of reprints and for purchase approvals. Several publishers asked if there is a difference in the procedures for buying reprints and original books, and a few wondered if there is a price ceiling (and what that is) over which a reprint purchase needs special authorization. A large number of publishers asked to what extent public librarians depend upon standard recommended booklists for reprint title selection.

By the end of the 1960s, many firms that acknowledged primary dependence upon the library market revealed their apprehension about the effect decreases in federal funds for the purchase of library materials would have on reprint sales. Although the facts are undocumented by solid research, subsequent events appear to have proved their fears justified. A large number of firms began to search for ways to diversify or broaden their publishing programs in order to take up the slack in reprint sales accompanying a falling-off of library support. In a backhanded way, perhaps this economic jolt to complacency points to a more creative, if smaller, reprint industry. More years must pass before one can assume a historical overview.

LIBRARY BUYING POWER

Let us look more at the magnitude of the reprint explosion. We are told that American book publication has been doubling in output faster than the population doubles.[3] The total number of titles published in the United States has roughly tripled in the past 15 years, rising from 12,589 titles in 1955 to 36,071 titles published in 1970.[4]

We are informed by Orne that nearly a billion dollars was spent on college and university library building in the five years from 1967–1971, providing accommodations for 127,377,821 volumes![5] There is no doubt that a significant percentage of the upsurge of titles published in this country in recent years are the products of the reprint sector, and that they were produced to occupy some of these newly created libiary shelves. Scholarly reprints accounted for about a third of the 1969 title output (see Chapter 5) and perhaps slightly more than a third of the "new" titles published in 1970 and 1971. These latter estimates are based on the number of reprints tagged on some Library of Congress MARC tapes and on projections of reprints entering the CIP Program.

Periodical publishing, which has traditionally catered to the demand for rapid access to specialized knowledge, has also proliferated so extensively that libraries cannot seriously consider buying and housing original copies of more than a small fraction of the current titles in a single collection.[6] Retrospective collections of periodicals and other long serial runs in microform are therefore increasingly appealing to libraries. Because of changing attitudes among librarians, reprint publishers have to acknowledge the following problems that affect their business.

Librarians now generally understand that it is impractical to make local collections self-sufficient. Building a comprehensive collection has become mostly an ideal, and some even question how ideal this ideal really is.[7] Yet, despite expanded interlibrary loans, networks for sharing educational resources, consortia, and other cooperative and centralized library systems, a considerable number of libraries do continue to build and maintain local collections of a size and variety that stimulates the publishing industry.[8] In addition, many institutions seek to strengthen or change their library collections to meet new missions, and they need to make critical acquisitions decisions.[9] Retrospective buying, while it might not approach the tremendous heights of the early sixties, is still necessary for special-purpose materials and for new libraries.

There are, unfortunately, no current, reliable figures that report how many reprints have been purchased by libraries, nor is the proportion of library budgets allocated to retrospective buying precisely known. In

1965, Goldwin Smith of Wayne State University remarked that our libraries were spending more than $7 million a year to purchase reprints.[10] Libraries certainly invested vastly larger amounts of money in the reprint market from the mid-sixties through 1970. There will probably be a lessening of library building and buying in the remaining years of the 1970s, but reprint buying should not, as some publishers glumly predict, bottom out.

In order to estimate roughly the amount of library money entering the reprint market, let us assume that 10,000 reprint titles are published annually. This is about a third of the annual U.S. title output. If every reprinter sells 100 copies of each of his hardcopy titles to libraries (probably high for a few reprinters, but low for most others), the number of hardcopy reprints bought by libraries in a year reaches a million. This estimate is believed to be at the low end of the curve. There are, as noted earlier, some similarities (and obvious differences) between scholarly reprint publishing and university press publishing. Herbert S. Bailey, Jr., director, Princeton University Press, estimates the library sale of a specialized historical monograph to be around 500–1,000 copies. He is speaking of new books, not reprints, but the kinds of audiences those books seek is similar—librarians and scholars interested in specialized subjects.[11]

At an estimated average retail price of $12 per copy (see Table 11), the magnitude of library reprint-buying-power becomes obvious. Based on these conservative figures, libraries have been spending at least $12 million annually for hardcopy reprints. In addition, libraries are the primary purchasers of other forms of reprinted works (periodical sets and the like) and they buy vast numbers of titles republished in microform.

In light of the significance of library purchasing to the reprint industry, it is important to recognize that librarians have developed very mixed attitudes towards the reprint industry.[12] Assiduous publishers earn praise for responding to library needs with more and better reprints,[13] but librarians take a dim view of those publishers suspected of gorging themselves at library troughs.[14] Harold E. Samuel, editor of *Notes: The Quarterly Journal of the Music Library Association,* pinpointed the issue. In a personal letter to the author (December 23, 1969), he wrote, "Some reprinters are making a marvelous contribution to the literature and others are proliferating junk."

REPRINT DISTRIBUTION CHANNELS

The availability of reprints through different kinds of distribution channels probably affects their purchase by libraries for several reasons. First, the way books are distributed seems to relate significantly to the methods publishers use to advertise and promote their wares. Second, certain kinds of libraries (e.g., schools and some public libraries) are either accustomed to purchasing through library jobbers or by law must buy library materials on a bid system.

Question 20 asked publishers through which of the following outlets their reprints are sold: by direct mail, through wholesalers, bookstores, or other methods, and, further, to rank these outlets.

All or part of this question was answered by 124 respondents. Two nonrespondents are printers who presumably "dispose" of their products, except for titles published under their own imprint, by direction of others who pay the printing bills.

The question attempted to determine *how many* firms utilize each type of sales outlet, the *relative importance* of each outlet to publishers who sell through more than one, and what *"other" sales outlets*, if any, publishers consider important.

The responses reveal that reprints are sold primarily by direct mail; 104 firms, or 84 percent of the respondents, identified this sales outlet as one of their choices. Of the 104 firms, 82 selected direct mail as their *primary* sales outlet, 15 sell primarily through bookstores, and 12 primarily through wholesalers. An unexpectedly large number of firms state that these two latter outlets, while not of primary importance, are significant. That is, 71 firms (57 percent) cite booksellers and 68 firms (55 percent) cite wholesalers as sales outlets. The relative importance (i.e., ranking) of each outlet indicates that, while only 10 firms specify that they do not sell by direct mail, 34 do not sell through wholesalers and 30 do not sell through bookstores.

Ten firms sell reprints primarily through "other" outlets, including their own sales force (six firms), and distribution through large trade houses (one firm). Also cited as "other" outlets are: "our own membership and individuals who see our titles in libraries," "personal calls," and "requests made by individuals to our company." Two firms that selected "other" outlets as a fourth choice cited "scholarly media advertising," and "over the counter sales." Three did not rank "other," but cited "individual book collectors who visit our workshop or studio," "word of mouth," and "advertising in professional and consumer magazines," especially the *Saturday Review* and *The New York Times*.

The only sales outlet other than direct mail cited by a significant number of publishers is the secondary dependence upon wholesalers, noted by 41 firms, or 32 percent of the respondents. A composite of this information revealed that the most frequently cited combination of sales outlets is direct mail, wholesalers, and bookstores, ranked in that order by 36 firms. The second most frequent pattern to emerge was exclusive dependence upon direct mail (25 firms.).

To determine whether or not a particular size firm tends to favor a single outlet or a particular combination of sales outlets, data were cross-tabulated. No definite sales pattern emerges as a function of company size, although the data suggest that both small publishers with fewer than 50 titles, and publishers with more than 5,000 titles, sell primarily by direct mail.

What do these figures mean? We know that a large proportion of the antiquarian booksellers are in the small-firm category, and that the majority of companies that publish more than 5,000 titles are micropublishers. One might assume therefore that these two types of publishers sell mostly by direct mail. These data, more suggestive than definitive, are interesting as a preliminary excursion into unexplored reprint distribution channels. It should be useful to publishers and prospective purchasers alike to collect and analyze more data about reprint distribution.

That the reprint industry is primarily a direct mail industry is significant for a variety of reasons. As Daniel Melcher and Nancy Larrick explain in their useful *Printing and Promotion Handbook,* the mail order industry is highly specialized, and selling books by mail is more difficult than the novice sometimes assumes. The authors wisely stress the importance of utilizing reliable mailing lists, noting that the difference between a 2 and a 3 percent return may make all the difference between loss and profit. And, they add, "It is hard to make ends meet on units of sale of less than $5.00 unless repeat business is expected."[15]

This last statement is particularly meaningful to reprint publishers and offers another explanation for the promotion of publishers' series and standing-order purchase plans. Mail-order selling also directly affects:

1. The relationship publishers establish and maintain with their customers. Do customers feel badgered by too-frequent mailings from publishers and by receipt of duplicate mailings, or is there a hunger for more or different kinds of information? How can publishers effectively assess the value of direct-mail promotion in terms of actual sales? In terms of building a favorable regard for their firms?

2. Competition among reprint publishers. With so many firms utilizing direct-mail techniques, are individual firms' efforts dissipated? Might cooperative catalogs be feasible or useful, perhaps something similar to the Dutch Reprint Publishers *Joint Catalogue?* (Volume I: 1967–1968, 99pp.; Volume II: 1969–1970, 72pp. Issued by the Associated Publishers, Amsterdam. Volume II states: ". . . issued by fourteen Dutch publishers, each specializing in one or more field, in order to furnish librarians and scholars with a guide to new scientific publications and a permanent work of reference. . . . The publishers mentioned . . . have decided to work in closer association. . . .")

3. Discount practices and schedules. Booksellers are increasingly discontent with some publishers who, by selling only by direct mail, bypass the retailer or create an embarrassing business climate between the bookseller and his customers. Bookstores (and some jobbers) obviously feel an economic hardship if they are obligated to supply books published by houses that grant inadequate discounts, or none at all.

Distributors who prefer not to handle, or who are not encouraged to handle, titles from no-discount publishers face discontented customers. "The Opinionated Man," G. Roysce Smith, who retired in 1971 from his position as book department manager, Yale University Co-op, and others have discussed these matters in spirited *PW* articles. The points they make need not be repeated here, but the need for publishers of special-ized scholarly titles to review and to be alert to the consequences of their marketing methods and policies is highlighted in Smith's remark:

> The abuses which have gradually proliferated in the use of direct mail threaten to undermine publisher-retailer and customer-retailer relations and to operate to the ultimate detriment of the entire industry. Therefore [he offers six suggestions] a more formal guide for the use of direct mail by a mature and responsible indus-try . . . is recommended.[16]

Paperback scholarly reprint houses that publish many titles of a fairly general nature (Dover, for example) frequently sell through bookstores and wholesalers, seeking the advantage of wide distribution and exposure that is not usually gained by direct mail selling alone. In interviews, several hardcover reprinters expressed hesitancy about utilizing outlets that would "force" them to allow discounts. They suggested that they would need to raise retail prices in order to give booksellers or other middlemen reasonable discounts. Perhaps this is a shortsighted view, since increased sales which could result from wider distribution might offset higher selling costs and still return a respectable profit. Most impor-tantly, as the *Times Literary Supplement* has often noted, more students and scholars would be given an opportunity to purchase reprints. These people might benefit by and enjoy owning their own copies of some reprints they now cannot afford, or which they may not even know exist.

WHOLESALING REPRINTS

At least 34 firms do not sell any reprints through wholesalers, yet 68 firms (55 percent) do. Some 20 of the publishers interviewed consider wholesalers important middlemen. While this study did not attempt to survey wholesalers in depth, a peripheral view of their industry makes it evident that in the 1970s more jobbers are handling reprints than was true in the 1960s. This trend points to a lessening of the distinction between reprinting and other kinds of publishing.

Richard Abel & Company, for example, includes reprint titles in its preprofiled selection plan for libraries. Abel does not automatically ship reprints on approval, as it does other books, but forwards notification slips for reprints to its library customers. According to Lyman Newlin, assistant to the president, Abel has been exploring the possibilities of expanding its efforts to distribute reprints from many publishers and to serve as a clearinghouse for reprint title availability information.[17] This latter program, if developed, would be an outgrowth of the firm's computerized listing of some 14,500 OP "wanted" titles. "Richard's Reference," a computer listing of OP desiderata titles, is a publication first issued by Abel in 1970, to be updated as books are acquired.[18]

At least some regular library jobbers now handle reprint titles, in most cases accepting orders for reprints from regular customers as a convenience to them, but not necessarily stocking the titles. A few firms, and this is new to the reprint scene, are specialists in jobbing reprints.

The Baker & Taylor Company, whose huge New Jersey warehouse was seen to contain large numbers of reprints (from AMS, Arno, and Greenwood, for example), estimated a 1,000 percent increase in requests for reprint titles over the past decade, particularly as part of package purchases from libraries.[19] Many requests are for books in series, especially titles listed in *Books for College Libraries*. Baker & Taylor, which purports to be "America's oldest and largest book wholesaler," was acquired by W. R. Grace & Company in 1970. One example of the firm's interest in the reprint market is evident in its publication, "Current Books for Academic Libraries," a well-organized monthly guide to new scholarly books. Under broad LC subject headings, scholarly reprints are designated by an asterisk, a handy device for rapid scanning. Each listing includes author, title, publisher, announced publication month, information source, and announced list price.

Bro-Dart, Inc. unveiled its computerized microform "Books in Print" inventory and sales system at the ALA conference in Detroit in July 1970. Company advertisements call the plan "Bro-Dart's Direct Input Ordering System," providing a master title file that records "every book in print, and noting recent out-of-prints." Scholarly reprints are included in this service, which appears to have the potential to capture and disseminate massive amounts of current data.

Herbert M. Johnson, vice-president and general manager of Walter J. Johnson, Inc., announced (by form letter dated September 8, 1970, mailed to about 1,000 libraries) his firm's new direction, to become a "Central Source Reference Supply Service," specializing in "accurate information and supply of reprints of serial reference works."[20]

Another firm, Reprint Distribution Service, Inc. (RDS) entered this specialized field in 1971. According to its first advertisement, the company is a "newly established library book-jobbing service . . . dealing exclusively in reprints of all publishers, domestic and foreign. . . ."[21] One particularly interesting service RDS offers its library clients, according to Robert Davis, president, is an automatic availability status report which tells the purchaser about unexpected delays in publication. This information is important to librarians who might lose encumbered funds if delivery dates carry over into a new budget period.

REPRINTERS' CATALOGS

Knowing that a majority of reprinters sell direct, it is not surprising to find that more than 75 percent of the firms who responded to the question, "Do you regularly issue catalogs, lists of flyers?" answered yes. Only 14 of the 126 respondents do not produce catalogs regularly, and 3 of them plan to begin doing so.

A majority of firms that had promotional literature available sent copies as requested, providing a rich and fascinating mine of reprint information (but one that occupies more than 15 feet of shelf space!). Reprinters create a wide variety of materials in their attempts to find their customers, inform them, and sell their wares. Reprinters' catalogs and brochures range in style and quality of content from overcrowded mimeographed sheets of pulpy paper to professionally prepared reference tools of enduring value.

Among the firms issuing high quality, informative catalogs obviously designed with the user's reference needs in mind are Gale, Readex, Kraus, Johnson, Hafner, Kelley, Garrett, Micro Photo, and University Microfilms. Other firms have prepared catalogs that are artistic and collectible, such as those of Burt Franklin, Benjamin Blom, and Garland. Traditional publisher catalogs, with descriptive lists of titles, some illustrated with pictures of books or title pages, are distributed by Peter Smith, Tuttle, Africana, and Humanities, among others. Because costs are high to produce and distribute catalogs, publishers try to find out about their effectiveness and use by librarians. In 1970, for example, Jerry A. Minnich, advertising manager of the University of Wisconsin Press, queried several thousand librarians for their opinion about the firm's advertising and promotion efforts. The results encouraged continuing circularization, but with modifications to meet librarians' expressed needs, particularly for more subject listings, batched mailings, and altered size and style of presentation.[22]

Some examples of catalog costs may be of interest. Gabriel Hornstein, president of AMS Press, noted that his firm's monthly newsletter alerting service costs about $12,000 a year to produce and distribute.[23] Albert Boni, President of Readex Microprint, reported that his 1969–1970 catalog cost about $16,000, and Fred Rappaport, Johnson Reprint's vice-president, estimated the cost of their 1969 "Red Dot" Catalogue at slightly more than $1.00 each, with a major catalog costing about $18,000 to $30,-000 to prepare, print, and mail.[24] With these costs in mind, publishers would seem well advised to heed librarians' reactions to a 1971 pre-conference on the topic "Publishers' and Wholesalers' Catalogs and Brochures." At this meeting, sponsored by the Association of American Publishers at the invitation of the New England Library Association, librarians said that they feel antagonized when they receive as many as five or more duplicate copies of a publisher's mailing; they prefer facts to frills, want the factual information presented in an organized manner and indexed for rapid retrieval, and are generally unimpressed with multi-colored, glossy, oversized catalog formats.

To summarize, publishers have shown that they want feedback from catalog users. Feedback that terminates in sales is preferred, of course, but publishers also want to know what kinds of information and style of presentation users prefer, or what features they find unsatisfactory. One may be reasonably assured that specific suggestions or comments about the organization, quality, contents or frequency of catalogs will be attended to at the executive level in most publishing houses. Book promotion pulls on publishers' purse strings, probably more than librarians realize.

Chapter 9

Acquiring Reprints

"The great, all-pervasive fact of our time is burgeoning knowledge."[1] For librarians responsible for building and maintaining useful collections, the impact of this statement is clear. The acquisition staff necessarily invests the major portion of its time and funds on current materials, in order to capture and make available at least a part of this vast outpouring of new knowledge. This policy affects, but does not obviate the need for libraries to acquire older material.[2]

The period 1960–1970 was a decade of (sweet) irony for acquisitions librarians. Probably never before has so much money been available to buy library materials, nor have librarians had to spend it as quickly in a marketplace fairly bursting with an abundance of print and nonprint media, much of which sold, however, at steadily increasing prices.

In the 1960s, librarians, especially those in new institutions, were seriously hampered by insufficient time to make careful decisions about each title selected for purchase, and by an acute shortage of personnel to handle the huge amount of paperwork generated by increased buying of books, including reprints.

It has been claimed that many librarians buy reprints for one reason primarily: because they are available.[3] Perhaps so. But clearly, different types of libraries have differing needs for reprints, and any one library probably has more than a single need.

In general, reprints are purchased as new copies for new libraries; as new copies for established libraries than are strengthening subject collections (e.g., black studies or foreign area studies); or to support newly unlocked curricula (e.g., the many "hyphenated" disciplines); as replacement copies for originals in poor physical condition; as additional copies in libraries where scarce or unique materials need to be preserved; and to fill gaps in existing library collections.

Hardcopy and micropublications serve some similar and some variant needs. Microforms are bought to save storage space, especially for little-used archival materials. Microforms help to preserve the textual content of works that rapidly deteriorate, such as newspapers (also a bulk-storage problem), and serve as protection copies of rare items. As a substitute for bound volumes, microforms enable libraries to share their resources more economically (i.e., mailing interlibrary loans). And certain titles may be selected in microform to take advantage of a lower initial-unit cost.

A text in microform generally is less expensive to purchase than in macroform, particularly if the title is one that a micropublisher might reasonably expect to sell in an "edition" (i.e., multiple copies, not a single or very few copies). This statement may seem insupportable in view of the fact that each copy or print made from a master negative costs as much to make as every other copy, but, in planning an edition, the front-end costs to produce the master negative may not be fully charged against each copy sold.

Hardcopies may be preferred for more popular titles, since the library's public still generally prefers what Wooster calls the "cuddly" book, to reading machines.[4] A hardcopy reprint may even be selected over an extant original copy if the physical quality of the reprint (paper, binding, print legibility, openability, cleaner pages) is superior. Or, both hardcopy and microform of a single title may be purchased, the hardcopy for circulation and the microform assuring a permanent record in the library. Allen B. Veaner of Stanford University has provided excellent guidelines for evaluating the quality of microforms and an explanation of the various forms, emphasizing the need for quality control.[5] Selection criteria for microforms were examined years ago at the conference of Eastern College Librarians at Columbia University, and the critical factors identified remain well defined.[6] Negative master microforms may also be utilized as an intermediary step toward in-house replication—unresolved copyright problems notwithstanding.[7]

Veenstra has pointed out some problems related to the accelerated pace of library buying of commercially produced micrographics in his perceptive review, "Microimages and the Library."[8] He cites mid-1969 statistics from the Association of Research Libraries, which describe the median ARL library with holdings of 1,286,159 book volumes and 355,490 units in microform.

The micropublishers interviewed for the present study enjoyed a continuous rise in sales to libraries over the past decade, particularly of filmed "runs" of serials and government publications. Generally these publishers are optimistic about the future of their programs, although there appear to be some storm clouds ahead for the private publishing sector if the Government Printing Office microreproduces government documents, as suggested in 1971.

With regard to reproducing (not necessarily in microform) government documents, there have been unpublicized charges that at least two companies are seriously abusing the public domain status of government publications by reprinting "free" materials and vending them under new titles, making it practically impossible for buyers to know that the works are straight reprints. Libraries might already own these works but have them cataloged under the original titles. The ALA Reprinting Committee is paying attention to this matter. The ALA Bookdealer-Library Relations Committee, under the chairmanship of Murray S. Martin, is known to have been in correspondence with at least one midwestern firm which has taken serious liberties in this direction. Not only is this form of publishing furtive, but the publishers add insult to injury by charging very high prices for their newly titled "reprints," so it is venal as well, and deserves to be exposed.

In the early 1970s a few publishers (e.g., The University of Toronto Press and Yale) began to advertise simultaneous publications of original titles in hardcopy and microform editions, usually offered for sale at the same price. It is still too soon to determine the long-range effects of such programs, but surely this trend (if it is a trend) has obvious implications for the reprint industry. Having their titles on film, trade publishers and university presses may be able to keep them alive longer. They will be able to offer copies of their own backlist titles on demand if they wish to, or reprint small editions, using film as an intermediary step to hardcopy, if they find a new market. Until such time as the copyright law revision is approved and international copyright is made more equitable, and until microforms are brought under improved bibliographic control, it is not possible to see clearly into the crystal ball. These are areas where emerging patterns will be watched by publishers and librarians alike.

LISTING AND CATALOGING REPRINTS

The inadequacy of bibliographic controls is not confined to reprinted library materials, nor are most of the problems new. "Bibliographic control" is meant here to include all kinds of published information sources which systematically record and describe the products of the reprint industry. By extension, the phrase includes directory-type reference sources that list and describe the publishers. Ray Astbury, who describes the need for quick and easy access to increasing amounts of information, notes that bibliography is an essential part of the communication process, bringing relevant information to those who need adequate listings, assembled into a logical and useful order.[9] The rapid growth and complexity of the reprint industry only compounds the problems and makes them more evident.

The large quantity and variety of scholarly reprints makes even a systematic listing of all titles a formidable task for each publisher and for producers of bibliographic and cataloging services. Reprint editions compete for entry in the bibliographic mainstream which is already swollen with new titles. According to Kochen and Segur, the number of titles in *Books in Print* for a given year grows at about 6.3 percent per year,[10] and it is known that not all U.S. publishers and titles are included in *BIP*. Some reprints are swept to the side, others emerge only through specialized reprint reporting channels, and a small number never seem to receive any formal bibliographic notice.

Many reprinters are uncertain about what specific descriptive information they should provide about their titles, in the works themselves, in catalogs, and for entry in national and trade lists. Some publishers are trying to learn what information librarians need and how the Library of Congress handles reprints.

DESCRIPTIVE CATALOGING

At the Library of Congress, according to Paul W. Winkler, principal cataloger in the Descriptive Cataloging Division, most current reprints are treated as new books.[11] Before the Cataloging in Publication Program was implemented in 1971, the only reprints which LC catalogers compared with the original volumes and for which they made cross-reference on LC cards were the relatively small number of works "intended by the publishers" to be "facsimiles," works in which the text, typography and physical design are made to resemble the original as closely as possible (i.e., same style of binding, paper, marginalia, and the like). The majority of reprints, those with a new or changed title page, are treated as any other new book, except that, since about 1969, LC policy has been to note the original publication date on the LC card. If the old title page is reproduced *and* a new one added, the book is still treated as a new work. (Until a few years ago, Winkler said, LC added the old imprint information to the card as a cataloger's note.) LC would like publishers to print as much information about their book as possible on the title page (and publishing history on the verso); LC will then put this information on the cards. This applies particularly to new matter, which the publisher should identify explicitly on the title page.

For participating CIP publishers, all titles that fall within the scope of the program will be checked against existing records, and reprints which were not previously cataloged by LC will be brought under control. Fortunately, many reprinters have been quick to realize the tremendous advantage CIP offers them and their customers and are cooperating with LC. It is interesting that LC found that it had cataloged all but 4 of the first 500 CIP reprint titles at an earlier date.[12]

The missing linkage between an old and new edition puts a heavy burden on users of the *National Union Catalog* (*NUC*), a "finding" record which is divided, physically and in published form, between pre-1956 and post-1956 entries.[13] Anyone searching *NUC* to locate copies of books must know to search both *NUC* sets, or he could be misled into thinking that very few (or no) copies of a particular title are available. When reprinters ask the LC staff to search *NUC*, the double-entry system makes the task time-consuming indeed! Until about 1970, the staff did search in *NUC* at the request of reprinters, but so many publishers sent such long lists of titles that these requests can no longer be accommodated. A few titles might be searched, but reprinters are urged either to hire free-lance searchers or to send their own staff to LC to do this reference work.[14]

Some of these problems may be alleviated by commercially reproduced copies of the Library's *NUC*. Mansell's republication of the *Pre-1956 National Union Catalog*, from library cards, is interesting, for the firm has copyrighted these works, which means that even the Library of Congress will need to buy copies (aside from the two given to it as copyright deposit copies). The price of the Mansell edition is about $9,000. The Library's own publications are generally reissued at the Library's request by the Government Printing Office, but many of LC's public domain titles (including LC cards) have been reprinted by commercial houses, without royalties. In the years to come it might well be necessary for the Library to try to work out some cooperative publishing ventures in order to gain remuneration to at least cover the costs of handling and storage of original materials which become commercial properties.

NATIONAL AND TRADE BOOKLISTS

One might assume that reprinters have the same responsibility to make *their* titles known to potential customers and users as regular publishers have, and that reprinters would eagerly submit information to national and trade bibliographies and specialized reference sources. Certain aspects of the industry alter this assumption. These are the noncopyrightability of many reprints; the fear some publishers harbor that title listing might encourage piracy; the expense of listing and promotion; and occasionally, one suspects, lack of interest in matters bibliographic.

Publishers are not required to submit information to any bibliographic service, of course, nor do many reprinters need to register copies with the Copyright Office. Whether or not reprinters send their titles to LC for cataloging (thus getting them listed in the LC *Catalogs*) is a matter for each firm to decide. Such action would assure a wider dissemination of information about their titles, and should be encouraged, but is not mandatory. Because each publisher must make these decisions about his own list, it is possibly unfair to generalize responses to this survey's questions about bibliographic practices and publishers' reactions to review media.

From the results reported below, however, it is clear that *no standard bibliographical service,* not even those of the Library of Congress, *can be assured that all titles from every reprint house are regularly reported.* This is an important and perplexing finding, for without each publisher's continuing cooperation, librarians, booksellers, other publishers, and scholars are denied access to comprehensive bibliographies, and to competently cataloged and recorded reprint information.

SURVEY FINDINGS

Publishers were asked to describe their bibliographic practices, problems, and needs. From a choice of seven bibliographies, the firms indicated those to which they regularly submit titles (see Table 16). The majority (94) of the 123 publishers who responded send information on a regular basis to LC. *PTLA-BIP* is a close runner-up, with 87 firms submitting. *PW* surprisingly ranked third, with only 62 percent of the respondents (77 firms) sending their titles regularly.

Five firms submit titles to "none," a significant admission from publishers, but probably not as dismaying as it might seem, for two of the firms publish 10 or fewer titles (of regional interest); two, between 10 and 49 titles (both music firms) and one, a micropublisher, stated that they "issue catalog cards for each title," presumably in lieu of bibliographical submissions.

It is significant that 29 firms do not submit titles to LC and 46 do not submit to *PW.* This suggests that only to the extent that LC, Bowker, and other national and trade bibliographic services make successful efforts to capture bibliographic information, rather than waiting for publishers to take the initiative, will users be able to find all reprints listed. Six firms list titles only in *PTLA,* which underscores the usefulness of this work as a finding aid to reprint titles. An effort was made to discover any significant correlations between bibliographic practice and the number of titles a firm publishes, but, as can be seen in Table 16, none can be considered consequential.

As the tabular data indicate, the NCR Guides, other than the *Guide to Microforms in Print,* do not seem to attract a large number of regular contributors, at least not among the responding publishers.[15] Oceana's *Reprint Bulletin* takes last place as a listing to which these respondents feel committed.[16] Several publishers remarked that they did not know that this journal exists.

Five firms mentioned "other" bibliographies or lists, including *Choice* (two firms); *Antiquarian Bookman* (two); *Library Journal, RQ (Reference Quarterly,* published by the ALA); the Music Library Association's

TABLE 16
BIBLIOGRAPHIES TO WHICH FIRMS REGULARLY SUBMIT TITLES, BY SIZE OF FIRM

No. of titles published	A 1–10 (N=45)	B 10–49 (N=58)	C 50–99 (N=14)	D 100–299 (N=35)	E 300–499 (N=6)	F 500–999 (N=12)	G 1,000–1,499 (N=10)	H 1,500–2,999 (N=3)	I 3,000–5,000 (N=4)	J Over 5,000 (N=9)	TOTAL[a] (N=201)
No. of firms responding	32	38	10	21	5	6	2	1	2	6	123
Percentage of total N firms responding	32%	65%	50%	60%	84%	50%	20%	33%	50%	66%	60%
BIBLIOGRAPHIES											
Library of Congress	21	33	7	20	4	5	1	0	2	2	94
Publishers' Weekly	16	27	7	18	4	3	0	0	2	0	77
Books in Print-PTLA	20	29	8	17	4	6	1	0	2	0	87
Guide to Reprints	8	10	3	9	3	4	0	0	1	0	38
Announced Reprints	4	7	2	8	2	2	0	0	1	0	26
Reprint Bulletin	1	6	1	6	1	1	0	0	1	0	17
Guide to Microforms in Print	1	4	1	0	1	0	0	1	0	6	14
Other	2	1	0	0	0	1	0	0	0	1	5
"None"	2	1	0	1	0	0	0	0	0	1	5
No answer	1	2	0	0	0	0	1	0	1	0	5

Source: Publisher's response to Question 22, cross-tabulated with responses to Question 9. The latter, the number of titles published, here determines the "size" of the firm.
[a] Column totals exceed total number of firms because firms submit to more than one bibliography.

Notes (two) and scholarly journals in general. Interesting for its omission is Wilson's *Cumulative Book Index,* which might have been a biased response, because *CBI* was not included in the question. This omission was unintentional. *CBI* was not thought of as a reprint information source, and no mention was made of it when the questionnaire was under construction. Several publishers discussed the value of *CBI* in personal interviews, but a few noted their resistance to filling out yet another data-collection form which asks a publisher to rearrange his title information, a complaint also made about submitting title information to NCR.

DESCRIBING REPRINTED BOOKS

Given the basic, obvious differences between reprints and original works, persons seeking reliable information in order to select, evaluate, or buy reprints need certain data other than is sought for new books. They need to know the date and edition of the original; the original place of publication (to help define the point of view of the textual content); the intended degree of fidelity between reprint and original in terms of contents, pagination, format, size, and binding; and what new matter is added or what textual or pictorial matter is deleted from the original. Other descriptive elements, i.e., publisher's name, place and date of publication, pagination, Library of Congress card number, International Standard Book Number (ISBN), and price, are the same ones that identify new books.

Many reprinters question the need to be involved with LC card numbers. Publishers who supply these in their advertising and mailing pieces and catalogs serve libraries well, especially small and medium-sized libraries that may lack book-trade reference tools, or libraries which do not order books preprocessed. LC card numbers are useful for ordering cards before the books are delivered, and libraries now save $.39 per card set (six cards cost $.36) if they order from the Card Division by number rather than by author and title (at $.75 per set).

Because the Library of Congress preassigns card numbers at a publisher's request, well in advance of publication date, it is a simple matter for publishers to include LC numbers in sales and promotion literature. According to Nathalie Wells, head of the Library's Preassigned Card Number Division, numbers were not preassigned for reprints until about 1964. Now they are. To answer an oft-repeated question, Miss Wells noted that if more than one publisher reprints the same title, each gets a separate number. There is no tie between the old and new LC card numbers.

In order to help librarians sidestep these pitfalls, some publishers deliver cards free, or at minimal costs, with their books or microforms. Scarecrow has done so for years. Kraus supplies cards, at least for some of its works; and Falls City Microcards provides cards for all its titles. Increased availability of CIP data printed in books should minimize these problems, and make it possible for the Library to offer LC cards much nearer (or before) publication date.

It is also hoped that efforts will be made to improve the present haphazard styling of cataloging entries for reprints. The multitude of styles used to describe reprints in a single listing service and the differences between one list and another make it extremely difficult for users to know certainly that the information they find is reliable or complete. It is considerably more difficult and time-consuming to locate accurate information about reprint titles than it is to learn about other new books. Inconsistencies in the wording on LC cards (and hence in *PW*'s Weekly Record) that is intended to identify works as reprints are apparent even in the few selected examples that follow. Some of the variations on LC cards include: "First published in . . . ," "A reprint of . . . ," "Unchanged reprint of . . . ," "Reprinted from . . . ," "Reprint of 1911 ed.," "Reprint of the edition published in . . . ," and "Photocopy in reduced size." To add to the confusion, this information may appear as a cataloger's note (sometimes buried in other text), or may only be inferred from the copyright or publication date. The reprint status of some titles may only be surmised by the fact that the author died a hundred years ago! In a few known cases, there is no way to discern from the information on the cards that a book is a reprint.

PUBLISHERS' BIBLIOGRAPHIC PROBLEMS AND PRACTICES

Reprint publishers are both suppliers and users of bibliographic reprint information. Therefore it is ironic that all reprinters do not voluntarily participate in normal book-trade bibliographic systems; yet a large number of publishers complain, publicly and privately, about the inadequate nature of the bibliographic apparatus that attends reprints.

In discussing these matters with publishers, it appears that some of the problems stem from habits acquired in earlier years when the reprinter was an antiquarian bookseller or back-issues periodicals dealer. One publisher said, "Many antiquarian bookmen-turned-publisher got into bibliographic trouble because of ignorance or inattentiveness to details that librarians and catalogers need." Browsing through old booksellers' catalogs, one finds many different bibliographic styles for reprints; probably a result of their being listed generally as "appendages" to the firm's primary business.

Over the years, many booksellers built valuable private mailing lists. When the bookseller became a publisher, he continued to use these lists of scholars and collectors to inform them of his reprints. Perhaps neither the buyer nor the seller felt a need for more formal communication when the industry was more personal than it is today.

One interesting by-product of the on-site interviews with reprinters has been the discovery of an unexpectedly large number of custom-built and privately maintained files of bibliographic information about reprints. Some reprint houses and dealers have amassed valuable reprint data banks containing information about competitive reprints, descriptions of titles for future reprint projects, and the like. The files are arranged in many ways: by author, title, subject, publisher, or publication due date. For obvious reasons, other publishers' announced reprint prices are often filed for ready reference. Book dealers build files in order to respond to customer requests with accurate order information, and to gather data for catalog preparation. The reference value of dealers' catalogs is the subject of an excellent short piece in *The Papers of the Bibliographical Society* 62 (second quarter, 1968), pp. 234–235. It is noted that the catalogs serve to amend basic bibliographies, but are difficult to use as reference tools because there is no comprehensive indexing system for retrieval. Some dealers' catalogs contain original bibliographic research unavailable elsewhere.[17]

Each firm obviously needs to keep its own proprietary information, but the wastefulness inherent in multiple efforts to collect the kinds of basic reprint industry information that should be readily available to all is apparent and appalling.

The precise number of reprint titles that find their way into standard national or trade bibliographies is not known. Utilizing computer capabilities, reprint information is being selectively retrieved from Library of Congress MARC Bibliographic Records in a variety of professional and commercial experiments. For example. in a project directed by Gerald L. Swanson, Systems Office, Columbia University Libraries, machine-manipulated data reveal how many titles entered on the MARC tapes are reprints, the original and reprint publication date, and more. This system, currently for internal use only, holds promise for the bibliographic future of reprints, if librarians and publishers are interested in and support such programs. Swanson, in a trial run, found 6,371 reprint titles, or 12 percent of the total file run.[18] Slightly more than 1,000 catalog entries in this run are reprints which lack original publication dates. These data are suggestive, not conclusive. They were compiled to assist in the development of the Columbia University Machine-Readable Cataloging System (CUMARC).

This study's findings generally support Reichmann's statement that "a great number of hardcover reprints are included in national bibliographies."[19] But importantly, some titles are *not* listed, and others appear only years after their reprint publication date. For example, *PW* Weekly Record of March 16, 1970, has an entry for *The Old Story Books of England* by William John Thomas, with the imprint (New York) Johnson Reprint, 1968. One must be cautious, of course, not to fault the bibliographic service without assurance that the delay is not publisher-caused.

Searching for reprint information in current book trade reference sources such as Bowker's *PW* Weekly Record and *Books in Print* (*BIP*),

Wilson's *Cumulative Book Index* (*CBI*), and Library of Congress catalogs reveals the existence of some reprints that must be "ghosts," or as Felix Reichmann calls these publishers' wishes, "bibliographic castles in Spain." These titles probably are picked up by the services from titles listed but not identified as "not yet published" in publishers' catalogs.

All titles in *PTLA* are transferred to *BIP*, according to Gertrude Jennings, head of Bibliographic Services at Bowker, a fact which could account for entries of titles that have never been published. (Publishers have to submit copies of their trade lists many months in advance of *PTLA* publication, and some titles a publisher might anticipate publishing have not yet come to life.) As one reprinter noted, this creates real problems, for many publishers have no wish to "fool" customers, yet need to include all potential titles in the trade lists they pay to enter in *PTLA*.

According to Nina Thompson, editor of *CBI*, fewer corrections of bibliographic information are made by *CBI* now than in previous years, mostly because of lack of staff time and increased title output. Information that publishers submit is what *CBI* generally lists. This may account for some of the inconsistencies in styling and reliability. If a publisher does not note what edition has been reprinted, neither does *CBI*, whose entries depend upon LC styling. In some cases, *CBI* will go back to the cataloging that LC did for the original edition, especially regarding subject analysis.

It is perplexing to find that stated policies of scope regarding the inclusion and exclusion of reprints are not consistently adhered to by some reference book publishers. This stems partly from the lack of standard definition of what is or is not a scholarly reprint.

It is interesting to speculate about what would happen if reprints were treated in the same bibliographic manner as all other kinds of new books. For example, does a government document, once available from the Government Printing Office (perhaps an unbound congressional committee report), become a different class of publication when reproduced by a commercial publisher and sold in hardcover? Are Sears Roebuck trade catalogs transformed into "books" when they are photographically reproduced and sold in hardcover? Are unrevised public domain dissertations no longer dissertations when sold in hardcover by library reprinters? Do radical or "little" magazines become "books" when bound and sold as a reprint collection? Many of these works, for example, appear in *PW* Weekly Record. There is no reason to doubt that the editors of the Weekly Record do try to offer, as the preface to every issue states, "a conscientious listing of current American book publication." But, the fact that the scope specifically excludes "federal and other government publications, subscription books, dissertations; new printings (as distinct from reprints, reissues, and revised or new editions); quarterlies, serials, and other periodicals; pamphlets under 49 pages; and specialized publications . . . of a transitory nature or intended as advertising," points to the lack of clear scope with regard to reprints.

Some titles that have been reprinted (particularly microforms) are not listed in any standard trade bibliographies, nor in specialized reprint finding aids. Generally, the titles are not included because the publisher has not provided the information. There have been reports from some publishers, however, that despite the fact that they have submitted title information in the form desired, their titles are omitted. After a while, according to one relatively new publisher who is trying to enter his titles into regular book-trade information channels, "you just sort of give up, because of all the paperwork and time spent with no results."

A few reprint publishers appear to consider the bibliographic situation with tunnel vision; they either lack a peripheral view or do not care. Several small "mom and pop" publishing houses are willing to participate more fully in national bibliographic systems but say they cannot afford to. Perhaps these firms could arrange to have their books returned after descriptive cataloging is completed. Several firms that publish huge "publishers' series" refuse to provide these expensive sets free to any agency, especially if the agency already owns the originals (e.g., the Library of Congress). Some publishers promote and sell complete sets only, not single volumes. Ironically, it is the separate title buried in a series that frequently gives catalogers nightmares, particularly if the publisher has created a new series title but neglected to provide complete bibliographic descriptions of each original work included.

The bibliographic road ahead may remain blocked a little longer by obstacles placed by a few reticent or unknowledgeable reprint publishers; but it is becoming increasingly evident to publishers, librarians, and scholars that none are served well if works rescued from oblivion are permitted to be lost again because they are not clearly identified. As Carter and Bonk observed some years ago, the paperback market "came of age when it developed its own in-print list, *Paperbound Books in Print*."[20] Possibly the reprint industry too is coming of age, approaching the phase when it will devote concerted attention to bibliographic and cataloging needs.

PUBLISHERS' VIEWS ABOUT REPRINT REVIEWS

Critical reviewing of reprints is improving; there is more of it, and the quality of the reviews is higher. If this trend continues, descriptive and evaluative information about reprints will help customers considerably. *The Reprint Bulletin* is specializing in publishing reviews. A Forthcoming Reprints section made its debut in *Library Journal*'s January 1, 1971, issue. Edited by Irene Land, this descriptive listing appears three times yearly. *Choice* has included reprints since its inception, although new book reviews remain the journal's primary emphasis. Two reprint publishers noted that reviews appear in *Choice* too long after the book's publication date to do them much good in terms of sales, but delayed reviews is a plight of most review journals. *Choice* reviews were singled out by several other reprint publishers as being especially helpful to them. Librarians generally find *Choice* reviews fair and accurate, so it is reasonable to assume that a publisher whose titles are reviewed in *Choice* will benefit.

It is generally assumed that every publisher wants his books reviewed. It is also known that only a fraction of all books published each year are reviewed. Even *The New York Times Book Review*, the major general review medium, is able to cover only about an eighth of the new books published. Competition among publishers of original materials to get books reviewed is keen.

Inside regular publishing houses, the birth of a new book is usually cause for celebration. Each title is subject to a degree of new-parent anxieties. Reviews generate interest and can make one book more successful than another in what the literary agent Jackinson calls "The Barnum-Cinderella World of Publishing."[21] The publisher and editor whose title is spotlighted are proud. The author is pleased. Authors like to have their books reviewed. Often it is they who urge publishers to distribute review copies widely; usually, one might add, in larger numbers than the promotion budget allows. Whether or not a review is favorable, publishers agree that its very appearance helps to sell books and gain a wider audience for the author.

Reprinters feel justified in considering reviews in a somewhat different light, mostly because a reprint is, in a manner of speaking, born old. In the relatively few reprint houses that distribute review copies, if the original author of a reprint is living he may play the author's traditional role of encouraging his publisher to send reviewers free copies. More often, the part is assumed by the author of a new introduction, be he faculty member, historian, genealogist, librarian, or publisher's brother-in-law! Many reprint reviews seem to be written by persons who also serve on reprint publishing editorial boards or as consultants to publishers. Usually the reviewer *does not* review titles from the house he serves. Probably he has developed an interest in the reprint field and a competence in his particular areas of interest. The question of who reviews reprints and with what evaluative criteria is a topic worth further study.

Scholars in all fields unquestionably appreciate having reprints brought to their attention, particularly if reviews are written by their peers. For librarians, however, the fact that a large majority of reprint reviews appear in subject-oriented journals has other, often frustrating, implications. It suggests that librarians may need to read or scan many more subject-oriented journals than they have time for, or risk missing some highly informative and evaluative reprint reviews.

Responses from 106 firms were analyzed further to compare established and new publishers' opinions about reprint reviewing, and to determine whether publishers of large numbers of titles receive proportionately more review attention than small houses. Older firms do have a slight edge over the new fellows insofar as getting reprints reviewed "often." Of the 70 firms in the "often" category, 39 began reprinting prior to 1960; 31 are newer firms. Interestingly, 3 more "old" than "new" firms "never" have titles reviewed (16 of the 29 "never" firms are established houses; 13 are new).

As to format, hardcover reprints traditionally have been reviewed more frequently than other kinds. Titles republished in microform, one firm noted, "hardly ever get reviewed, mostly because we cannot afford to give away free copies for the purpose of review." The 1971 birth of the important new journal, *Microform Review* (published by Alan M. Meckler, Rogues Ridge, Weston, Conn. 06880), should change this attitude. With Allen B. Veaner as editor-in-chief and Hubbard Ballou, head of Photographic Services, Columbia University, as technical editor, this publication could be the needed focal point for communications about micropublishing projects, for librarians, publishers, and the education community.

Publishers were also asked to indicate the frequency with which reviews of their titles appear in various kinds of review media. Their responses appear in Table 17.

Because the wording of the question was considered ambiguous by several publishers ("our titles" shoud have read "our reprint titles," as was intended), a low level of statistical reliability is assumed. Still, the findings indicate some industry patterns. The only surprise is that a relatively large percentage of thse 115 respondents (61 percent, or 70 firms) find their titles reviewed "often" in some media. (It should be noted that the "no answer" responses possibly mean "never," but this cannot be assumed.)

Subject-oriented journals, according to the publishers, are more hospitable to reprints than other review media, as might be expected. For example, music reprints are reviewed in journals such as the MLA *Notes* (cited earlier); Western Americana is reviewed in *The American Book Collector;* relevant titles are reviewed in "A Critical Checklist of Current Southwestern Americana," compiled at the University of Arizona Library, Tucson; genealogical reprints are reviewed in specialized journals, history in historical journals, and so forth.

TABLE 17
FREQUENCY OF REVIEWS

Total (N = 115) Percentage of N	Often (N = 70) 61%	Seldom (N = 60) 52%	Never (N = 29) 25%	No Answer
National media	22	37	26	30
Local or regional journals	36	26	17	36
Subject-oriented journals	53	20	14	28

In talking about reviews, most reprint publishers say they do not send review copies because of their typically small printings. Several small firms seemed reticent about having their titles reviewed, perhaps reflecting a lack of confidence in their own title selection. One major New York reprinter summed up some of the other reasons for not sending review copies. First, he noted, books sent for review frequently are not reviewed. Second, the delay between the book's publication date and the appearance of the review may be as long as two years. By the time the review appears, the book may be out of stock. A potential customer who reads a review, requests a copy of the book, and is told that the book is "no longer available" is led to believe that the firm is either very inefficient or unreliable. Going into a second printing to satisfy the orders that might be triggered by a review, this publisher said, generally is uneconomical and further delays delivery of the book to an already dissatisfied customer. If the customer happens to be a librarian, and begins to doubt the company's credibility, the problems created far outweigh the benefits of the review.

With some of these finndings in mind, Table 18, summarizing the responses of 118 publishers to a question concerning reviews, is interest-

TABLE 18
OPINIONS ON REVIEWING

	Yes	No	No Answer
Coverage in library journals should be extended	80	10	28
Specialized journal is needed	61	17	37
Adequate ways now exist to locate reviews of older titles	25	33	60

ing. The results, however, are probably less significant at the present time than they might have been before the announcements of the new reprint-review media mentioned above.

The majority of the respondents favor increased coverage for reprints, with extended coverage in existing journals preferred slightly over establishing new review media. Perhaps of most interest are the responses which indicate that reviews really do not matter much to a firm. It is not possible to know all the factors that influence such decisions, but it is rather interesting to conjecture about what some might be.

LIBRARIES AS PUBLISHERS

The tremendous activity in the reprint industry during the latter part of the sixties, the apparent success of some reprint firms, the close ties between the industry and libraries, and the rapidly changing photographic technology reveal a trend toward increasing publication by libraries of their own materials. How far this kind of reprinting might spread is anyone's guess, but clearly it carries important implications for librarians and for publishers.

This subject is only briefly discussed here, not because it is taken lightly but rather because its full potential is only now beginning to emerge.

Columbia University is a good example. The following information appeared in the *Annual Report of the President for the Year 1968–1969*.

> Librarians . . . combed the book markets of the world for current and retrospective materials. . . . Approximately 126,000 volumes have been added to the catalogued collections this year, a figure exceeding that of most prior years and equal to all library acquisitions by the University during the first 145 years of its existence . . . the university research library . . . is really a creature of the twentieth-century developments in research and scholarship. Half the collections have been acquired since 1952, a quarter of them since 1961.[22]

The magnitude of these acquisitions and its implications clarify, in part, the desire of library administrators to offset some of the expenses incurred in building collections. More important is the concern of some university librarians to retain master negatives of works from their collections, to assure quality control, and to make it possible for libraries to publish (perhaps cooperatively) those specialized works that even short-run scholarly reprinters would not consider.

Many libraries, perhaps especially the Library of Congress, have "personal" bibliographic information sources that have been developed for local use over long years. Some of these collections (e.g., Southeast Asia, regional and local history, college catalogs) would be useful to a few other libraries but have not been commercially published. These and similar items may be appropriate for microform publication, and some libraries have embarked upon such programs.

Lowell A. Martin, in the report of his masterful survey of the Chicago Public Library, states:

> In the future, multiple duplication of materials will play a role in building collections. The Library in a sense will become printer and issue publications in short runs, these to be derived either from already published items (duplication of a valuable pamphlet no longer available from the original source, for example) or from manuscripts prepared within the library . . . the Chicago Public Library should function as a small-scale and special purpose publisher and printer.[23]

As hardware and software costs are reduced and as even newer audiovisual technological feats are accomplished, there is little doubt that libraries will assume some role as reprographers. Speed of access to hard-copies from microforms and convenience in satisfying local requests for specialized materials seem almost a mandate to many persons in the library world.

In this world so accustomed to rapid change, it is perhaps worth a short pause to consider that the modern library has evolved in a seesaw action from an early custodial role as the keeper of the books through a transitional stage when copyists abounded and the scribes produced the books. For many years following, the warehouse function seemed the most important. Now, and again, libraries are considering their potential role as mechanical scribes—and perhaps booksellers. Publishers are librarians; librarians are publishers. All things are possible. While *this* work was in progresss, man walked on the moon. He really did.

Chapter 10

Mutual Concerns of Reprinters and Librarians

The juxtaposition of viewpoints about reprinting might suggest cross-purposes, but the dual route leads to a single goal: to encourage a more symbiotic relationship between reprint publishers and librarians. There are so many and good reasons for librarians and publishers to do business rather than battle that a sharper awareness of each other's problems should result in increased tolerance, and who knows, perhaps even in mutual benefits.

LIBRARY ASSOCIATIONS AND REPRINT PUBLISHING

Reprint publishing did not receive effective, coordinated attention from the library world until the mid-1960s. This is not to say that librarians did not try to communicate with reprinters in years past. Some of these efforts were reviewed in Chapter 4. Christopher Samuels has described a whole slew of American Library Association explorations in the reprint field, going back into the 1920s.[1] Most of these ended with librarians discovering individual OP titles to suggest for reprinting. Communications were predominantly of a suggestion-box nature, conducted in an impersonal atmosphere. The proposals were not widely supported. Most were abortive or only of limited value. The lack of a reprinters' association has seriously hampered librarians' efforts to discuss such matters with a representative publisher's group.

The need for more and better communications grew as the industry grew. In the 1960s, as libraries began buying vast numbers of reprints, they also became increasingly aware of problems created by requests from reprinters to borrow library-owned materials.

In the mid-1960s, the ALA Reprinting Committee (Acquisitions Section, Resources and Technical Services Division) assumed a new, vital role as a channel of direct communications with the industry. Face-to-face discussions between interested librarians and reprint publishers were, and continue to be, encouraged. In 1967, the first of a series of this committee's meetings brought librarians and representatives of some major reprint houses together to exchange information and opinions about title selections, business ethics, lending policies, and other important matters. Avis G. Zebker, then chairman of the Reprinting Committee, also chaired the highly successful 1969 ALA Atlantic City Preconference Institute cosponsored by the American Book Publishers Council/RTSD Joint Committee. The topic, "New Dimensions in Acquisitions," attracted a large, responsive audience. A session on the "Acquisition of Serials, Scholarly Reprint Editions and OP Books" gave the audience an opportunity to learn about reprinting directly from highly respected publishers: John Mlandinich, then with Barnes & Noble, Henry Schlanger of Octagon, and Harry Lubrecht of Stechert-Hafner.

The fact that 36 reprint publishers and a score of micropublishers exhibited their products at the conference, many for the first time, signified an awareness of common interests. The reprint meeting at the July 1970 ALA Conference in Detroit, previously mentioned, attracted even more reprinters. At long last, reprinters were openly soliciting their primary market. Librarians seemed pleased to stop and shop at the exhibit booths. They saw that reprinters are "real live people." Equally significant, and more amusing to watch, were the furtive visits one reprinter made to another's booth, and the busyness of a few peripatetic reprinter's "consultants." The ALA Reprinting Committee (under the strong leadership of Alfred H. Lane, chairman) continues to represent a constructive influence. The ALA/RTSD Bookdealer-Library Relations Committee (Murray S. Martin, chairman) is also concerned with reprints, particularly as they affect the book trades. These two committees work in close harmony.

Another group that is ardently working to resolve reprint industry-related problems is the Rare Book Section of the Association of College and Research Libraries (ACRL), a division of the ALA. A Rare Book Libraries' Conference on Facsimiles was convened for the first time at the Folger Library on October 25, 1969, in response to concerns created by the rapid growth of the reprint industry. The conference has met since then at the Beinecke Library (Yale), the Newberry Library (Chicago), and the Clark Library (Los Angeles). Interim reports on editorial and technical standards have been distributed for review and comment. A final report is planned for 1972. One recommendation set forth in their "Recommendations for Control of Editorial Quality" is that "the reprint shall be plainly identified as a reproduction of a particular original copy at the library of origin." Another states that "Unless otherwise indicated, the original copy thus identified shall be the only source of the reproduction." From these it is clear that research libraries fully intend to continue to lend their originals for copying, but with provisos to protect their scholarship.

The rare-book librarians also passed an interim "Resolution Concerning Cost and Permission Fees for the Facsimile Reproduction of Books and Other Library Materials." In 1970, they distributed copies to various ALA committees for endorsement. As of late 1971, this resolution had not been unanimously endorsed. The resolution attempts to assure that libraries, by royalty arrangements or fees, will recover expenses incurred for photoduplication service to individuals, the full costs for service to commercial firms *and* compensation for the use of the materials. Reprinters should be aware of these conferences and communicate their views. Again, if reprinters belonged to a trade association, it would be possible to inform all of them of these very significant works in progress.

Other library and trade associations with committees concerned with reprinting include the Medical Library Association, American Association of Law Libraries, American Theological Library Association, American Educational Theatre Association, the Children's Services Division of the ALA, and the Music Library Association.

LIBRARY SPECIAL COLLECTIONS

Many original works which appeal to reprinters are unique or rare. Libraries acquire, process, and house these and other special collections only with a great investment of professional expertise, money, and time. Administrators of special collections generally agree that each library has a traditional right, even a duty, to place protective restrictions on its materials. Most libraries do so. These collections are kept intact to benefit scholars and to attract and encourage new donors to add private collections to existing library strongholds.

A few publishers have openly objected to being denied copying privileges for certain materials. They argue that the very act of reprinting allows for wider distribution of copies, which should benefit scholars. For some scholarly research, this seems to be a valid argument. Not so for other books, where the original paper, binding, illustrations, endpapers, marginalia, broken typefaces, and other peculiarities of rare works are essential points.

Librarians are rightly concerned about damage or loss of original materials. Librarians lend reprinters some materials knowing that the original will be destroyed. But there are other cases when careless reprinters have caused irreparable and unanticipated damage to library properties. Even photographing rarities on-site at the library has not prevented their occasional destruction, however unintentional. The final say about which works may be copied, librarians believe, must rest with the owner of the material. Most responsible reprinters recognize these difficulties and respect the library viewpoint. A few, perhaps with good reason, feel that certain publishers have been given preferential treatment. For example, during a 1970 meeting, Earl Coleman, president of Plenum Publishing Company, of which DaCapo is the reprint division, suggested that some librarians were giving unfair advantage by choosing to lend to some firms but not to others.[2] Connie R. Dunlap (head, Graduate Library, University of Michigan), then president of the Acquisitions Section of RTSD, replied that selectivity was a fair and proper businesslike stance for librarians, who should be dealing only with responsible businessmen in order to protect library collections and the rights of their clientele, and to assure the safe and timely return of materials for use by patrons. Several reprinters in the audience openly agreed with Mrs. Dunlap. How many might agree with Mr. Coleman was not ascertained.

The point is that librarians will undoubtedly continue to enter into business contracts which are most rewarding to the library, as they should. Librarians are not obligated to do business with every publisher.

PRESERVATION OF LIBRARY MATERIALS

The preservation and conservation of library materials is an urgent matter, and one recognized as serious even before it became fashionable in the 1970s for professionals to express concerns about pollution and ecology. The Council on Library Resources, Inc. (CLR), by its attention to these problems and financial support of investigations seeking solutions, has made an inestimable contribution to scholarship. In the late 1950s, CLR began to support studies conducted by the late William J. Barrow to determine the causes of book-stock deterioration. Barrow conducted a number of important investigations, including the development of so-called permanent/durable book paper capable of being manufactured from chemical wood pulp within the normal price range of book papers. These studies have been reported by W. J. Barrow Research Laboratory in a landmark series under the title, Permanence/Durability of the Book.[3]

CLR funds the laboratory, quartered in Richmond since 1961 by the Virginia Historical Society. Dr. Forestier Walker is director of the laboratory as of November 1971.

Preservation of a library collection has been clearly defined by Friedman as "The maintenance of the resources in lasting physical condition through retention, restoration and replacement of library materials based on a clearly defined policy."[4]

Libraries with holdings of significant works published on paper stock manufactured in the late nineteenth and early twentieth centuries are particularly concerned with preservation problems, for many of these materials are already brittle and deteriorating rapidly. In 1966, Williams reported that the materials in American libraries requiring preservation attention numbered (in single copies) about three billion pages.[5]

In 1969 it was estimated that 2 million of the 5.5 million books in the Research Libraries of the New York Public Libraries (NYPL) were in a deteriorating state. In an effort to preserve and restore original materials, NYPL in 1971 established a conservation laboratory, under the supervision of H. Wayne Eley, Jr.

The Library of Congress faces preservation problems of tremendous magnitude. Its Preservation Microfilming Office (the name changed from the Brittle Books Projects Office) prepared and microfilmed a total of 1,639,500 pages of brittle and deteriorating materials in fiscal year 1969,[6] some 400,000 more pages than they filmed in 1968, according to Shaffer.[7]

REPLACEMENT DECISIONS

A library's replacement policy is based on the uses to be made of the replacement copies. Shaffer also noted that these decisions must take into consideration the cost of positive microfilm as opposed to hardcopy reprints. A positive microfilm, he stated, can be purchased for about one fourth the cost of a reprint.

Hardcopy reprints will be useful to libraries as long-term replacement copies only if they are produced on acid-free, permanent/durable paper stock and printed with margins adequate for rebinding. Equally useful, one assumes, are well-made microproductions, i.e., archival films produced with attention to quality controls and to standards recommended by the Standards Committee of the National Microfilm Association and the U.S. National Bureau of Standards.

McGraw-Hill was the first major trade publisher to announce, in 1968, a policy of printing its books on so-called permanent (acid-free) paper. According to an article in *PW* (March 4, 1968), University Microfilms has a policy of using acid-free paper for its reprints. A large number of reprinters' catalogs carry a statement describing the quality of paper the firm uses for its products. Examples may be found in catalogs from Arno Press, Garland Publishing, Garrett Press, Kraus Reprint, Johnson Reprint, and others.

Reprints manufactured to low quality specifications will have short-range appeal to some libraries based on their textual content, but these works must be considered expendable. As librarians become increasingly hard-nosed about budgetary decisions, reprints which are expensive but expendable will probably be much more selectively purchased by libraries.

BORROWING AND LENDING ORIGINALS

We have seen that the mushrooming growth of the reprint industry has placed heavy demands on publishers and librarians to borrow and lend materials for republication. It is axiomatic that publishers must have access to reprintable originals in order to produce copies. We know that publishers can and do propose reprints. They can and do describe their selected titles in promotional literature. They can and do accept orders; but without a useable original to copy they are left high and dry.

Obtaining this original is the first tangible step in the reprinter's production process, similar to a regular publisher's acquisition of a manuscript. The obvious contrast is that a regular publisher deals with an author or his agent; the reprinter, with bookstores, private collectors, and libraries.

In 1968, reacting to the need expressed by librarians for guidelines on lending to reprinters, the ALA Reprinting Committee prepared a policy statement, developed from a sampling of 72 major U.S. and Canadian libraries. These have been widely distributed, but are not uncontested. Within the past several years, reprinters' requests to libraries to borrow materials and for bibliographic checking and searching have put a noticeable strain on some library staffs and budgets. This strain is felt mostly in large research libraries with rich and unique collections, such as the Research Libraries of the NYPL, the Newark Public Library, and Columbia University Libraries.

It is interesting that, while the number of requests is high, the number of requestors is relatively small. For instance, in 1969 the NYPL received requests to borrow about 800 titles from only 35 hardcopy reprinters and 5 or 6 micropublishers.[8] The library's policy has been to cooperate fully with reprinters, for "reprinting is of mutual benefit to all research libraries and benefits our [NYPL] preservation program."[9] Because the cost to the library for handling special requests from publishers and their scouts has increased beyond the cost of regular patron service, library administrators are taking a closer look at the economics and desirability of their lending policies.

Some of the special tasks typically performed in a large research library in order to service reprinters' requests include:

Searching for and delivering materials, examining and approving each loan; processing incoming requests, preparing work sheets; searching the official catalog, preparing borrowers' records, estimating charges; retrieving books from stacks; matching books with records; notifying publishers that books are ready to be picked up; sending overdue notices and rebinding, reshelving, and entering reprints into the collection.

To accomplish these tasks (and there are more) one library assistant probably will spend about 38 hours each week; an administrator, 14 hours; other personnel, from department heads to library pages, are also involved.

This brief listing demonstrates that a large number of man-hours are needed to satisfy the unique requests reprinters make to libraries. Man-hours equal money in libraries as well as in commercial enterprises. To offset some of these costs, many libraries now charge reprinters borrowing fees, and the amount of these fees appears to be on the increase. Library attitudes toward supporting what appear to be lucrative commercial ventures are considerably less Pollyanna-like than they were some six or seven years ago when the reprint industry was smaller and the problems less evident.

At certain research libraries (Columbia University is a good example), library policy-makers are deeply concerned about commercial use of library holdings, particularly if there is no promise of reasonable immediate and long-term remuneration. The fact that master negatives of certain library-owned originals end up in publishers' vaults is a practice that is under critical library review as libraries operate under mounting financial pressures. Large universities are seeking ways to bring funds into their institutions for preservation programs and maintenance of library collections for future scholars. At Columbia University, the book collection is estimated to be a $100 million asset. The library administration feels that, within the philosophical, legal, and social parameters of the university, such a remarkable asset must be protected and made as profitable for the university as is feasible.[10]

Those large research libraries which are frequently asked for materials are members of the Association of Research Libraries. In 1970, ARL's Committee on Availability of Resources queried its members about "Reprinting Library Resources." The ARL Board of Directors asked the committee to study "the problems associated with providing copies of library materials for the use of reprinters and microfilmers and to look toward the formulation of a model statement of practises [*sic*] which might be recommended to university libraries."[11] In a cover letter accompanying the questionnaire form, it is noted that an earlier ARL committee had considered this problem, but that increasing reprinting and filming "makes it a whole new ball game."

The ARL survey asked libraries to estimate the number of reprinters who requested library materials during 1968–1969. Of 56 libraries questioned 50 responded (see Table 19).

These ARL findings correlate highly with the findings from the present survey. It may be concluded that relatively few firms are frequent

TABLE 19
REPRINTERS BORROWING FROM LIBRARIES

No. of Libraries	No. of Reprinters' Requests
1	0
34	1–5
5	5–10
7	10–15
3	15–30

library borrowers. The general subject of abuse of borrowing privileges probably has been adequately exposed. It should be noted, however, that since eight publishers specifically mentioned that the costs of searching and securing originals is figured into their production costs, this might be a typical industry practice. Should library fees continue to increase, as they did during the 1970s when Yale raised its borrowing fee to $100 a volume and Columbia from $25 to $50, the retail price of reprints probably will follow suit. Borrowing fees that reimburse one library will thus tend to increase reprint prices for all others. One major New York reprinter noted these increases with alarm. He said that if such a practice becomes a trend, reprinting is a "doomed industry."

RETRIEVING BORROWED ORIGINALS

A contentious point in library relations with reprinters concerns publisher's delinquency in returning borrowed materials—in some cases overdue for as long as two years.

Reprinters have tried to explain delayed returns by blaming their printers and binders, who, they say, hold materials long past promised delivery dates. True or not, librarians find this an unacceptable excuse. To a librarian such apologies sound like the rationalization of the library borrower who says, "Don't blame me for these damaged books; my dog ate the pages." Concerned librarians believe that reprint publishers must make more extensive efforts to uphold their end of the contractual agreements they enter into with the library. Publishers could take positive remedial action by notifying the library in advance of the due date that books will be returned late. Such simple but polite consideration on the part of the publisher would put the responsibility for costly follow-up paperwork where it properly belongs—with the borrower—and thus gives librarians one less reason to be at odds with the industry.

On the other side of this "to lend/to borrow" coin, some reprinters resent the fact that (1) they must pay for borrowing materials which they feel they have as much right to use as other library patrons; (2) even when they offer to pay the required library charges and meet other borrowing requirements, some libraries will not lend specific materials to them, but might lend them to other reprinters; and (3) certain materials are purposely kept out of commercial channels in order to maintain the uniqueness of a library's collections. When this is true, publishers feel that scholars who cannot come to the library to use the materials are "unjustly denied access" to works which the reprinter could make available to them. These are strong accusations and some sound pompous and overly altruistic, but the issues are complex.

Because of this generally confused background publishers were asked, in Question 14, how frequently they borrow library copies to reprint. The responses of 142 publishers (about 51 percent of all firms) indicate that 45 borrow library copies "often," 53 "seldom," and 44 "never" borrow.

From these data it appears that a relatively small number of firms borrow library copies—on the order of 31 percent of the 142 respondents. It is highly probable that even fewer than 45 firms borrow a disproportionately large part of all materials libraries lend to reprinters.

Publishers who "never" borrow prefer to purchase their own copies to avoid being beholden to the owners, to eliminate the worry and expense of rebinding after they have removed the pages from the casing in order to photograph, and to avoid other special care and handling and the need to return borrowed properties by a specified time.

Several reprinters remarked that originals are generally bought with great difficulty and expense. Others, mostly antiquarian bookmen, have access to the copies they need from stock or know where and how to locate copies on the used-book market.

Fifteen publishers personally commented that they believe libraries are entitled to remuneration for the actual expense incurred in lending to reprinters. Not all reprinters agree, especially not microrepublishers. Some of them are concerned about having to pay the same borrowing fees as hardcopy reprinters. The cost of lending is the same for libraries regardless of the kind of firm that borrows. The microrepublishers say, however, that it might take them years before the sale of a title returns the amount of the fee, if ever. In the meantime, investment capital is tied up.

LIBRARY SELECTION AND ACQUISITION OF REPRINTS

Some libraries have had to set up special procedures in acquisitions departments to deal with reprints. At the Columbia University Libraries, for example, a separate division had to be created to review, research, select, order, and receive reprints. This division also serves as liaison with reprint publishers, handling matters relating to lending materials to reprinters and seeing to the safe return of these materials to the collection.

Ellsworth has said that libraries can "no longer afford to buy specific titles to meet newly existing needs; there simply isn't time to do things that way anymore."[12] The proliferation of publishers' and wholesalers' standing-order and other automatic-shipment plans appears to reinforce Ellsworth's theory. Librarians have been buying more titles in publishers' series and in other "package" plans, generally preprofiled to match the library's anticipated needs.

An informative interview with the librarian of a large public library system provided an example, probably a representative one, of a library buying reprints directly from a publisher through the firm's standing-order plan.[13] Some years ago, when the number of titles reprinted by one particular firm was "moderate," the plan seemed desirable. Library staff time was saved. Books were delivered by the publisher once a month, each delivery consisting of some dozen titles. The books were shelved in the acquisition department upon arrival and held for staff review, and selected titles were then sent through regular library book-entry processes. A majority of the titles were retained, for the library either did not own copies or needed additional ones. In certain subject fields, such as Africana and Asian studies, and for timely topics (war, black studies, women's rights), reprints were extremely useful to strengthen the collections. Unwanted titles were simply returned to the publisher.

As the number of reprints from this house burgeoned and new reprint programs were initiated, the standing order plan started to be more a burden than a relief for the staff. The number of delivered titles increased greatly, because the company automatically extended the original standing order plan to all its new series. Suddenly, reprints were arriving two or three times each month. The books in each delivery filled some nine feet of shelf space! Additional paraprofessional staff was employed just to do the preliminary bibliographic search in the library's catalogs. More professional staff time was needed to help the searchers, for reprints are difficult to check bibliographically, due to title changes and new matter added.

Librarians would prefer to select, order, acquire, and catalog reprints with the same library procedures and criteria they apply to other new books. Because reprints are frequently treated out of the mainstream of bibliographic control, this is not always possible.

The identification and acquisition of reprints is inextricably tied to the antiquarian and used-book markets.[14] Many librarians are untrained insofar as dealing wisely in these markets.[15] Reprints of some titles available as original copies in the OP market appear to be excessively high priced.[16] Listed below are a few examples of original copies examined on booksellers' shelves during the course of the present investigation. The prices noted are the bookseller's 1969 retail price for the original, and the reprint edition price listed in reprint publishers' catalogs of corresponding date.

Hunt, William and Poole, Reginald, eds. *The Political History of England.* Original volumes at $110.00 per set; reprint at $225.00.

Smith, William, ed. *Dictionary of Greek and Roman Biography and Mythology.* 3 volumes. Original volumes at $47.00; reprint at $125.00.

Smithsonian Institution, *Annual Reports.* Original bound volumes, 1863–1958 (lacking 1952) at $300.00 the set; reprint edition 1846–1932 in 82 volumes (plus cumulative index) at $2,750.00 (with check) or $2,915.00 (billed).

Turgenev, Ivan. *The Novels of Ivan Turgenev.* Original at $90.00; reprint at $195.00.

Some interesting speculations arise. Two experienced used-book dealers stated privately that the high price of reprints has inflated, not depressed, the price for some used originals. For example, the Smith title noted above had been selling for $20 until the reprint was advertised at $125. In some bookstores, contrary to the plaints of a few booksellers, titles in stock and not selling at any price suddenly come to life again when the title is selected for reprinting and marketed to libraries.

Many librarians are aware of this pricing discrepancy. Libraries that decide to buy "packages" of reprints directly from publishers or from jobbers generally believe that they will save money in the long run by not spending time to locate and acquire individual titles.

In the past several years, British booksellers, like their American counterparts, have been carefully watching customer requests. Their stock of American titles is being more heavily promoted to libraries in this country. Requests for titles not in stock are sometimes recommended for copublishing with an American firm, which generally guarantees a minimum purchase (perhaps 1,000–1,500 copies) of the edition for distribution in this country. The money advanced or guaranteed provides the working capital for the edition to be manufactured abroad. Each publisher inserts his own title page or affixes the appropriate imprint label.

Librarians accustomed to dealing with the foreign market have reported that they sometimes can order copies of needed U.S. titles from British booksellers when they are reported OP or out of stock by the original publisher in this country. Several librarians have noted their increasing dependence upon *British Books in Print* as a finding aid, which they check before they place an order for an American reprint.

In general, policies with regard to standing orders for reprints have had to be reviewed to determine whether the time spent in checking, reviewing, and perhaps returning a large number of reprints automatically shipped by the publisher is justified, or whether the library must again become more personally involved in individual title selection or very careful pre-profiling by subject fields and levels of interest. Several librarians have recently suggested that they may prefer to pay somewhat higher prices for single titles purchased, or lose out on prepublication prices, in order to avoid the reprint deluge.

Chapter 11

Conclusions and Recommendations

In the latter part of the 1960s when this survey began, the big unspoken question inside the reprint realm was, "How can I get a piece of the library spending pie?" or perhaps, "How big a piece can I get?" At the start of the seventies funding programs for education and libraries were threatened or diminishing. Some reprint publishers showed signs of uncertainty about their programs. Others, more confident in their role as publisher, or dedicated to survival, sought innovative ways to meet the new challenges. Changes are evident in the increasing amount of original publishing by reprint specialists, in creative reprint programs, in more stringent title selection, in more microform publishing by firms previously committed only to paper reprints, and in obvious efforts to find out more about customers' needs and wants. It is an ironic twist that the economic squeeze of the 1970s probably has fostered the growth of a better reprint industry. Let us examine some of these statements in more detail.

After a series of intermittent beginnings, reprint publishing achieved unprecedented heights in the late 1960s. Obviously, when this study of the ongoing industry was begun, it was not known that the timing would coincide with the greatest period of growth and change the industry has ever enjoyed. The vast number of educational, social, and economic factors that converged while the study was in progress helped to generate the so-called reprint explosion.

Will the crest reached in the affluent years be maintained during the more troubled seventies? Probably not. It seems reasonable to predict that the world of reprinting will shrink, both in terms of numbers of publishers involved and in the quantity of titles produced. The smaller sphere probably will be comprised, however, of more experienced publishers who will produce higher quality reprints. Because publishing production and selling costs are rising in general, publishers will need to be cost and quality conscious. So will librarians.

A key element of success in reprint publishing appears to lie in the publisher's understanding of the marketplace before he plans his publishing programs. The haphazard, hit-or-miss nature of title selection which some publishers practiced during the sixties probably developed because many reprinters did not start out to *be* publishers. Rather, they were printers, booksellers, collectors, librarians, or teachers. Unfortunately, the industry also attracted a small band of piratical copycats. Publishing projects frequently did not have end uses defined thoroughly before publication.

Successful reprint publishing in the seventies will depend more upon well-conceived, continuing publishing programs and less on single titles offered for sale in random order. Too many dollars need to be invested in these atomized programs. Publishers will find it increasingly difficult to gain the institutional purchaser's attention with a title-at-a-time approach. Hardcopy reprints will need to be described clearly, microforms will need to be identified precisely and indexed. Reprint publishers' products and promotional activities of the sort that waste librarians' time and money will be high-risk ventures in the 1970s.

Many of the findings presented and analyzed in the previous chapters point to the interaction of reprint publishers and librarians. It is evident that "as libraries go, so goes scholarly reprint publishing." What does this suggest about the future of reprint publishing? First, that the economic health of the industry is a function of the economic strength of libraries. Second, that reprinters and librarians must recognize their interdependence and come together for more planned discussions of specific nuts-and-bolts topics of mutual concern.

In recent years, many regular publishers, aware of the implications of strong library budgets for building collections, have volunteered to help gain support for libraries through legislation. Very significant library funding programs have resulted. Reprinters generally have not participated in these efforts. They should, because they share immediate and long-term benefits.

One might reasonably assume that the public will one day again encourage and fully support these vital funding programs. In the meantime, the level of reprint activity—and scholarly publishing generally—appears to be diminishing somewhat, and is likely to become further depressed. The directional signals to which reprinters look for guidance seem to be tilted downward, but the picture is not all one of gloom and doom.

APPROACHES TO PROBLEM-SOLVING

Most of the problems we have identified and discussed seem solvable, although the solutions sound sanctimonious. For example, librarians could be urged to help good reprinters to success and let the culprits who sour the industry find other means of support. But, who can judiciously sort the good from the bad without accepted guidelines, and what safeguards can be built in to prevent unintentional boycotting? One could recommend a laissez-faire attitude towards the industry, placing burdens squarely upon individual librarians and publishers. This is proper in a competitive society, but then, somehow, librarians and other reprint customers must be able to gain access to factual information about each publisher, his works, and his methods of doing business. The lack of a reprinters' association and the present unsatisfactory bibliographic control of reprints makes this route an obstacle course.

The answers appear to lie in purposeful efforts made by those publishers and librarians who care about ensuring a viable reprint publishing industry. If a large number of people do care, they should seriously attempt to encourage mutual respect, the kind that comes with understanding. (In the words of a once-popular melody, they should "accentuate the positive.") To "respect" is to hold in high esteem. This trait is generally missing in the relationship between the industry and the library world. Librarians do not generally respect reprinters. Reprinters frequently speak negatively about librarians. Reprinters do not respect each other. And, not least, some reprinters do not even seem to hold themselves in high regard. From awareness of these attitudes comes a simple recommendation.

Reprinters who deserve praise should hear it often and clearly, from their customers and from their colleagues. Librarians and scholars should call attention to meritorious reprint programs and reputable reprinters, and they should point out those which they find worthless. This can be accomplished by carefully prepared professional reviews, by descriptive articles in professional journals, in speeches at conferences and meetings, and by word of mouth.

Publishers who create reprints in which they can take pride should not have to continue to bear the cross from others who downgrade the industry. This is precisely what has created a disconcertingly high level of defensiveness within the industry. Like a disease the trait has spread into the library world. With collective wisdom certainly publishers and librarians can act more constructively now than they have in the past.

The rising tide of questions asked by librarians and reprinters alike indicates that anything less than open and continuing efforts to explain their needs to each other, be they procedural, intellectual, or whatever, could result finally in the demise of reprint publishing houses. Although in a few cases this might be beneficial, the overall effect would be to cut off the supply of a great deal of useful library materials—and livelihoods.

THE FUTURE OF REPRINTING

A considerable number of reprinters, especially those who have built substantial lists of scholarly titles, continue to be confident about the future of their programs. Established libraries will continue to need some of these works as replacement and additional copies. New libraries will need to stock their shelves. (There will, of course, be fewer new libraries built until adequate funds become available again.) Reprint firms that have gained experience in publishing titles in both hardcopy and microforms probably will fare best in the long pull, for they will be able to adjust to changes in institutional buying patterns.

At least a few highly creative and innovative people have been recruited into the publishing industry over the reprint threshold. Since the general publishing industry is criticized for its bigness and impersonality, this small new corps of individuals may add another and refreshing dimension to publishing, and thus help publishing remain what it has characteristically been, a socially responsive and responsible industry. On the other hand, several printer-publishers and bookseller-publishers have already turned their energies and resources back to their original pursuits. Probably these firms will continue to publish occasional reprints, but it is unlikely that they will go so far afield as they did when the reprint bandwagon was rolling speedily through the sixties.

Survival Tactics

Reprinting has become more and more a risky business. Some small firms are known to be searching for working capital. In the tight money market of the early 1970s, some are finding security and continuance under a larger corporate umbrella. Mergers and acquisitions in the reprint field are increasingly commonplace. As the large firms become larger and the small houses lose their identity, the same kind of bigness that attends general publishing could engulf reprinting. Those reprinters who do retain their specialist status are likely to grow in their understanding of library selection and acquisition processes. Title selection decisions will be more intelligent. Reprint sales and promotion practices will improve (i.e., become more efficient). These changes should aid librarians.

It is reasonable to conclude that reprinting may one day be viewed as an intermediary step in publishing history. That day will come when the photographic and electronic technologies can economically be adapted to serve specialized needs for small editions. There are many important factors to be considered before this can occur, not the least of which is the matter of copyright and protection for authors and owners of original works. Scholarly reprint publishing, conducted responsibly, will continue to serve useful purposes for the near and foreseeable future.

Some reprinters are improving their marketing methods. They are telling it like it is. As a result, there appears to be less vindictiveness and bickering inside the industry than there was in the pioneer days. Not all the problems are solved yet. Some reprinters continue to market their wares deceptively. Their promises are suspect and deserve to be. Probably friction and jealousy will be evident so long as a large number of independent entrepreneurs each seek a piece of a relatively small market. Rival reprint editions (i.e., when the same title is reprinted by more than one firm), continue to plague the industry. Intentional duplication of titles diminishes sales for each shortrun publisher and creates ill will among purchasers. There are signs that this practice is lessening, mostly because this kind of below-the-belt rivalry is being thwarted, as it should be, in the marketplace.

College and research libraries, the industry's major customers, are operating with severely curtailed budgets. More stringent expenditure for library resources means decreased retrospective buying. This factor has obvious, serious implications for reprinters. Publishers of very large and expensive sets, or esoteric titles, are likely to be seriously affected by cutbacks in library reprint purchasing. There is evidence that at least a few reprinters are beginning to exercise restraint in the numbers of titles they are publishing. For example, one major house which published about 500 titles in 1970 intended to produce about half that number in 1971 and 1972. Another firm with 390 titles listed in 1971 scheduled about 300 for 1972. And, one New York firm is known to have canceled some 200 preassigned Library of Congress card numbers, indicating that they dropped that many titles from their forthcoming lists.

The reprint industry, in the latter years of the 1960s and the beginning of the present decade, has been responsible for a significant percentage (almost one third) of the titles published annually in this country. Even assuming a curtailment in reprint-title output, the industry deserves to be considered a significant publishing sector.

COMMON GOALS OF REPRINTERS

It is clear from the nature of the findings that reprint publishers do not form a "distinct group of productive enterprises," Webster's definition of an "industry." It is therefore concluded that there is no one reprint industry. Rather there are about 300 publishers who are more or less involved in numerous kinds of reprint programs. As individual publishers, reprinters vary tremendously. Their lists differ, the format and quality of their reprints differ, and their publishing philosophies differ. Their financial resources are reported to be vastly different. Their talents as businessmen and as bookmen run a wide gamut indeed. There are publishers who contribute to efficient bibliographic control and others who seem not to care. The majority of firms sell their reprints directly by mail while others also distribute through bookstores and wholesalers. This litany could easily be extended, but the point is that reprint publishing is unquestionably fragmented. This means that there is now no efficient way for publishers and purchasers to deal with overall problems. Any attempt to effect widespread changes must now depend upon approaching each reprinter, or upon efforts to communicate in a one-at-a-time mode through journals.

The one thread that does appear to run through the variety of cloaks is the publishers' intent to bring back into print works that are not generally available. Their success depends on knowing what is available, what is needed, and what other publishers have already produced. Therefore it is recommended that the bibliographic control of reprints be studied further and improved. Publishers must do their part in this. They must understand the need to cooperate with national and trade bibliographic systems. This is happening in part as a by-product of the Cataloging in Publication (CIP) Program through which the Library of Congress is helping reprinters to understand how and why they need to catalog and describe their titles consistently and correctly. The appropriate Z39 subcommittee of the American National Standards Institute, the ALA Reprinting Committee, and other concerned and interested groups or persons should continue to consider problems relating to increased access to standard descriptors for reprints and microforms. One particular area that must be tackled is the proper identification and cataloging of reprinted government publications. It seems likely that the CIP project, which intends to include government documents as soon as possible, will effectively help bring order to this confused subject. Continuing support for the CIP project as a part of the Library of Congress' regular annual budget is therefore essential.

COMMON GOALS OF LIBRARIANS

Librarians are increasingly concerned with preservation and conservation of library materials. Their focus will encourage reprinters to improve the quality of their products. However, it is equally clear that the economics of shortrun publishing makes it difficult for publishers to accommodate these needs without seriously affecting list prices. Some reprinters have hedged their bets so considerably that they probably do have room to make pricing adjustments and still come away with a reasonable profit. There are a few reprinters who now sell their reprints at low prices. These publishers will need to decide whether to maintain low prices and perhaps compromise on physical quality, or publish better books at higher prices. This is a problem area of reprinting that needs to be discussed by librarians and publishers. Do librarians want certain titles in expendable editions to serve immediate needs? Does a particular book need to be manufactured to long-lasting specifications so that it may endure for several hundred years? There is an alternative. If larger quantities of books in specialized fields could be sold, unit costs (and prices) might come down. The only conclusion one can reach about reprint prices, from the data collected for this study, is that there is a wide variety of pricing practices and policies among publishers. The only realistic and legal recommendation is that the price that one is willing to pay to purchase a reprint needs to be determined in the marketplace. Decisions about what titles to publish and which to buy should be based upon informed professional judgment.

A considerable number of publishers and other persons who have been observing the reprint scene closely are expressing doubts that reprint publishing will survive as a specialized sector of the publishing industry. While this view does not seem to be held by a majority of the active publishers, there is some evidence that lends support to the doubters. This may be found in publishers' responses about long-range title availability. There are further hints in the general shift and blurring of lines in other parts of the publishing industry. It is becoming much more difficult to separate general publishing from educational publishing, for example, or higher-priced paperbound publishing from mass-market paperbound publishing or university press publishing from high-quality trade and scholarly reprint publishing. Micropublishing is a growing field. But seen as a printing technology, it is an option open to all sectors of the industry. Micropublishing remains a specialty. At one time it was possible to distinguish classes of publishing rather sharply. Now the traits formerly characteristic of one category are in transit to another. Many firms engage in a variety of publishing endeavors: trade titles are adapted for supplemental reading in schools; university presses are considering major fiction programs; microforms are produced by (or for) many kinds of firms; hardcover books are published by microform firms; and, as noted, more reprinters are publishing original titles and microforms.

In addition to these industry fusions, there are also many new and different kinds of publishing going on inside the houses. Parts of books and periodicals are published as spin-off programs. These appear under new titles and new names. There is enrichment in this diversity, and there is confusion. Reprint publishing is affected by changes that take place in other kinds of publishing houses. It is probable that reprinters will increasingly come into direct competition with publishers from other sectors, some of whom are known to be exploring the potential for reproducing titles on demand, in a kind of custom publishing.

Much of the interaction between reprinters and other publishers has to do with copyright matters and with securing rights and permissions. The copyright revision bill has been before Congress for more than five years. Copyright legislation is at the forefront of the thinking of some astute reprinters. In 1971, for example, some houses were known to be pump-priming, in order to be ready to reprint titles published between 1906 and 1915, titles that would have automatically dropped into the public domain on December 31, 1971, if another one-year extension bill had not been passed. It was passed, in a skin-of-the-teeth measure, in November 1971. The copyright revision bill is a piece of legislation of major significance to the entire publishing world and to libraries. It is likely that in 1972 or 1973 a new copyright bill will be enacted into law. The new law is expected to protect copyright property for the author's lifetime plus 50 years. Any such law will have serious implications for reprinters who concentrate on copying public-domain materials.

MUTUAL GOALS

Libraries are expressing increasing interest in reproducing some works in their collections which do not seem to be viable commercial publishing projects, or which, for other reasons, the library prefers to publish itself. The subject of libraries as publishers is one to which reprint and microform publishers will pay close attention. Indeed there may be some anxiety about competition between the for-profit and the not-for-profit interests. How libraries might be able to surmount the complex book distribution problems that deeply concern all publishers is a matter which calls for careful study in the library world. It is strongly urged that libraries and publishers work together to sift and to sort out which kinds of programs each might do best, and to agree to whatever remunerative and cooperative plans will satisfy their particular needs and the needs of the readers they serve. There can only be bad consequences for all concerned if any permanent wedge is allowed to come between these two worlds.

Publishers and librarians must make serious efforts to come to equitable agreements concerning reprinters' borrowing privileges and fees. Publishers need to understand library policies and the rationale behind charges and restrictions. Librarians must realize that high charges for copying may be detrimental to the library world generally. Arguments set forth by each side seem perfectly justified; yet a common meeting ground should be sought. It seems unquestionable that libraries have the right to try to assure their own financial security. They must, for the future of scholarship is at stake. On the other hand, increased charges to reprinters could finally result in an industry that consists only of giant-sized firms, for many small publishers say they find it impossible to pay $50 or $100 for each volume borrowed for copying without increasing the price of their works. These complex matters call for careful deliberations. It is recommended that this topic be taken up again as an order of business by the ALA reprinting committees, and by relevant committees of other professional associations. Reprint publishers, including micro-publishers, should be invited to present their views before the various committees.

In a similar vein, it is recommended that the many committees of professional organizations now concerned with reprint publishing establish formal liaisons or other channels to communicate and share opinions and findings in order to prevent duplication of efforts.

SUGGESTIONS FOR THE FUTURE

There is one area where the industry-that-is-not-quite-an-industry can be discussed as an entity. There is clear evidence that the reprint publishers, splintered and competitive as they are, would benefit by belonging to a trade association. This writer has long been an advocate of a more cohesive industry. The reasons for advocacy stem from years of viewing unmet, but common, needs. An association of publishers can, within established legal boundaries, help its members in such important social and legislative areas as copyright, postal rates and regulations, encouragement of standard advertising practices, marketing research, and more. It can help to lobby in support of funding programs, and perhaps help gain support for bibliographic standards. Responsible publishers should be willing to share some of the burden for effective industry actions which are helpful to libraries and publishers generally.

Therefore, reprint publishers are urged to discuss the possibility of associating as a reprinters' council or preferably, to consider joining the existing Association of American Publishers. There are some who will read this recommendation and doubt that reprinters will ever sit down peaceably, with proper legal counsel, to discuss such matters. This writer can attest to its possibility, for there were also some who said that the present research survey was not feasible because reprinters would not talk. A great many reprinters want to talk. They also seem ready to listen.

Appendix A

Definitions of "Reprint"

The term "reprint," and by extension, "reprinter," "reprint publisher," and "facsimile reprint" have been variantly defined. The chronological arrangement of definitions cited below reveals the changing nature of reprint technology. The effort to apply the same term to newer technologies probably contributes to the vagaries of current usage. (Italics have been supplied throughout, for emphasis.)

A "reprint" has been defined as:

1. A second or new impression or edition of any *printed* work; the *publication in one country of a work* previously printed *in another.* In the printing trade a printed article cut from one paper and reproduced in another is called reprint copy, as distinguished from manuscript or written copy.

Reprint copy is more easily composed than manuscript, and is more profitable alike to the journeyman, the employer and the publishers. The latter is able to estimate exactly the size and the cost of the work which he proposes to issue; the employer gets a much quicker return of the matter which he sets up, the journeyman has better profits and less loss of time on his copy. . . ."

Source: *American Dictionary of Printing and Bookmaking.* 1894. Reprinted, 1967.

2. Copy for a book or other work which *has already been printed,* in distinction from written manuscript. A second or new printing of a work. Reprint copy, is, naturally, easier to handle than manuscript, on account of its legibility. A reprint of a work may be done in different type and style from the original; *when an exact reprint* is meant it is *facsimile.*

Source: Hugo Jahn, compiler. *The Dictionary of Graphic Arts Terms.* 1928.

3. A new printing of a book; 2, A term used for *an edition in cheaper form* than the original and often issued *by another publisher* who specializes in such popular editions. Also called REBINDS and POPULAR COPYRIGHTS.

Source: John A. Holden. *The Bookman's Glossary.* 1931.

159

4. A subsequent printing of a work, not as a new edition, but as a re-rendering of text. Reprints may be divided into two classes: (1) literary reprints, which may be either a re-rendering of the text of a selected original, or an intercollation of various copies or editions combined into a perfected reading; (2) typographic reprints, which present a selected original in a new setting of type, frequently attempting, through the type-designs, arrangement, spelling, punctuation, etc., to suggest as far as possible, the appearance of the selected original.

Source: Stillwell. *Incunabula and Americana: 1450–1800*, 1931.

5. A reproduction in print of any matter already printed; a new impression of a work previously printed, without alteration of the matter. 2. Typog: Printed matter used as copy to be set up and printed again. a) to print a work again in a new edition; to print (matter) a second time; b) to print again in a different form. . . .

A reprinter is "one who reprints, *or who publishes* a reprint."

Source: *Oxford English Dictionary*. 1933.

6. A *new printing*, without material alteration, *from new or original type or plates*, as distinguished from copies made by typing, or reproductions made by a mechanical or a photomechanical process. Prefer the specific terms, EDITION, IMPRESSION, ISSUE, OFFPRINT, etc.; A textual reprint is one whose text follows exactly that of a particular edition.

Source: *ALA Glossary of Library Terms*. 1943.

7. A new printing from unchanged plates, *in cheaper form* than the original and often issued by a *specialized "reprint publisher."* . . . often collectively applied to reissues and later editions in general as "reprint literature," "reprint series," "reprint publishing."

The fact that publication of paper-bound reprints continues to increase and publication of hard-bound reprints continues to decrease makes a serious problem for librarians.

Note: Haines also discusses "Popular Reprints," issued in the nineteenth and twentieth centuries, in series such as "Bohn's Library," and "Everyman's Library."

Source: Haines. *Living with Books*. 2nd ed. New York: Columbia University Press, 1950, pp. 221–24.

8. Strictly defined, a reprint is a new printing from the original plates in cheaper form than the original. This definition has been expanded within recent years to include books printed from newly set or re-set plates, not necessarily cheaper in price or form than the original.

Source: Whitten and Fessler. "Hard-cover Reprint Publishing." *Library Trends*, July 1958, p. 82.

9. A book reprinted from the original plates. This definition has been enlarged to include also volumes with text unchanged (sometimes with minor corrections) but which are newly reset to conform with the publisher's policy for the series. A third type is the volume made up of collections from any sources, such as the anthology, which may be entirely original and brand new in scope, but the contents of which have been taken from earlier publications, both book and periodical.

Source: Orton. *Catalog of Reprints in Series*. Preface. 1967 Supplement.

10. A reprint is not a new printing or edition reprinted from original type or plates, or reset completely; it is almost always a facsimile of the original edition, usually but not always the first edition; it usually but not always has been out of print for some

time, and there has been a slow but steady demand for the title, not from the general public, but from librarians, collectors and specialist dealers; it is usually but not always the same size, photo-offset from the original, but may be increased photographically for legibility, or several copies used to produce the 'best' reproduction; it may sometimes—though rarely—be reduced in size, but then the type must be readable by the naked eye without use of any soft- or hardware; it may contain—and often does—new introductory matter, updated bibliographies, corrected indexes, references to later researches . . . ; it is usually but not always hardbound; . . . it may be in paperback, portfolio, etc. . . . usually but not always in a small edition, from 200 to 2000, but averages from 250 to 1000, but . . . may go to 5000 and above . . . and only a thousand copies may be bound at one time by even the most optimistic publisher. . . .

Source: Sol M. Malkin. 1969 AB *Bookman's Yearbook,* pp. 2–3.

11. Reprints "must have two minimal factors . . . (1) the original publication should serve as the direct source for the new publication, whether via photography, photolithography, photo-offset or any other process so that the two items, page for page, are identical, and (2) the new product must be published by someone other than the original publisher."

Source: Frederick Freedman. *Choice,* October, 1969, p. 978.

In addition to the above meanings, conferred and inferred, a "facsimile" is specifically defined as:

1. A lithographic or a photomechanical reproduction of an original, or some portion of it, made for the purpose of presenting an accurate picture of the original. In modern times, the term is applied to those made by one or another of the mechanical processes that are based, fundamentally, upon some form of photographic reproduction.

Source: Stillwell, *op. cit.,* p. 179.

2. "An exact copy or reproduction." (From the Latin: *factum simile,* something made like.)

Source: Funk & Wagnalls. 1948.

A "type facsimile" is defined as:

1. "An edition in which types of similar founts to those used in the original are set to follow the original setting as closely as possible."

Source: Pollard. *The Library,* 4th Series, 6 (1926) p. 305.

Appendix B

Identifying Titles for Reprinting: A List of Sources Cited by Publishers

AMERICA IN FICTION by Otis W. Coan and Richard G. Lillard. 5th ed. (Palo Alto, Calif.: Pacific Books, 1967).

AMERICAN AUTHORS, 1600–1900: A Biographical Dictionary of American Literature by Stanley J. Kunitz and Howard Haycraft. (New York: Wilson, 1938).

AMERICAN BIBLIOGRAPHY,1639–1800 by Charles Evans. (Chicago: printed for the author, 1903–59; v. 14 edited by Roger P. Bristol.)

THE AMERICAN HISTORICAL FICTION by Arthur T. Dickinson. 2nd ed. (New York: Scarecrow, 1963).

THE AMERICAN HISTORICAL NOVEL by Ernest E. Leisy. (Norman: University of Oklahoma Press, 1950).

THE AMERICAN NOVEL 1789–1959: A Checklist of Twentieth-Century Criticism by Donna L. Gerstenberger and George Hendrick. (Denver: Alan Swallow, 1961).

THE AMERICAN NEGRO REFERENCE BOOK by John P. Davis. (Englewood Cliffs, N.J.: Prentice-Hall, 1966).

ANNIVERSARIES AND HOLIDAYS by Mary Emogene Hazeltine. 2nd ed. rev. (Chicago: American Library Association, 1944).

A BASIC GEOGRAPHICAL LIBRARY: A Selected and Annotated Book List for American Colleges by Martha Church, Robert E. Huke, and Wilbur Zelinsky. (Washington: Association of American Geographers, 1966).

BASIC RUSSIAN PUBLICATIONS: An Annotated Bibliography on Russia and the Soviet Union by Paul L. Horecky. (Chicago: University of Chicago Press, 1962).

BEST BOOKS: A Reader's Guide and Literary Reference Book by William S. Sonnenschein. 3rd ed. (London: Routledge, 1910–1935).

BIBLIOGRAPHICAL GUIDE TO THE HISTORY OF CHRISTIANITY by Shirley Jackson Case and others. (Chicago: University of Chicago Press, 1931).

BIBLIOGRAPHY OF AMERICAN LITERATURE by Jacob Nathaniel Blanck. (New Haven: Yale University Press, 1955).

BIBLIOGRAPHY OF COMPARATIVE LITERATURE by Fernand Baldensperger and Werner P. Friederich. (Chapel Hill: University of North Carolina Press, 1950).

A BIBLIOGRAPHY OF NORTH AMERICAN FOLKLORE AND FOLKSONG by Charles Haywood. 2nd rev. ed. (New York: Dover, 1961).

BIBLIOGRAPHY OF THE NEGRO IN AFRICA AND AMERICA by Monroe N. Work. (New York: Wilson, 1928).

BOOKMAN'S GUIDE TO AMERICANA by Joseph Norman Heard. 2nd ed. (New York: Scarecrow, 1960).

BOOKS FOR COLLEGE LIBRARIES compiled by Melvin J. Voigt and Joseph H. Treyz. (Chicago: American Library Association, 1967).

BRITISH AUTHORS OF THE NINETEENTH CENTURY by Stanley J. Kunitz and Howard Haycraft. (New York: Wilson, 1936).

CATALOG OF THE LAMONT LIBRARY, HARVARD COLLEGE prepared by Philip J. McNiff. (Cambridge: Harvard University Press, 1953).

CHILDREN'S LITERATURE: A GUIDE TO REFERENCE SOURCES prepared under the direction of Virginia Haviland. (Washington: U.S. Library of Congress, 1966).

CIVIL WAR BOOKS: A Critical Bibliography by Allan Nevins, James I. Roberton, and Bell I. Wiley. (Baton Rouge: Louisiana State University Press, 1967).

CLASSIFIED LIST OF PERIODICALS FOR THE COLLEGE LIBRARY by Evan I. Farber. (Boston: F. W. Faxon Co., 1957) (New edition to be published in 1972).

THE CLASSIFIED LIST OF REFERENCE BOOKS AND PERIODICALS FOR COLLEGE LIBRARIES by W. Stanley Hoole. (Atlanta: Southern Association of Colleges and Secondary Schools, Commission on Colleges and Universities, 1955).

CRITICAL BIBLIOGRAPHY OF FRENCH LITERATURE edited by David C. Cabeen. (Syracuse: Syracuse University Press, 1947–1961).

CYCLOPEDIA OF WORLD AUTHORS by Frank N. Magill. (New York: Harper, 1958).

DICTIONARY OF AMERICAN BIOGRAPHY edited by Allen Johnson and Dumas Malone. (New York: Scribner, 1928–1937).

DICTIONARY OF AMERICAN LITERATURE compiled by Jacob N. Blanck. (New Haven: Yale University Press, 1955–.)

DICTIONARY OF BOOKS RELATING TO AMERICA, From Its Discovery to the Present Time by Joseph Sabin and Wilberforce Eames. (New York: Sabin, 1868–1892).

A DICTIONARY OF UNIVERSAL BIOGRAPHY: Of All Ages and of All People by Hyamson. 2nd ed. rev. (New York: Dutton, 1951).

ENCYCLOPEDIA OF PHILOSOPHY edited by Paul Edwards. (New York: Macmillan, 1967).

ENCYCLOPAEDIA OF THE SOCIAL SCIENCES edited by Edwin R. A. Seligman. (New York: Macmillan, 1930–1935).

THE ENGLISH NOVEL, 1578–1956: A Checklist of Twentieth-Century Criticisms by Inglis F. Bell and Donald Baird. (Denver: Alan Swallow, 1959).

ESSAY AND GENERAL LITERATURE INDEX (New York: Wilson, 1934–.)

FICTION CATALOG by Estelle A. Fidell and Ester V. Flory, 7th ed. (New York: Wilson, 1961).

GUIDE THROUGH THE ROMANTIC MOVEMENT by Ernest Bernbaum. 2nd ed. (New York: Ronald, 1949).

GUIDE TO AMERICAN LITERATURE AND ITS BACKGROUNDS SINCE 1890 by Howard Mumford Jones and Richard M. Ludwig. 3rd ed. rev. & enl. (Cambridge: Harvard University Press, 1964).

GUIDE TO ART REFERENCE BOOKS by Mary Chamberlain. (Chicago: American Library Association, 1959).

GUIDE TO HISTORICAL LITERATURE edited by George F. Howe. (New York: Macmillan, 1961).

GUIDE TO REFERENCE MATERIAL edited by Albert John Walford. (London: Library Association, 1959).

GUIDE TO REFERENCE BOOKS by Constance M. Winchell. 8th ed. (Chicago: American Library Association, 1967, and supplements).

GUIDE TO THE STUDY OF MEDIEVAL HISTORY by Louis J. Paetow. Rev. ed. (New York: Crofts, 1931).

A GUIDE TO THE STUDY OF THE UNITED STATES OF AMERICA. (Washington, D.C.: U.S. Government Printing Office, 1960).

HARVARD GUIDE TO AMERICAN HISTORY edited by Oscar Handlin and others. (Cambridge: Belknap Press of Harvard University Press, 1954).

A HISTORY OF AMERICAN MAGAZINES by Frank Luther Mott. (Cambridge: Harvard University Press, 1968).

INTERNATIONAL ENCYCLOPAEDIA OF THE SOCIAL SCIENCES edited by David L. Sills. (New York: Macmillan, 1969).

LAW BOOKS RECOMMENDED FOR LIBRARIES edited by the Association of American Law Schools. (South Hackensack, N.J., Rothman, 1967).

A LIST OF BOOKS FOR COLLEGE LIBRARIES by Charles B. Shaw. (Chicago: American Library Association, 1931).

LITERARY HISTORY OF THE UNITED STATES edited by Robert E. Spiller and Willard Thorp. (New York: Macmillan, 1948).

THE LITTLE MAGAZINE: A HISTORY AND A BIBLIOGRAPHY by Charles Allen, F. J. Hoffman, and Carolyn F. Ulrich. (Princeton, 1947, reprinted by Kraus, 1967).

MANUAL DE BIBLIOGRAPHIE by Louise-Noelle Malclès. (Paris: Presses Universitaires de France, 1963).

MODERN DRAMA: A CHECKLIST OF CRITICAL LITERATURE ON TWENTIETH CENTURY PLAYS by Irving Adelman and Rita Dworkin. (Metuchen, N.J.: Scarecrow Press, 1967).

A PACIFIC BIBLIOGRAPHY by Clyde R. H. Taylor. (Wellington, New Zealand: Polynesian Society, 1951).

POETRY EXPLICATION: A Checklist of Interpretation Since 1925 of British and American Poems Past and Present by Joseph Marshal Kuntz. (Denver: Alan Swallow, 1962).

READER'S ENCYCLOPAEDIA OF AMERICAN LITERATURE by Max J. Herzberg. (New York: Crowell, 1962).

RELIGIONS, MYTHOLOGIES, FOLKLORES: An Annotated Bibliography by Katherine Diehl. (Metuchen, N.J.: Scarecrow, 1962).

SCIENTIFIC SERIALS: Characteristics and Lists of Most Cited Publications in Mathematics, Physics, Chemistry, Geology, Physiology, Botany, Zoology, and Entomology by Charles Harvey Brown. (Chicago: American Library Association, 1956).

SELECT BIBLIOGRAPHY: Asia, Africa, Eastern Europe, Latin America. (New York: American Universities Field Staff, Inc., 1960–63–67).

SHORT FICTION CRITICISM: A Checklist of Interpretation Since 1925 of Stories and Novelettes (American, British, Continental) 1800–1958 by Jarvis A. Thurston and others. (Denver: Alan Swallow, 1960).

A SHORT GUIDE TO CHEMICAL LITERATURE by Malcolm G. Dyson. (London: Longmans, Green and Company, 1951).

THE SOUTH IN AMERICAN LITERATURE, 1607–1900 by Jay B. Hubbell. (Durham, N.C.: Duke University Press, 1954).

STANDARD CATALOG FOR HIGH SCHOOL LIBRARIES edited by Dorothy H. West and others. 8th ed. (New York: Wilson, 1962).

U.S.-IANA (1650–1950) by C. Wright Howes. 2nd ed. (New York: Bowker, for the Newberry Library, 1962).

VICTORIAN FICTION: A Guide to Research by Lionel Stevenson and others. (Cambridge: Harvard University Press, 1964).

VICTORIAN POETS: A Guide to Research by Frederick Everett Faverty (Cambridge: Harvard University Press, 1956).

THE WORLD OF CHILDREN'S LITERATURE by Anne Pellowski. (New York: Bowker, 1968).

Appendix C

List of Interviews with Publishers and Persons in the Book Trades and Library World; April 1968–August 1970

Organization	Interviewee and Title	Date
AB Bookman's Weekly	Mary Ann O'Brian Malkin, Editor	10/30/68*
Abercrombie & Fitch (R)	Charles A. Pearce, Publisher[1]	4/15/69
Africana Publishing Corp. (R)	Hans M. Zell, Editor-in-Chief	6/13/69
Agathon Press, Inc. (R)	Burton Lasky, President	8/19/69*
American Book Prices Current	Edward A. Lazare, former Editor	3/27/69
American Book Publishers Council	M. Ann Heidbreder, Senior Associate[2]	10/29/68
AMS Press, Inc. (R)	Gabriel Hornstein, President	2/25/69*
Arno Press, Inc. (R)	Arnold Zohn, President	2/1/69*
Assn. of Research Libraries	Stephen A. McCarthy, Executive Director	4/23/69
Award Books	Michael deForrest, Editor	4/28/69
Baker & Taylor Company	Harold L. Roth, Vice-President[3]	3/19/69
Barnes & Noble, Inc. (R)	John Mladinich, Vice-President[4]	4/16/68 7/18/69*
Benjamin Blom, Inc. (R)	Anthony Santaniello, Editor	6/26/69
Bergman Publishers (R)	Peter M. Bergman, Publisher	7/20/69
Books for Libraries, Inc. (R)	Harvey P. Roth, President	2/7/69
R. R. Bowker Company (R)	John Berry III, Editorial Dept.[5]	5/3/69
Brooklyn Public Library	Avis Zebker, Coordinator, Book Order Dept.	4/19/68
Carrollton Press, Inc. (R)	William Buchanan, President	5/25/69*
CCM Information Sciences, Inc.	Jeffrey Norton, President	6/12/69
Central Book Company (R)	Milton Hirschman, President	1/6/69*
Collectors Editions, Ltd. (R)	David M. Block, Publisher	11/5/69

Key: (R) following company name indicates publisher of reprints.
Asterisk following date indicates additional information supplied by telephone or correspondence.
T following date of interview indicates all data supplied by telephone.

Organization	Interviewee and Title	Date
Columbia University Libraries	James E. Fall, Assistant Head Acquisitions Dept.	4/17/68
Columbia University Libraries	Alfred H. Lane, Head, Gifts & Exch: Chrmn., ALA Reprinting Committee	4/16/68*
Columbia University Libraries	Earl Kemp, Head, Acquisitions Dept.	6/17/70
Columbia University Libraries	Walter M. Barnard, Bibliographer —Acquisitions Dept.	6/17/70
Columbia University Libraries	Warren J. Haas, Director of Libraries	6/22/70
Columbia University Press	Carl B. Hansen, Assistant Director	4/28/69
Cornell University Libraries	Felix Reichmann, Assistant Director[6]	7/27/68*
Council on Library Resources, Inc.	Melville J. Ruggles, Program Officer	7/8/69
Crescendo Publishing Company (R)	Robert Bell, Publisher	6/26/69
DaCapo Press (R)	Alan J. Marks, Executive Editor	3/10/69
Dover Publications, Inc. (R)	Hayward Cirker, President	1/14/69
Edwards Brothers, Inc. (R)	Joseph W. Edwards, President	3/12/69
Howard Fertig, Inc. (R)	Howard Fertig, President and Editor-in-Chief	8/22/69
Burt Franklin, Publisher (R)	Burt Franklin, President	5/27/69
Gale Research Company (R)	Frederick G. Ruffner, President	3/11/69*
Gale Research Company (R)	James M. Ethridge, Editorial Director	3/11/69
Garnet Reprint Corp. (R)	Rosalyn T. Badalamenti, Publisher[7]	8/8/69
Garrett Press, Inc. (R)	Daniel C. Garrett, President	5/26/69*
Garrett Press, Inc. (R)	Thomas T. Beeler, Editorial Director	5/26/69*
Genealogical Publishing Corp. (R)	Jules Chodak, President (deceased)	4/24/69
Genealogical Publishing Corp. (R)	Barry Chodak, President	7/1/70
Greenwood Publishing Corp. (R)	Harold J. Mason, Co-President	9/27/68*
Greenwood Publishing Corp. (R)	Harold Schwartz, Co-President	4/24/70
Gregg Press (R)	Fred Sawyer, Editor	6/26/69
Hafner Publishing Company (R)	Harry Lubrecht, Vice-President	5/14/69
Harper & Row, Publishers	Alfred E. Prettyman, Editor-Manager, J & J Harper Editions (R)[8]	10/2/69
Harper & Row, Publishers	Frank Scioscia, Marketing Coordinator[9]	10/30/69*
Haskell House Publishers, Ltd. (R)	Nachman Halberstadt, President	10/14/69
Humanities Press, Inc. (R)	Lothar Simon, Sales Manager	6/26/69
Johnson Reprint Corp. (R)	Albert Henderson, Editor[10]	6/19/68*
Johnson Reprint Corp. (R)	Fred Rappaport, Vice-President	12/9/69*
Walter J. Johnson, Inc.	Herbert M. Johnson, Vice-President & General Manager	9/16/70*

continued

Organization	Interviewee and Title	Date
Augustus M. Kelley, Publishers (R)	Augustus M. Kelley, Publisher	5/12/69
Kennikat Press, Inc. (R)	Cornell Jaray, President	7/10/69*
Kraus Reprint Company (R)	Jens Christoffison, Assistant Manager	4/16/70
Library Editions, Ltd. (R)	Sol Lewis, President	8/20/70
Library Editions, Ltd. (R)	J. T. Clairborne, Jr., Chairman of Board	8/20/70
Library Editions, Ltd. (R)	David Glotzer, Production Manager	8/20/70*
Library of Congress	Richard S. Angell, Chief, Technical Processes Research	4/22/69
Library of Congress	Roy P. Basler, Chief, Mss. Division	4/22/69
Library of Congress	John Cole, Technical Assistant to the Asst. Dir. for Development of Collections, Reference Dept.	4/22/69
Library of Congress	Jean B. Metz, Selection Officer, Processing Dept.	4/22/69
Library of Congress	Mary E. Kahler, Assistant Chief, Union Catalog Division	4/22/69
Library of Congress	George Schwegmann, Chief Union Catalog Division	4/22/69
Library of Congress	Nathalie Wells, Head, Pre-assigned Numbers, Card Division	4/22/69
Library of Congress	Paul W. Winkler, Principal Cataloger, Descriptive Cataloging Division	4/22/69
McGrath Publishing Co. (R)	Daniel McGrath, Publisher	4/24/69
McGraw-Hill, Inc.	Dan M. Lacy, Senior Vice-President	7/2/68*
MicroPhoto Division, Bell & Howell (R)	Larry Block, Manager, Project Operations	10/9/69
Mikro-Buk, Inc. (R)	Marvin Lipper, Vice-President, Publishing	8/18/70
NCR Microcard Editions (R)	Albert J. Diaz, Executive Director	1/28/69*
New York Public Library	Sam P. Williams, Librarian & Editor, *The Reprint Bulletin*	6/18/68
New York Public Library	Christopher Samuels, Ref. Librarian[11]	7/31/69
New York Public Library	Hannah Friedman, Collections-Preservation Coordinator, The Research Libraries	6/8/70
Octagon Books (R)	Henry G. Schlanger, Editor-in-Chief	8/28/69*
Princeton University Library	Helen Welch Tuttle, Assistant Librarian for Preparations	10/31/69
Queens Borough Public Library	Eileen Rowland, Librarian, New Books Section, Assistant Superintendent, Acquisitions	5/7/69
Readex Microprint Corp. (R)	Mark Levine, Editor	6/26/69
Readex Microprint Corp. (R)	Nathan Cohen, Editor	6/26/69

Organization	Interviewee and Title	Date
Readex Microprint Corp. (R)	Albert Boni, President	11/24/69
Research Reprints, Inc. (R)	Jo-ann Jacobs, Publisher	1/14/70
Bernard M. Rosenthal, Inc.	Bernard M. Rosenthal, Owner	4/4/69
Russell & Russell (R)	Sidney A. Russell, Managing Editor	4/28/69
William Salloch	William Salloch, Owner	4/2/69*
Scholarly Press, Inc. (R)	R. John Oliver, Vice President & Assistant to the President	6/26/69
Shoe String Press, Inc. (R)	Frances T. Ottemiller (Rudder), President	6/3/69
Shoe String Press, Inc. (R)	Lewis T. Wiggin, Editorial Director	6/3/69
Patterson Smith Publishing Co. (R)	Patterson Smith, President	5/25/69*
Patterson Smith Publishing Co. (R)	Thomas Kelley, Sales Manager	5/25/69*
Charles E. Tuttle Company (R)	Tom Fagan, Promotion Director	11/18/68
Charles E. Tuttle Company (R)	Charles E. Tuttle, President	7/2/69
University Microfilms, Inc. (R)	Eugene B. Power, Chairman of Board[12]	3/11/69
University Microfilms, Inc. (R)	Robert F. Asleson, President	7/2/70
Ye Galleon Press	Glen C. Adams, Owner[13]	1/13/69*

Note: The following changes have been noted since interviews were conducted. An effort has been made to be current to March 1971.

[1] Deceased—February 1, 1970.
[2] Assn. of American Publishers, Inc., as of July 1970.
[3] Director, Nassau County Reference System, as of 1970.
[4] Managing Director, Rowman & Littlefield, as of March 1971.
[5] Editor, *Library Journal.*
[6] Retired, 1971.
[7] Out of business, as of November 1969.
[8] Publisher, Emerson Hall, as of 1970.
[9] Sales Manager, Children's Books, as of 1970.
[10] General Manager, Maxwell Reprint Corp., as of 1970.
[11] Research Administrator, McKinsey & Co., 1971.
[12] Retired, 1970.
[13] Correspondence with Mr. Adams has been so extensive and informative that it serves in lieu of a personal interview.

Appendix D

Request for Information from Scholarly Reprint Publishers in the United States

FIRM NAME:

ADDRESS:

SCHOLARLY REPRINTS are titles generally issued in small editions (less than 5000 copies) intended for a specialized audience, often of works that have been out of print or scarce. Probably most bound books will be produced by photo-offset, but any production methods are admissible. Excluded are reprints of titles from a publisher's own backlist, and most mass-marketed "popular" titles.

NUMBER OF TITLES: Following UNESCO and Publishers' Weekly practice, count each volume in a multi-volume set separately only if each volume has a different title and forms a separate whole. Please count an imported title only if your firm financially participated in its production, or if you are the sole distributor of the title in the United States.

---

1. The head of our
   organization is: _____
   Name   Title

2. Our primary business is that of:

   a. publisher   a. _____
   b. bookseller   b. _____
   c. printer   c. _____
   d. professional association or society   d. _____
   e. library   e. _____
   f. other (please specify)   f. _____

3. Our organization was founded in the year   _____

4. Reprints were first published in the year   _____

5. In our publishing program, reprints constitute:
   a. our entire list   a. _____
   b. about 75% of our list   b. _____
   c. about 50% of our list   c. _____
   d. about 25% of our list   d. _____
   e. a very small part of our list   e. _____

6. Our reprints are issued under the following imprints: (please supply)

7. We reprint in the following format(s): (If more than one kind,
   please note approximate percent of production)

                                                Percent
   a. hardcover books   a. _____
   b. paperbound books   b. _____
   c. microfilm (16mm & 35mm rolls)   c. _____
   d. microfiche   d. _____
   e. ultramicrofiche   e. _____
   f. microprint   f. _____
   g. electrostatic prints   g. _____
   h. other (please specify)   h. _____

8. The original form(s) of material we reprint is: (If more than one,
   please give the approximate percent of your total program)

                                                Percent
   a. books (monographs & books in series)   a. _____
   b. periodicals   b. _____
   c. newspapers   c. _____
   d. government documents   d. _____
   e. maps, sheet music or other separates   e. _____
   f. other (please specify)   f. _____

9. The number of titles we have reprinted is:
   (Please note explanation on first page)
   a. Less than 10   f. 500– 999   a. _____   f. _____
   b. 10–49   g. 1000–1499   b. _____   g. _____
   c. 50–99   h. 1500–2999   c. _____   h. _____
   d. 100–299   i. 3000–5000   d. _____   i. _____
   e. 300–499   j. Over 5000   e. _____   j. _____

10. New matter is added to our editions:

                             Usually   Sometimes   Never
    a. introduction   a. _____   a. _____   a. _____
    b. index   b. _____   b. _____   b. _____
    c. updated bibliography c. _____ c. _____   c. _____
    d. updated biography d. _____   d. _____   d. _____
    e. critical notes   e. _____   e. _____   e. _____
    f. other (please specify) f. _____ f. _____   f. _____

11. Please express your opinion about the *policy* of adding new matter to reprinted
    editions.

12. Our subject specialties are: (prefer specific to general terms. e.g., Botany rather
    than Science)
    a.   d.
    b.   e.
    c.   f.

13. Titles are selected for our programs primarily on the basis of:
    a. personal knowledge of subject field(s) and needs   a. _____
    b. awareness of unmet demands for copies on the used book market   b. _____
    c. appearance of title on recommended book list   c. _____
    d. advice from paid consultants   d. _____
    e. advice from faculty, librarians, scholars   e. _____
    f. other (please describe)   f. _____

14. We borrow a library copy to reprint   __often__seldom__never

15. Our editions are manufactured under outside contract   __yes__no

16. We use the following method(s) of production: (e.g., photo-offset, letterpress, etc.) Please list.

17. Please list (discuss if you wish) particular production problems you encounter in publishing reprinted editions. (e.g., delivery dates, quality control, etc.)

18. The size of our usual initial pressrun is:
    a. Less than 100   a. _____
    b.   100 – 249   b. _____
    c.   250 – 499   c. _____
    d.   500 – 749   d. _____
    e.   750 – 999   e. _____
    f.   1000 – 2000   f. _____
    g.   Over   2000   g. _____

19. Please indicate which of the following markets is your primary, secondary, etc. by ranking on a scale of 1–7, where 1 = primary. Insert a zero if you do not now sell a particular market.
    a. college and university libraries   a. _____
    b. wholesalers (jobbers)   b. _____
    c. secondary schools and libraries   c. _____
    d. public libraries   d. _____
    e. bookstores   e. _____
    f. individual customers   f. _____
    g. other (please specify)   g. _____

20. Our reprints are sold: (If more than one outlet, indicate primary, secondary, etc. using scale 1–4, where 1 = primary. Insert zero if not applicable)
    a. by direct mail sales   a. _____
    b. through wholesalers (jobbers)   b. _____
    c. through bookstores   c. _____
    d. other (please specify)   d. _____

21. We regularly issue catalogs, lists and/or flyers   __yes__no
    (If you do, kindly send me a sample copy)

22. Our titles are regularly submitted for listing in the following bibliographies:
    a. Library of Congress   a. _____
    b. Publishers' Weekly   b. _____
    c. Books in Print—PTLA   c. _____
    d. Guide to Reprints   d. _____

e. Announced Reprints   e. _____
f. Reprint Bulletin   f. _____
g. Guide to Microforms in Print   g. _____
h. Other (please specify)   h. _____

23. Reviews of our titles appear in:

	often	seldom	never
a. national media	a.	a.	a.
b. local or regional journals	b.	b.	b.
c. subject-oriented journals	c.	c.	c.

24. Concerning reviews, we feel that:

	yes	no
a. coverage in library journals should be extended to include more reprinted editions	a. ___	___
b. a review journal devoted to reprints is needed	b. ___	___
c. adequate ways now exist to find reviews of older titles	c. ___	___
d. they are not of particular importance to us	d. ___	___
e. other (please comment)	e. _____	

25. The approximate number of titles on our list that are in the public domain is:

a. all or most   a. _____
b. more than half   b. _____
c. less than half   c. _____
d. few   d. _____
e. none   e. _____

26. Please express your opinion about the payment of royalties on titles which are not copyrighted.

27. Please react to the statement, "the well is running dry" as it applies to availability of titles of merit yet to be reprinted and the future of your publishing programs.

28. How do you feel about discussing with other publishers the possibility of forming some kind of an association of reprint publishers?

a. would probably join in a discussion   a. _____
b. would probably not join in a discussion   b. _____
c. other (please comment)   c. _____

29. If your firm is an affiliate or subsidiary of another company in the United States or abroad, kindly note the name of the firm(s) and your relationship.

Please share with me any further ideas about any of the above or about your future programs or the future of the industry. If you prefer to have any of your remarks kept "off the record" please note your request, which will be honored. It is important for me to know your program so that I can draw a composite picture of the industry.

Thank you for your help. You have my personal wishes for a successful publishing season.

(Mrs.) Carol Nemeyer
Columbia University
October 1969

_____
Name and Title of Respondent

Appendix E

Directory of
Reprint Publishers

SCOPE AND ARRANGEMENT

All firms and institutions known to publish reprints of titles that are not from their own backlists are included. Efforts have been made to include reprint publishers identified after the survey was completed, and to keep the directory current. Corrections and additions will be gratefully received.

Reprint publishers are listed alphabetically by firm name. The company code which precedes each entry serves as a finding aid for references in the Index to Subject Specialties.

Firms entered by name only, preceded by an asterisk, are *not* reprint publishers according to this survey's definitions. These firms are included as a reference aid only because they have been listed as reprint publishers in other sources.

SYMBOLS AND ABBREVIATIONS

Founded: A single year indicates that the firm began reprinting the year it was founded. If two dates are given, the first is the founding date, the second, in parentheses, is the date the program reprint was initiated.

Type: The firm is primarily an: ASSN (association or society); BKSL (bookseller); COMM (commercial publisher); FNDT (foundation); LIBY (library); MICR (micropublisher); PRTR (printer); UNIV (university press).

Format: Reprints are published as: EL (electrostatic or xerographic prints); HC (hardcover books); MC (microcards); MF (microfilm reels); MI (microfiche); MP (microprints); UM (ultra-microfiche).

174

Forms: The firm primarily publishes reprints of works that originally appeared as: AN (anthologies or collections); BK (books [monographs and books in series]); GD (government documents); JL (journals, magazines, and other serials); MS (manuscripts); NP (newspapers); RP (reports, including annual reports, travel accounts, and the like); SH (sheet music, separate maps, and other separate materials).

Titles: The approximate number of titles published from the beginning of the firm's reprint program through 1970. If no numerical range is given, either the firm prefers not to provide this information and the figure could not be ascertained through secondary sources.

Subjects: The firm's primary or major fields of interest are given. Individual firms' catalogs should be checked for additional areas of interest.

Comments: The comment "No further information supplied" indicates that the firm did not respond to the request for information; data given are primarily from secondary sources. "No further information requested" indicates that the firm was located too late for a formal interview to be conducted. Data given for these firms are compiled from catalogs, descriptive literature, and secondary sources.

*: An asterisk preceding a name-only entry indicates that the firm is *not* currently a reprint publisher, as explained in the Scope and Arrangement note above, or that the firm could not be contacted at its last known address.

CIP: Reprint publishers participating in the Library of Congress' Cataloging in Publication Program, as of March 1972.

ISBN: The International Standard Book Number code for each firm is given where available.

Please note that if the headings described above are omitted from an entry, it has not been possible to report reliable information for these items.

---

*ABBOTSFORD PUBLISHING COMPANY

*RICHARD ABEL & COMPANY

A1 ABERCROMBIE & FITCH LIBRARY, Madison Avenue & 45th Street, New York, N.Y. 10017

Head: Henry Geis, Treasurer; Donald F. Smith, Director of Gallery. *Founded:* 1892 (R 1966). *Type:* BKSL. *Format:* HC. *Forms:* BK; JL; RP. *Titles:* 10–49. *Subjects:* Health, physical education, & recreation; exploration & travels. *Comments:* Publishing division of sporting goods firm.

A12 ACADEMIC INTERNATIONAL, P.O. Box 666, Hattiesburg, Miss. 39401

Type: BKSL. *Format:* HC; PB. *Forms:* BK. *Titles:* 10–49. *Subjects:* Russian Studies; Asian Studies. *Comments:* Name changed from University Prints and Reprints; Issue "The Russian Series." No further information supplied. *ISBN:* 0–87569

A14 ACADEMIC PRESS, INC. *See* Johnson Reprint Corp.

A16 ACME BOOKS, P.O. Box 1706, Oakland, Calif. 94604

Head: James L. Taylor, Owner. *Type:* BKSL. *Format:* HC. *Forms:* BK. *Titles:* Fewer than 10. *Subjects:* Journalism. *Comments:* Bookseller specializing in "The Literature of Journalism."

A18 ACOMA BOOKS, P.O. Box 4., Ramona, Calif. 92065

Head: Gerald S. O'Neal, Owner. *Founded:* 1959 (R 1969). *Type:* BKSL. *Format:* PB. *Forms:* JL. *Titles:* Fewer than 10. *Subjects:* Archeology. *Comments:* Bookseller specializing in new and used books on the Southwest.

A2 AFRICANA PUBLISHING CORPORATION, 101 Fifth Avenue, New York, N.Y. 10003

Head: Max J. Holmes, Publisher. *Founded:* 1969. *Type:* BKSL. *Format:* PB. *Forms:* AN; BK; JL; RP. *Titles:* 10–49. *Subjects:* African studies; African languages. *Comments:* Division of International University Booksellers, Inc. *ISBN:* 0–8419

A22 AFRO-AM BOOKS, INC. *See* Afro-Am Press.

A24 AFRO-AM PRESS, 133 South Racine Avenue, Chicago, Ill. 60607

Head: David Ross, Jr., President. *Founded:* 1969. *Type:* COMM. *Format:* HC; PB. *Forms:* BK; MS. *Titles:* 100–299. *Subjects:* Black studies; African studies; ethnic studies. *Comments:* Division of Afro-Am Books, Inc.

A26 AGATHON PRESS, INC., 150 Fifth Avenue, New York, N.Y. 10011

Head: Burton Lasky, President. *Founded:* 1959 (R 1967). *Type:* COMM. *Format:* HC. *Forms:* BK.

Titles: 10–49. *Subjects:* Criminology; education; economics; sociology. *Comments:* Reprint specialists, with plans for some British co-publishing. *ISBN:* 0–87586

*ALDINE PUBLISHING COMPANY

A28 ALPHATEC PRESS, INC., 2150 Guardian Building, Detroit, Mich. 48226

Subjects: Poetry; Black studies; bibliography & reference. *Comments:* In 1969, announced six multi-volume reprint "Libraries." No further information supplied.

A29 AMERASIA RESOURCES, INC., 165 West 66 Street, New York, N.Y. 10023

Head: Yoshio Kishi. No further information requested.

*AMERICAN ASSOCIATION FOR THE ADVANCEMENT OF SCIENCE

*AMERICAN BAR FOUNDATION

A3 AMERICAN CHEMICAL SOCIETY, Special Issues Sales Department, 1155 Sixteenth Street, N.W., Washington, D.C. 20036

Head: B. R. Stanerson, Executive Secretary. *Founded:* 1876. *Type:* ASSN. *Format:* MF. *Subjects:* Chemistry; life sciences. *Comments:* No further information supplied. *ISBN:* 0–8412

A32 AMERICAN ENTOMOLOGICAL INSTITUTE, 5950 Warren Road, Ann Arbor, Mich. 48105

Head: Henry Townes, Director. *Founded:* 1961 (R 1968). *Type:* ASSN. *Format:* HC. *Forms:* BK. *Titles:* Fewer than 10. *Subjects:* Entomology. *Comments:* Thirteen original and one reprint title published, with more planned.

*AMERICAN INSTITUTE OF BIOLOGICAL SCIENCES

*AMERICAN JEWISH PERIODICAL CENTER

A34 AMERICAN LIFE FOUNDATION & STUDY INSTITUTE, Old Irelandville P.O., Watkins Glen, N.Y. 14891

Head: Dr. G. Laverne Freeman, Executive Director. *Founded:* 1959. *Type:* FNDT. *Format:* HC; PB. *Forms:* AN; BK; SH. *Titles:* 10–49. *Subjects:* Americana; literature— U.S.–19th century; children's books; art. *Comments:* Publish "American Life Collector's Annual;" affiliated with Century House, Inc.

A36 AMERICAN MATHEMATICAL SOCIETY, P.O. Box 6248, Providence, R.I. 02904

Head: Oscar Zariski, President, *Founded:* 1888. *Type:* ASSN. *Subjects:* Mathematics. *Comments:* No further information supplied. *ISBN:* 0–8218. CIP

A38 AMERICAN ORIENTAL SOCIETY, 329 Sterling Memorial Library, New Haven, Conn. 06520

Head: Ferris J. Stephens, Secretary-Treasurer. *Founded:* 1842. *Type:* ASSN. *Format:* HC; PB. *Forms:* BK; MS; RP. *Titles:* 50–99. *Subjects:* Oriental languages; Asian Studies. *Comments:* Some of Society's out-of-print titles issued by Kraus Reprint.

A4 AMERICAN SCHOLAR PUBLICATIONS, INC., 485 Lexington Avenue, New York, N.Y. 10017

Head: Angelo Torrisi, President. *Founded:* 1964. *Type:* COMM. *Format:* HC. *Forms:* BK. *Titles:* 10–49. *Subjects:* Literature–English; history; Shakespeare. *Comments:* 25 titles are in the Furness New Variorum Edition of Shake-

speare with supplementary bibliography. *ISBN:* 0–87260

A42 AMERICAN THEOLOGICAL LIBRARY ASSN., 409 Prospect Street, New Haven, Conn. 06511

Comments: No further information supplied.

A44 AMERICANA REVIEW, 725 Dongan Avenue, Scotia, N.Y. 12302

Head: Mrs. Dorothy Johnson, Owner. *Founded:* 1960. *Type:* COMM; BKSL. *Format:* PB. *Forms:* BK. *Titles:* 10–49. *Subjects:* Americana; advertising & advertisements. *Comments:* Collected illustrations from Nineteenth Century trade and children's literature.

A46 AMERICANIST PRESS, THE, R.D. 2, Pottstown, Pa. 19464

Head: Norman Kane, Proprietor. *Founded:* 1961 (R 1967). *Type:* COMM; BKSL. *Format:* PB. *Forms:* BK. *Titles:* Fewer than 10. *Subjects:* Americana; literature— U.S.; American studies; history— U.S. *Comments:* Bookseller specializing in "Literary and Historical Americana." *ISBN:* 0–910120

A48 AMS PESS, INC., 56 East 13th Street, New York, N.Y. 10003

Head: Gabriel Hornstein, President. *Founded:* 1963. *Type:* COMM. *Format:* HC; MF; PB. *Forms:* AN; BK; JL; MS; RP. *Titles:* 3000– 5000. *Subjects:* Bibliography & reference; history; exploration & travels; language; Shakespeare; social sciences; Americana; literature–English; literature–Classical; Judaica & Hebraica; Germanic studies; periodicals. *Comments:* Paladin Press is a division; associated with Abrahams Magazine Service. *ISBN:* 0–0404. CIP

A5 AMTEL, INC. *See* Barnes & Noble, Inc.

A51 ANDRONICUS PUBLISHING COMPANY, INC., 666 Fifth Avenue, New York, N.Y. 10019

Head: Robert P. DuBois, Publisher; John Haldi, President. *Founded:* 1970. *Type:* COMM. *Format:* HC; MF; MI. *Titles:* 10–49. *Comments:* No further information requested.

A52 ANTIQUARIAN PRESS, LTD. *See* Argosy-Antiquarian, Ltd.

A53 ARCATA NATIONAL CORPORATION. *See* Atlantic Microfilm Corp.

A54 ARCHIVE PRESS, THE, P. O. Box 480, New York, N.Y. 10024

Head: William E. Boggs, President. *Founded:* 1964 (R 1965). *Type:* COMM. *Format:* HC. *Forms:* BK. *Titles:* Fewer than 10. *Subjects:* Antiques–furniture. *Comments:* President reports company is inactive as of 1969.

A56 ARCHON BOOKS. *See* Shoe String Press, Inc.

A58 ARGONAUT, INC., PUBLISHERS, 737 North Michigan Avenue, Chicago, Ill. 60611

Head: A. N. Oikonomides, President. *Founded:* 1963. *Type:* BKSL. *Format:* HC. *Forms:* BK. *Titles:* 100–299. *Subjects:* Classical studies; numismatics; history–world–ancient; archeology; bibliography & reference; folklore; medals; art history & reference; African studies; Asian studies. *Comments:* U.S. representative for publications of the Institute for Balkan Studies, Greece. Firm not related to Argonaut Press, Ltd. *ISBN:* 0–8244

A59 ARGONAUT PRESS, LTD. *See* Arno Press.

A6 ARGOSY-ANTIQUARIAN, LTD., 116 East 59th Street, New York, N.Y. 10022

Head: Louis Cohen, President. *Founded:* 1963. *Type:* COMM. *Format:* HC. *Forms:* BK; SH. *Titles:* 10–49. *Subjects:* Biography; history; Americana; medicine. *Comments:* In 1965, firm acquired from Sol Lewis.

A62 ARIZONA SILHOUETTES. 1730 East Greenlee Road, Tuscon, Ariz. 85719

Head: George Chamberlain, Publisher. *Comments:* No further information supplied.

A64 ARNO PRESS, 330 Madison Avenue, New York, N.Y. 10017

Head: Arnold Zohn, President. *Founded:* 1963 (R 1966). *Type:* COMM. *Format:* HC; PB. *Forms:* BK; GD; JL; NP; RP; SH. *Titles:* 1000–1499. *Subjects:* Black studies; art; humanities; social history; journalism; literary history & criticism; Americana; immigration; environmental studies; business & finance. *Comments:* Acquired Argonaut Press, Ltd. from Sol Lewis in 1965; Arno became a publishing and library service of the New York Times in 1968. *ISBN:* 0–405. CIP

A66 ART GUILD REPRINT, INC., 2844 Spring Grove Avenue, Cincinnati, Ohio 45225

Head: Okey J. Hatcher, President. *Titles:* 10–49. *Subjects:* Archeology Asian studies; exploration & travels. *Comments:* Information from advertisements.

A68 ASIA PUBLISHING HOUSE, INC., 420 Lexington Avenue, New York, N.Y. 10017

Head: P. S. Jayasinghe, President; C. Krumble, Director. *Founded:* 1943 (R 1955). *Type:* COMM. *Format:* HC; PB. *Forms:* BK. *Titles:* 100–299. *Subjects:* Engineering; mathematics; economics; history; sociology; anthropology. *ISBN:* 0–210

A7 ASSOCIATION FOR ASIAN STUDIES, INC. *See* Chinese Materials and Research Aids Service Center, Inc.

A72 ATHENEUM PUBLISHERS. *See* Russell & Russell.

A74 ATLANTIC MICROFILM CORPORATION, 700 South Main Street, Spring Valley, N.Y. 10977

Type: COMM. *Format:* MF. *Comments:* Merged with Arcata National Corp. in 1969. No further information supplied.

A76 ATLANTIC PRINTERS & LITHOGRAPHERS, 653 Washington Avenue, Miami, Fla. 33139

Comments: No further information supplied.

A78 ATTIC PRESS, INC., THE, P.O. Box 1156, Greenwood, S.C. 29646

Titles: Fewer than 10. *Subjects:* Religion & theology. *Comments:* Publish original and reprinted titles and some translations of German studies. No further information supplied. *ISBN:* 0–910178

A8 AUDAX PRESS, 3110 Fillmore Street, San Francisco, Calif. 94123

Head: Joseph Rubinstein, Owner. *Founded:* 1964. *Type:* COMM. *Format:* HC. *Forms:* BK. *Titles:* Fewer than 10. *Subjects:* History; bibliography & reference; literature–Medieval & Renaissance. *ISBN:* 0-910180

A82 AUGUSTAN REPRINT SOCIETY, THE, William Andrews Clark Memorial Library, University of California, Los Angeles, 2520 Cimarron Street, Los Angeles, Calif. 90018

Head: William E. Conway, George R. Guffey, Maximillian E. Novak, Bd. of General Editors. *Founded:* 1946. *Type:* ASSN. *Format:* PB. *Forms:* BK. *Titles:* 100–299. *Subjects:* Literature–English; rare books & manuscripts. *Comments:* Primarily facsimile reproductions of rare Restoration and eighteenth-century works: Society's out-of-print titles issued by Kraus Reprint.

A84 AUTO BOOK PRESS. *See* Large-print Publications.

B1 BAKER BOOK HOUSE, 1019 Wealthy Street, S.E., Grand Rapids, Mich. 49506

Head: Herman Baker, President; Richard Baker, Vice President. *Founded:* 1939. *Type:* COMM. *Format:* HC; PB. *Forms:* BK. *Titles:* 300–499. *Subjects:* Religion & theology. *Comments:* "Twin Brooks," & "Notable Books on Preaching," Series. *ISBN:* 0–8010

B13 BALD EAGLE PRESS, 273 Woodland Drive, State College, Pa. 16801

Head: Joseph Jay Rubin, Publisher. *Founded:* 1950. *Type:* COMM. *Format:* HC. *Forms:* BK; JL; NP. *Titles:* 10–49. *Subjects:* History–U.S.; literature–U.S.; newspapers. *Comments:* Monument Editions is an imprint. *ISBN:* 0–910196

B16 BALTICA PRESS, PUBLISHERS, 820 Kentucky Home Life Building, Louisville, Ky. 40202

Format: EL. *Titles:* Fewer than 10. *Subjects:* Religion & theology. *Comments:* No further information supplied. *ISBN:* 0–910198

B19 BANNER PRESS, P.O. Box 20180, Birmingham, Ala. 35216

Subjects: Genealogy; history–U.S. –Alabama; religion & theology; history–U.S.; science–history. *Comments:* Distributes publications of Dawsons of Pall Mall, England. No further information supplied. *ISBN:* 0–87121

°BANTAM BOOKS, INC.

B22 BARNES & NOBLE, INC., 105 Fifth Avenue, New York, N.Y. 10003

Head: Warren Sullivan, President. *Founded:* 1873 (R 1938). *Type:*

COMM. *Format:* HC. *Forms:* BK. *Titles:* 500–999. *Subjects:* Literary history & criticism; anthropology; history; African studies; exploration & travels; history—U.S.; history—Medieval & Renaissance. *Comments:* U.S. publisher of many British titles; acquired by Amtel, Inc., in 1969; Facsimile Library, Inc. is an inactive reprint imprint. *ISBN:* 0–389. CIP

B25 BAY MICROFILM, INC. 4009 Transport Street, Palo Alto, Calif. 94303

Type: MICR. *Format:* MF. *Comments:* No further information supplied.

B28 BEACON PRESS, 25 Beacon Street, Boston, Mass. 02108

Head: Gobin Stair, Director. *Founded:* 1902. *Type:* COMM. *Format:* HC; PB. *Subjects:* Sociology; psychology; education; history; literary history & criticism; religion & theology. *Comments:* Publish mostly original titles. No further information supplied. *ISBN:* 0–8070. CIP

B31 BELKNAP PRESS (THE) OF HARVARD UNIVERSITY PRESS. *See* Harvard University Press.

B34 BELL & HOWELL COMPANY. *See* Micro Photo Division, Bell & Howell Co.

B37 BELL PUBLISHING COMPANY. *See* Crown Publishers, Inc.

*MATTHEW BENDER

B4 BENIN PRESS LTD., 5225 South Blackstone Avenue, Chicago, Ill. 60615

Head: Herbert Biblo, President. *Founded:* 1964 (R 1965). *Type:* COMM. *Format:* HC. *Forms:* BK. *Titles:* Fewer than 10. *Subjects:* African Studies. *Comments:* Reprints constitute entire list. *ISBN:* 0–910216

B43 ROBERT BENTLEY, INC., 872 Massachusetts Avenue, Cambridge, Mass. 02139

Head: Robert Bentley, President. *Founded:* 1949. *Type:* COMM. *Format:* HC. *Forms:* BK. *Titles:* Fewer than 10. *Subjects:* Education—Montessori method. *Comments:* Also sells new British hardbound copies of fiction titles from Wilson's Fiction Catalog which are OP in the U.S. *ISBN:* 0–8376

B46 N. S. BERG, "Sellanrann," Dunwoody, Ga. 30338

Head: Norman S. Berg, Publisher. *Founded:* 1962. *Type:* COMM. *Format:* HC. *Forms:* BK. *Titles:* 10–49. *Subjects:* Fiction; literature —U.S.; history—U.S.—regional. *Comments:* List includes 8 Pulitzer Prize titles. *ISBN:* 0–910220

B49 BERGMAN PUBLISHERS, 224 West 20th Street, New York, N.Y. 10011

Head: Peter M. Bergman, Publisher. *Founded:* 1966. *Type:* COMM. *Format:* HC. *Forms:* BK; RP. *Titles:* 10–49. *Subjects:* History; Black studies; bibliography & reference. *Comments:* Some reprints issued as "reconstituted books;" also publish original titles. *ISBN:* 0–87503

B52 BIBLO & TANNEN BOOKSELLERS & PUBLISHERS, INC., 63 Fourth Avenue, New York, N.Y. 10003

Head: Jack Biblo, President; Jack Tannen, Secretary-Treasurer. *Founded:* 1928 (R 1956). *Type:* BKSL. *Format:* HC. *Forms:* BK. *Titles:* 100–299. *Subjects:* Archeology; anthropology; literature—Classical; history. *ISBN:* 0–8196

B55 BINFORDS & MORT, PUBLISHERS, 2505 S. E. 11th Avenue, Portland, Oreg. 97242

Head: Thomas P. Binford, President. *Founded:* 1891 (R 1930).

Type: PRTR. *Format:* HC; PB. *Forms:* BK. *Titles:* 100–299. *Subjects:* History—U.S.—regional; history—U.S.—Pacific Northwest. *Comments:* Reprints account for about 25% of the firm's publishing program. *ISBN:* 0–8323

B58 BISON BOOKS. *See* University of Nebraska Press.

B61 BENJAMIN BLOM, INC., 2521 Broadway, New York, N.Y. 10025

Head: Benjamin Blom, President; Dr. Anthony Santaniello, Editor. *Founded:* 1963. *Type:* COMM. *Format:* HC. *Forms:* BK. *Titles:* 500–999. *Subjects:* Architecture & decorative arts; art; general; drama & dramatics. *ISBN:* 0–8118

B64 BLACK & GOLD LIBRARY. *See* Liveright Publishing Corporation.

B65 BLOCH'S BOOK SHOP AND PUBLISHING COMPANY, 31 West 31st Street, New York, N.Y. No further information requested. *ISBN:* 0–8197

B67 BONANZA BOOKS. *See* Crown Publishers, Inc.

B7 BOOK CLUB OF CALIFORNIA, THE, 545 Sutter Street, No. 202, San Francisco, Calif. 94102

Head: Albert Shumate, M.D., President; Dorothy L. Whitmak, Executive Secretary. *Founded:* 1912 (R 1916). *Type:* ASSN. *Format:* HC. *Forms:* BK; GD; JL. *Titles:* 10–49. *Subjects:* History—U.S.—California; fiction; graphic arts. *Comments:* Membership limited. Non-commercial, non-profit association of collectors interested in Pacific Coast literature and fine printing.

B73 BOOKS FOR LIBRARIES, INC., 50 Liberty Avenue, Freeport, N.Y. 11520

Head: Harvey P. Roth, President; Samuel Hauben, Chmn. of Bd.

Founded: 1964. *Type:* COMM. *Format:* HC. *Forms:* AN; BK. *Titles:* 1000–1499. *Subjects:* Literature; poetry; history. *Comments:* Selected titles from Essay & General Literature Index, Granger's Index to Poetry, and other standard bibliographies and book lists. Library Press is trade publishing imprint. Acquired assets of New World Press, Inc., Hallandale, Fla., April 1970; Solomon Roskin is President of New World Book Manufacturing Co., Inc., a wholly owned subsidiary; acquired NASH Publishing Corp., Los Angeles trade book publisher, in 1972. *ISBN:* 0–8369. CIP

B76 BOSTON BOOK AND ART SHOP, INC., 657 Boylston Street, Boston, Mass. 02116

Head: Abraham Bornstein, Owner. *Comments:* No further information supplied. *ISBN:* 0–8435

B79 BOTANIC PUBLISHING COMPANY, THE, P.O. Box 724, Cincinnati, Ohio 45201

Subjects: Botany. *Comments:* No further information supplied. *ISBN:* 0–910274

B82 BOUNTY BOOKS. *See* Crown Publishers, Inc.

B85 R. R. BOWKER COMPANY, 1180 Avenue of the Americas, New York, N.Y. 10036

Head: Richard P. Zeldin, President. *Founded:* 1872. *Type:* COMM. *Format:* HC. *Forms:* BK; JL. *Titles:* 50–99. *Subjects:* Book industries & trade; bibliography & reference; libraries & librarianship; periodicals. *Comments:* Part of Xerox Education Group, Xerox Corporation. *ISBN:* 0–8352. CIP

B88 BRAMHALL HOUSE. *See* Crown Publishers, Inc.

*CHARLES T. BRANFORD COMPANY

*BROADMAN PRESS

B91   BROUDE BROTHERS, LTD., 56 West 45th Street, New York, N.Y. 10036

Head: Irving Broude, President. *Founded:* 1939. *Type:* COMM. *Format:* HC. *Forms:* BK. *Titles:* 100–299. *Subjects:* Music. *Comments:* Publish also soft cover music scores and choral works.

B94   WILLIAM C. BROWN COMPANY, PUBLISHERS, Reprint Library, 135 South Locust Street, Dubuque, Iowa 52001

Head: William C. Brown, President. *Founded:* 1962. *Titles:* 50–99. *Subjects:* Bibliography & reference; philosophy. *Comments:* Primarily publishers of college textbooks. No further information supplied. *ISBN:* 0–697

B97   BUFFALO HEAD PRESS. *See* James F. Carr.

C1   CALIFORNIA BOOK CO., LTD., 2310 Telegraph Avenue, Berkeley, Calif. 94704

Titles: Fewer than 10. *Subjects:* History–U.S.–California. *Comments:* No further information supplied. *ISBN:* 0–910310

C12   CAMBRIDGE UNIVERSITY PRESS, 32 East 57th Street, New York, N.Y. 10022

Head: Jack Schulman, Manager, American Branch. *Founded:* 1521. *Type:* COMM. *Titles:* 100–299. *Format:* HC. *Subjects:* History; literature; general. *Comments:* Many reprints are from presses' own backlist, especially titles in CUPLE (Cambridge University Press Library Edition), published since 1945. No further information supplied. *ISBN:* 0–521

C14   J. S. CANNER & COMPANY, 49–65 Lansdowne Street, Boston, Mass. 02215

Head: Marshall Lebowitz, General Manager. *Type:* BKSL. *Format:* HC; MC. *Forms:* BK; JL; RP. *Titles:* 100–299. *Subjects:* Americana; periodicals. *Comments:* Division of IFI/Plenum Data Corporation; discontinued book department in 1967. Primarily suppliers of back files and sets of scholarly journals. Reprint periodicals in microcard format. Affiliated with Microcan, Inc. *ISBN:* 0–910324

C16   JAMES F. CARR, 277 East 81st Street, New York, N.Y. 10028

Head: James F. Carr, Owner. *Founded:* 1959 (R 1965). *Type:* COMM; BKSL. *Format:* HC. *Forms:* BK. *Titles:* 10–49. *Subjects:* History–U.S.; art–American. *Comments:* Buffalo Head Press and J Bar M Publishers, Inc. are imprints. *ISBN:* 0–87181

C18   CARROLLTON PRESS, INC., 1647 Wisconsin Avenue, N.W., Washington, D.C. 20007

Head: William W. Buchanan, President. *Founded:* 1968. *Type:* COMM. *Format:* HC; PB. *Forms:* BK; GD; JL; RP. *Titles:* Fewer than 10. *Subjects:* Science; technology; humanities; social sciences; patents; periodicals-indexes; government documents. *Comments:* Over 2000 volumes of Smithsonian Institution and American Historical Association annual reports and reprinted cumulative indexes to periodicals. *ISBN:* 0–8408. CIP

C2   CATHOLIC UNIVERSITY OF AMERICA PRESS, 620 Michigan Avenue, N.E., Washington, D.C. 20017

Head: Rt. Rev. Msgr. James A. Magner, Director. *Founded:* 1939. *Type:* UNIV. *Comments:* No further information supplied. *ISBN:* 0–8132

C21   CAYUCOS BOOKS, P.O. Box 524, Cayucos, Calif. 93430

Comments: Limited edition of OP Robinson Jeffers' poetry. No further information requested.

C22 CCM INFORMATION SCIENCES, INC., 909 Third Avenue, New York, N.Y. 10022

Head: Jeffrey Norton, President. *Founded:* 1967. *Type:* COMM. *Format:* EL; MI; PB. *Forms:* GD; RP. *Subjects:* Slavic studies; government documents; social sciences; education. *Comments:* Division of Crowell, Collier and Macmillan, Inc. licensed publishers of translations and other publications of Research and Microfilm Publications, Inc. *ISBN:* 0-8409

C24 CENTER FOR CHINESE RESEARCH MATERIALS, ASSOCIATION FOR RESEARCH LIBRARIES, 1527 New Hampshire Avenue, N.W., Washington, D.C. 20036

Head: Ping-Kuen Yu, Director. *Founded:* 1968. *Type:* ASSN. *Format:* EL; HC; MF; PB. *Forms:* BK; GD; JL; NP. *Titles:* 100–299. *Subjects:* Asian studies; newspapers; social sciences; Chinese studies. *Comments:* Titles listed in "Newsletter" and special announcements; ARL administers the Center.

C26 CENTRAL BOOK COMPANY, INC., 850 DeKalb Avenue, Brooklyn, N.Y. 11221

Head: Milton Hirschman, President. *Founded:* 1919. *Type:* COMM; BKSL. *Format:* HC. *Forms:* BK; GD; RP. *Titles:* 10–49. *Subjects:* Government documents; patents; law. *Comments:* The Luther M. Cornwall Co. is an affiliate selling O.P. government publications. Central also publishes original law, patent, & trademark texts.

C28 CENTURY HOUSE, INC., Watkins Glen, N.Y. 14891

Head: Dr. G. Laverne Freeman, Publisher. *Founded:* 1940. *Type:* COMM. *Format:* HC; PB. *Forms:* AN; BK; SH. *Titles:* 100–299. *Subjects:* Antiques; architecture & decorative arts; art; Americana; hobbies; music; children's books; psychology. *Comments:* Primarily publish original books reprints are "reorganized," issued in limited editions; distribute for American Life Foundation & Study Institute; operate Antiques Book Club. *ISBN:* 0-87282

C3 CHANDLER PUBLISHING COMPANY, 124 Spear Street, San Francisco, Calif. 94105

Head: Howard Chandler, President. *Founded:* 1960. *Type:* COMM. *Format:* HC; PB. *Forms:* AN; EK; RP. *Titles:* 100–299. *Subjects:* Political science; education; literature–U.S.; general law; literary history & criticism. *Comments:* Science Research Associates, Inc. is exclusive distributor of Chandler College Books. Purchase of Chandler by Intext, announced August, 1969. *ISBN:* 0-910348. CIP

C32 CHEDNEY PRESS, 230 East 61st Street, New York, N.Y. 10021.

Comments: No further information supplied.

C34 CHELSEA HOUSE PUBLISHERS, 70 West 40th Street, New York, N.Y. 10018

Head: Harold Steinberg, President. *Founded:* 1965 (R 1966). *Type:* COMM. *Format:* HC; PB. *Forms:* BK; GD; JL; NP; SH. *Titles:* 10–49. *Subjects:* History–U.S.; government–U.S.; social history; advertising & advertisements; government documents; periodicals. *Comments:* Also reproduce National Archive film in 8 mm. cassettes; books distributed by McGraw-Hill, Inc., Random House, Inc., and R. R. Bowker Co. *ISBN:* 0-910358

C36 CHELSEA PUBLISHING COMPANY, INC., 159 East Tremont Avenue, Bronx, N.Y. 10453

Head: Aaron Galuten, President. *Founded:* 1944 (R 1945). *Type:* COMM. *Format:* HC; PB. *Forms:* BK; JL; *Titles:* 100–299. *Subjects:* Mathematics; mathematical physics; logic; physics. *Comments:* About 75% of list are reprints, mostly in hardcover editions. *ISBN:* 0–8284

C38 CHEROKEE PUBLISHING CO., P.O. Box 1081, Covington, Ga. 30209

Subjects: History–U.S.–Georgia. *Comments:* No further information supplied. *ISBN:* 0–87797

C4 CHESAPEAKE BOOK COMPANY. *See* Virginia Book Company.

C42 CHINESE MATERIALS AND RESEARCH AIDS SERVICE CENTER, INC., University of Michigan, 48 Lane Hall, Ann Arbor, Mich. 48104

Head: Robert L. Irick, Managing Director. *Founded:* 1964. *Type:* ASSN; BKSL. *Format:* HC; PB. *Forms:* BK; JL; SH. *Titles:* 1000–1499. *Subjects:* Asian studies; Chinese studies; newspapers; periodicals. *Comments:* Subsidiary of the Association for Asian Studies, Inc.; publishing handled by Ch'eng-Wen Publishing Co., and other Taiwan publishers; Taipei representative office: P.O. Box 22048, Taipei, Taiwan, The Republic of China.

C44 CHRISTIAN CLASSICS, INC., 205 Willis Street, Westminster, Md. 21157

Titles: 10–49. *Subjects:* Religion & theology. *Comments:* Major program is a 42-volume reprint of the complete works of Cardinal Newman. No further information supplied. *ISBN:* 0–87061

C46 CITADEL PRESS, INC., 222 Park Avenue South, New York, N.Y. 10003

Head: Morris Sorkin, President; Allan Wilson, Editor. *Founded:* 1939 (R 1946). *Type:* COMM. *Format:* HC; PB. *Forms:* BK. *Titles:* 300–499. *Subjects:* Psychology; Black studies; occultism; sex education & hygiene. *Comments:* 90% of the titles are paperbound, issued in editions over 2000 copies. Wholly-owned subsidiary of Lyle Stuart, Inc. *ISBN:* 0–8065

C48 ARTHUR H. CLARK COMPANY, 1264 South Central Avenue, Glendale, Calif. 91204

Head: Arthur H. Clark, President. *Founded:* 1902 (R 1903). *Type:* BKSL. *Format:* HC *Forms:* BK. *Titles:* 10–49. *Subjects:* History–U.S.–regional; Americana–Western. *Comments:* Reprints are a small part of bookselling-publishing program. *ISBN:* 0–87062

*COBBLE HILL PRESS, INC.

C5 CODA PUBLICATIONS. *See* Auto Book Press.

C52 COLLECTORS EDITIONS LTD., 185 Madison Avenue, New York, N.Y. 10016

Head: David M. Block, Publisher. *Founded:* 1968 (R 1969). *Type:* COMM. *Format:* HC. *Forms:* BK; JL. *Titles:* Fewer than 10. *Subjects:* Art history & reference; Art–Catalogues Raisonne's; bibliography & reference. *Comments:* Wholly-owned subsidiary of Consolidated Fine Arts, Ltd., New York. Source Book Press is a division. *ISBN:* 0–87681

C54 COLLEGE BOOK STORE. *See* Renzi's College Bookstore.

C56 COMPACT EDITIONS. *See* Readex Microprint Corporation.

C58 COMPASS PUBLICATIONS, INC., P.O. Box 568, Peter Stuyvesant Station, New York, N.Y. 10009

Head: Jean Karsavina, President. *Founded:* 1965. *Type:* COMM. *Format:* PB. *Forms:* AN; GD; JL; NP. *Subjects:* Slavic Studies; economics; Communism; Socialism; Russian studies–Soviet economics; government documents. *Comments:* Issue bi-weekly magazine, "Reprints From the Soviet Press."

C6 COMPUTER APPLICATIONS, INC. *See* Tudor Publishing Company.

C62 CONSOLIDATED FINE ARTS, LTD. *See* Collectors Editions Ltd.

C64 CONTINENTAL BOOK COMPANY., P.O. Box 267, Marietta, Ga. 30060

Type: BKSL. *Titles:* 10–49. *Subjects:* History–U.S.–regional; Americana. *Comments:* Continental also sells reprints originally published by the late Walton Folk, Americana Publisher, Kennesaw, Georgia.

C66 COOPER SQUARE PUBLISHERS, INC., 59 Fourth Avenue, New York, N.Y. 10003

Head: Henry Chafetz, President. *Founded:* 1961. *Type:* BKSL. *Format:* HC; PB. *Subjects:* History; literary history & criticism; anthropology; Classical studies; literature–English; Latin American studies. *Comments:* No further information supplied. *ISBN:* 0–8154

C67 CORNELL MARITIME PRESS, INC. *See* Tidewater Publishers.

*CORNELL UNIVERSITY. Southeast Asia Program.

C68 THE LUTHER M. CORNWALL COMPANY. *See* Central Book Company, Inc.

C7 CRACKER BARREL PRESS, P.O. Box 1287, North Sea Road, Southampton, N.Y. 11968

Head: Malcolm A. Rogers, Jr., Publisher. *Founded:* 1968. *Type:* BKSL. *Format:* PB. *Forms:* BK; RP. *Titles:* Fewer than 10. *Subjects:* Antiques–American. *Comments:* Company also sells antiques and operates "country store." *ISBN:* 0–911750

C72 CRANE DUPLICATING SERVICE, INC., P.O. Box 487, Barnstable, Mass. 02630

Head: William W. Durrell, President; Priscilla Crane, Director and Consultant. *Founded:* 1954 (R 1963). *Type:* PRTR. *Comments:* Printer specializing in pre-production reader's proofs for publishers and reprints of journal articles. Print enlarged-type books under contract. Plan expansion in small edition reprinting.

C74 CRESCENDO PUBLISHERS, 48–50 Melrose Street, Boston, Mass. 02116

Head: Robert Bell, Publisher. *Founded:* 1967. *Type:* COMM. *Format:* HC; PB. *Forms:* BK. *Titles:* 10–49. *Subjects:* Music; history–U.S.–Virginia. *Comments:* Also co-publish with European publishers. *ISBN:* 0–87597

C76 CRESCENT BOOKS. *See* Crown Publishers, Inc.

C78 CROWELL, COLLIER AND MACMILLAN, INC. *See* CCM Information Sciences, Inc. and Hafner Publishing Co.

C8 CROWN PUBLISHERS, INC., 419 Park Avenue South, New York, N.Y. 10016

Head: Nat Wartels, President; Joseph H. Reiner, Vice President. *Founded:* 1933 (R 1935). *Type:* COMM. *Format:* HC; PB. *Forms:* BK. *Titles:* 1000–1499. *Subjects:*

General. *Comments:* Bonanza Books, Bell Publishing Co., and Gramercy Publishing Co. are reprint divisions. Allied firms are Clarkson N. Potter, Outlet Book Co., Living Language, Bounty Books, Bramhall House, Lenox Hill Press. Reprints account for about 50% of Crown list. *ISBN:* 0–517

C82   CUMBERLAND PRESS. *See* The Bond Wheelwright Company.

D1   DA CAPO PRESS, 227 West 17th Street, New York, N.Y. 10011

Head: Earl M. Coleman, President; Alan J. Marks, Vice President, Publisher. *Founded:* 1964. *Type:* COMM. *Format:* HC. *Forms:* BK; JL. *Titles:* 100–299. *Subjects:* Music; architecture & decorative arts; graphic arts; art; medicine; photography; history–U.S.; politics; literature–English; history–Australia; law. *Comments:* "Library of American Art" is a joint publishing venture with Kennedy Galleries, Inc., N.Y. Also co-publish with European publishers. A division of Plenum Publishing Corporation. *ISBN:* 0–306. CIP

D18   DAKOTA, 9655 West Colfax Avenue, Denver, Col. 80215

Head: Wynn D. Crew, President. *Type:* PRTR. *Format:* ES; HC; MF. *Forms:* BK; JL; NP. *Titles:* 50–99. *Subjects:* Musicology; general; children's books; education; periodicals; newspapers. *Comments:* Dakota Microfilm Service Centers also in Orlando, Fla. and St. Paul, Minn., specializing in hardcover editions in enlarged print from microfilm of hundreds of general titles for the visually handicapped; see also Microtech Press.

D26   DANCE HORIZONS, INC. 1801 East 26th Street, Brooklyn, N.Y. 11229

Head: A. J. Pischl, President. *Founded:* 1965. *Type:* COMM. *Format:* PB. *Forms:* BK. *Titles:* 10–49. *Subjects:* Dance. *Comments:* All titles are reprints. *ISBN:* 0–87127

D34   DARBY BOOKS, P.O. Box 148, Darby, Pa. 19023. *See* Folcroft Press.

D42   DAWSONS OF PALL MALL, ENGLAND. *See* Banner Press.

D5   DAWSON'S BOOK SHOP, 535 North Larchmont Boulevard, Los Angeles, Calif. 90004

Head: Glen Dawson, Muir Dawson, Partners. *Founded:* 1905 (R 1950). *Type:* BKSL. *Format:* HC. *Forms:* BK. *Titles:* Fewer than 10. *Subjects:* Americana–Western; art–Oriental. *Comments:* Primarily antiquarian booksellers. Reprints constitute a small part of publishing program. *ISBN:* 0–87093

D55   DENNIS & COMPANY, INC., 251 Main Street, Buffalo, N.Y. 14203

Comments: No further information requested. *ISBN:* 0–87452

D58   DIABLO PRESS, 440 Pacific Avenue, San Francisco, Calif. 94133

Head: Joseph Houghteling, President. *Founded:* 1963. *Type:* COMM. *Format:* PB. *Forms:* AN; BK. *Titles:* Fewer than 10. *Subjects:* Art history & reference; etiquette; History–U.S.–California. *Comments:* Edited reprints; anthologies of articles.

D66   DIVINE WORD PUBLICATIONS, Techny, Ill. 60082

Head: Rev. John P. McHenry, S.V.D., Publisher. *Founded:* 1821. *Type:* BKSL. *Format:* PB. *Forms:* BK. *Subjects:* Religion & theology; education. *Comments:* Primarily booksellers; an "Apostolate of the

Society of the Divine Word." Information from advertisements. *ISBN:* 0–87298

D74 R. R. DONNELLEY & SONS COMPANY, 350 E. 22nd Street, Chicago, Ill. 60616

Head: Gaylord Donnelley, Chmn. of Bd.; Harold W. Tribolet, Department manager. *Founded:* 1864 (R 1903). *Type:* PRTR. *Format:* HC. *Forms:* BK; MS. *Titles:* 50–99. *Subjects:* History–U.S. *Comments:* Lakeside Classics is an imprint for reprints produced, one title a year, by Lakeside Press. Books are not sold, but given as gifts to firm's customers and friends.

D82 DOVER PUBLICATIONS, INC., 180 Varick Street, New York, N.Y. 10014

Head: Hayward Cirker, President. *Founded:* 1945. *Type:* COMM. *Format:* HC; PB. *Forms:* BK. *Titles:* 1500–2999. *Subjects:* Science; music; literature; social sciences; humor; architecture & decorative arts; general; art; history; mathematics; photography; children's books; hobbies. *Comments:* Primarily paperbound reprint editions. Some hardcover and original works are published. Many titles rebound for library use by Peter Smith, Publisher. *ISBN:* 0–486

D83 DOWDEN, HUTCHINSON & ROSS, INC., P.O. Box 129, 10 North Seventh Street, Stroudsburg, Pa. 18360

Head: Albert M. Dowden, Charles S. Hutchinson, Jr., and James B. Ross. *Founded:* 1970. *Type:* COMM. *Format:* HC. *Forms:* JL. *Subjects:* Biological sciences; chemistry; engineering; physics. *Comments:* No further information requested. *ISBN:* 0–87933

D9 DUOPAGE. *See* Micro Photo Div. Bell & Howell Co.

E1 EAKINS PRESS, THE, 155 East 42nd Street, New York, N.Y. 10017

Head: Leslie Katz, Publisher. *Founded:* 1966. *Type:* COMM. *Format:* HC. *Forms:* BK. *Titles:* 10–49. *Subjects:* Literature; art; poetry. *Comments:* Some of the "few titles published each year" are reprints. No further information supplied. *ISBN:* 0–87130

E2 EBONY CLASSICS. *See* Johnson Publishing Co., Inc.

E3 EDWARDS BROTHERS, INC. *See* J. W. Edwards, Inc.

E4 JOHN EDWARDS, PUBLISHER, 61 Winton Place, Stratford, Conn. 06497

Head: J. Edmund Edwards, President. *Founded:* 1967. *Type:* COMM; BKSL. *Format:* HC. *Forms:* BK. *Titles:* 100–299. *Subjects:* History–U.S.; literature–U.S. *Comments:* Also rare book dealer; all titles are reprints. *ISBN:* 0–910544

E5 J. W. EDWARDS, INC., 2500 South State Street, Ann Arbor, Mich. 48104

Head: Joseph W. Edwards, President. *Founded:* 1893. *Type:* PRTR. *Format:* HC, *Forms:* BK; JL. *Titles:* 100–299. *Subjects:* Library catalogs; science; music. *Comments:* Contract printing and book manufacturing done by affiliate, Edwards Brothers, Inc. Major reprint under Edwards' own imprint now is the National Union Catalog. *ISBN:* 0–910546

*ENCINO PRESS

E6 ENCYCLOPAEDIA BRITANNICA, INC. *See* Library Resources, Inc., and Frederick A. Praeger.

E7 ENTOMOLOGICAL REPRINT SPECIALISTS, P.O. Box 77971,

Dockweiler Station, Los Angeles, Calif. 90007

Head: Julian P. Donahue, Partner. *Founded:* 1968 (R 1969). *Type:* BKSL. *Format:* HC. *Forms:* BK. *Titles:* Fewer than 10. *Subjects:* Entomology. *Comments:* Reprint monographs issued in periodical series; agent for E. W. Classey, Ltd., England. *ISBN:* 0–911836

E8 ERASMUS PRESS, INC., 225 Culpepper Street, Lexington, Ky. 40502

Head: Lawrence S. Thompson, President. *Founded:* 1964. *Type:* MICR. *Format:* ES; MF; MI. *Forms:* BK; GD. *Titles:* More than 5000. *Subjects:* Folklore; African studies; Latin American studies; incunabula–European; incunabula –Russian. *Comments:* Catalog cards supplied for all microform editions including those published by Falls City Microcards. Press also publishes "Germanic Notes."

E9 EUGRAMMIA. *See* Frederick A. Praeger.

F1 FACSIMILE LIBRARY, INC. *See* Barnes & Noble.

F16 FACTS ON FILM. *See* Race Relations Information Center.

F22 FALLS CITY MICROCARDS, 1028 Cherokee Road, Louisville, Ky. 40202

Head: C. R. Graham; Lawrence S. Thompson, Partners. *Type:* MICR. *Format:* MC; MF. *Forms:* BK; GD. *Titles:* More than 5000. *Subjects:* Drama & dramatics; incunabula; exploration & travels; government documents–U.S.–state. *Comments:* Catalog cards available from Erasmus Press, Inc.

F28 FARRAR, STRAUS & GIROUX, INC. *See* Octagon Books.

°FERNHILL HOUSE, LTD.

F34 HOWARD FERTIG, INC., PUBLISHER, 80 East 11th Street, New York, N.Y. 10003

Head: Howard Fertig, President. *Founded:* 1966. *Type:* COMM. *Format:* HC. *Forms:* BK. *Subjects:* History; political science; international relations; history–Europe–modern; sociology; Fascism. *ISBN:* 0–8335. CIP

F4 FIRESIDE PRESS. *See* Gale Research Company.

F46 N. FLAYDERMAN AND CO., INC., Squash Hollow, New Milford, Conn. 06776

Head: E. Norman Flayderman, President. *Founded:* 1952 (R 1961). *Type:* COMM. *Format:* HC. *Forms:* BK. *Titles:* 10–49. *Subjects:* Arms & armament; military history; medals; history–U.S. *Comments:* Company is also an arms and weapons dealer. *ISBN:* 0–910598

F52 FOLCROFT PRESS, P.O. Box 182, Folcroft, Pa. 19032

Head: Dr. Ralph Weinman, President. *Type:* BKSL. *Format:* HC. *Forms:* BK. *Titles:* 1000–1499. *Subjects:* Literature–English. *Comments:* Darby Books, Landsdowne Press, Library Services, Inc., Quality Books, Ridgeway Books, and West Books appear to be associated companies or imprints. Operate printing, binding, and warehousing facilities. Information from secondary sources. No further information supplied.

F58 WALTON FOLK, AMERICANA PUBLISHER. *See* Continental Book Company.

F64 FOLKLORE ASSOCIATES. *See* Gale Research Company.

F7 BURT FRANKLIN, PUBLISHER. *See* Lenox Hill Publishing & Distributing Corporation.

F76 FRASER PUBLISHING COMPANY, 283 South Union Street, P.O. Box 494, Burlington, Vt. 05401

Head: James Leon Fraser, President. *Founded:* 1962 (R 1963). *Type:* COMM. *Format:* HC; PB. *Forms:* BK. *Titles:* 10–49. *Subjects:* Economics; business & finance; psychology. *Comments:* A division of Fraser Management Associates, a financial services company. *ISBN:* 0–87034

*FREE LIBRARY OF PHILADELPHIA

F8 FRESHET PRESS, 90 Hamilton Road, Rockville Centre, N.Y. 11570
Comments: No further information requested.

F82 IRA J. FRIEDMAN, INC. *See* Kennikat Press, Inc.

F88 FRONTIER BOOK COMPANY, PUBLISHER, Fort Davis, Texas 79734

Head: Ed Bartholomew, Owner-Publisher. *Founded:* 1939 (R 1951). *Type:* BKSL. *Format:* HC; PB. *Forms:* BK. *Titles:* 50–99. *Subjects:* Americana–Western; antiques–collecting. *Comments:* Long-time antiquarian one-man business. Issues limited editions of original and reprinted "books published in the West, of the West, by Western writers and researchers."

G1 GALE RESEARCH COMPANY, Book Tower, Detroit, Mich. 48226

Head: Frederick G. Ruffner, Jr., President; James M. Ethridge, Editorial Director. *Founded:* 1955 (R 1965). *Type:* COMM. *Format:* HC. *Forms:* BK. *Titles:* 1000–1499. *Subjects:* General; genealogy; history; folklore; Americana; bibliography & reference; literature; literary history & criticism; rare books & manuscripts; journalism; library

catalogs; libraries & librarianship. *Comments:* Singing Tree Press, Fireside Press and Tower Books are imprints; Folklore Associates and its imprint "Tradition Press" acquired as an affiliate in 1969. Also publish original reference works. *ISBN:* 0–8103. CIP

G15 GARLAND PRESS, INC., 24 West 45th Street, New York, N.Y. 10036
Head: Gavin G. Borden, President. *Founded:* 1969. *Type:* COMM. *Format:* HC. *Forms:* BK. *Titles:* 100–299. *Subjects:* Literary history & criticism. *Comments:* First series due for completion by Dec., 1970. Individual volumes are not offered for sale. *ISBN:* 0–8240. CIP

G2 GARRETT PRESS, INC., 250 West 54th Street, New York, N.Y. 10019
Head: Daniel C. Garrett, President; Thomas T. Beeler, V.P. and Editorial Director. *Founded:* 1967. *Type:* COMM. *Format:* HC; MF; PB. *Forms:* BK; JL. *Titles:* 100–299. *Subjects:* Literature–U.S.; literary history & criticism; history–U.S.; biography; philosophy; sociology; humor; social history; fiction; periodicals; little magazines. *Comments:* Reported out-of-business, January 1972. *ISBN:* 0–512

G25 GENEALOGICAL PUBLISHING COMPANY, INC., 521–23 St. Paul Place, Baltimore, Md. 21202
Head: Barry Chodak, President. *Founded:* 1936 (R 1952). *Type:* COMM. *Format:* HC; PB. *Forms:* BK; GD; JL. *Titles:* 300–499. *Subjects:* Genealogy; History–U.S.–regional; heraldry; government documents. *Comments:* Regional Publishing Company is an affiliate. *ISBN:* 0–8063. CIP

G3 GENERAL MICROFILM COMPANY, 100 Inman Street, Cambridge, Mass. 02139
Head: Richard W. Loud, Chmn. of Bd.; John P. Eustis II, Manager

Library Services Division. *Founded:* 1947 (R 1953). *Type:* MICR. *Format:* EL; MF; MI. *Forms:* BK; JL; NP. *Titles:* More than 5000. *Subjects:* General; rare books & manuscripts; folklore; exploration & travels; African studies; history–world; history–U.S.; history–Canada. *Comments:* Firm also specializes in contract short-run printing.

G35 GLANVILLE PUBLISHERS, INC. *See* Oceana Publications, Inc.

G4 GLENN BOOKS, INC., 1227 Baltimore, Kansas City, Mo. 64105

Comments: No further information supplied. *ISBN:* 0–910656

G45 GODFREY MEMORIAL LIBRARY, 134 Newfield Street, Middletown, Conn. 06457

Head: Mrs. Edith B. Grant, Director. *Founded:* 1930 (R 1949). *Type:* LIBY; MICR. *Format:* MC; MI. *Forms:* GD; RP. *Titles:* 300–499. *Subjects:* Genealogy; history–U.S.–regional; biography. *Comments:* All titles except The American Genealogical-Biographical Index are reprints.

G5 GORDIAN PRESS, INC. 85 Tompkins Street, Staten Island, N.Y. 10304

Head: John Corta, Editor. *Type:* COMM. *Format:* HC. *Forms:* BK. *Titles:* 100–299. *Subjects:* Literary history & criticism; history; humanities; literature–translations into English. *Comments:* Distributors for Phaeton Press, Inc. *ISBN:* 0–87752

G55 GRAMERCY PUBLISHING COMPANY. *See* Crown Publishers, Inc.

G6 GRAND RAPIDS INTERNATIONAL PUBLICATIONS. *See* Kregel Publications.

G65 GRAPHIC ARTS TECHNICAL FOUNDATION, 4615 Forbes Avenue, Pittsburgh, Pa. 15243

Founded: 1924. *Type:* FNDT. *Titles:* 10–49. *Subjects:* Graphic arts; photography. *Comments:* GATF out of print titles available from Micro-Photo Division, Bell & Howell Company. No further information supplied.

G67 STEPHEN GREENE PRESS, P.O. Box 1000, Brattleboro, Vermont 05301

Comments: No further information requested. *ISBN:* 0–8289

G7 GREENWOOD PRESS, INC., 51 Riverside Avenue, Westport, Conn. 06880

Head: Dr. Harold Mason, President. *Founded:* 1967. *Type:* COMM. *Format:* HC; MF; MI; PB. *Forms:* BK; GD; JL; MS; NP. *Titles:* 1000–1499. *Subjects:* Black studies; exploration & travels; Americana; social history; government documents; periodicals; political science; history; anthropology; music; protest literature, library catalogs; general. *Comments:* A subsidiary of Williamhouse-Regency. Greenwood Press, Inc. reprints books; Greenwood Reprint Company reprints periodicals; Greenwood Publishing Company publishes only original works; Negro Universities Press, a subsidiary company, publishes original and reprint materials relating to Black studies. *ISBN:* 0–837. CIP

G75 GREGG PRESS, THE, 121 Pleasant Avenue, Upper Saddle River, N.J. 07458

Head: Charles S. Gregg, President. *Founded:* 1963 (R 1966). *Type:* COMM. *Format:* HC. *Forms:* BK. *Titles:* 100–299. *Subjects:* African languages; art; bibliography & reference; history; music; literary history & criticism; Asian studies; religion & theology; history–Pacific; history–U.S.–New York; humor; architecture & decorative arts; fiction; philosophy. *Comments:* Literature House is an imprint. *ISBN:* 0–8398. CIP

G8 GROLIER, INC. *See* Scarecrow Press, Inc.

H1 HACKER ART BOOKS, 54 West 57th Street, New York, N.Y. 10019
Type: COMM. *Format:* HC; PB. *Titles:* 10–49. *Subjects:* Art history & reference. *Comments:* No further information supplied. *ISBN:* 0–87817

H14 HAFNER PUBLISHING COMPANY, P.O. Box 2000, 260 Heights Road, Darien, Conn. 06820
Head: Harry Lubrecht, Vice President. *Founded:* 1946 (R 1954). *Type:* COMM. *Format:* HC; PB. *Forms:* BK; JL. *Titles:* 500–999. *Subjects:* Life sciences; botany; medicine; periodicals; literature—U.S. *Comments:* Subsidiary of Stechert-Hafner, Inc., acquired by Crowell Collier and Macmillan in 1969. *ISBN:* 0–7173

H18 G. K. HALL & CO., 70 Lincoln Street, Boston, Mass. 02111
Type: COMM. *Subjects:* Library catalogs; general. *Comments:* Acquired by ITT in 1969. No further information supplied. *ISBN:* 0–8161. CIP

H20 HANGMAN PRESS. *See* Superior Publishing Company.

H22 HARCOURT BRACE JOVANOVICH, INC. *See* Johnson Reprint Corp.

H26 HARLEM BOOK COMPANY, INC. *See* Tudor Publishing Company.

H3 J. & J. HARPER EDITIONS, 49 East 33rd Street, New York, N.Y. 10016
Head: M. L. Arnold, President; Hugh Van Dusen, Manager. *Founded:* 1817 (R 1970). *Type:*

COMM. *Format:* HC. *Forms:* BK. *Titles:* 50–99. *Subjects:* History—U.S.; history—Europe; sociology; music; Russian studies; political science. *Comments:* Hardcover reprint dept. of Harper & Row, Publishers.

H34 HARPER & ROW, PUBLISHERS. *See* J. & J. Harper Editions.

H38 HARVARD UNIVERSITY PRESS, 79 Garden Street, Cambridge, Mass. 02138
Founded: 1913. *Type:* UNIV. *Format:* HC; PB. *Forms:* AN; BK; RP. *Comments:* More than 250 books have been issued under the Belknap Press of Harvard University Press imprint, established in 1954. First John Harvard Library Books issued in 1960. No further information supplied. *ISBN:* 0–674

H42 HASKELL HOUSE PUBLISHERS, LTD. 280 Lafayette Street, New York, N.Y. 10012
Head: Herbert Knobler, Director; Herbert C. Roseman, Editor. *Founded:* 1964. *Type:* COMM; PRTR. *Format:* HC. *Forms:* BK. *Titles:* 500–999. *Subjects:* Literature—English; literature—U.S.; history; biography; genealogy; Black studies; bibliography & reference; music; literary history & criticism. *Comments:* Company also owns and operates a printing facility on premises. *ISBN:* 0–8383. CIP

H46 HEALTH RESEARCH, 70 Lafayette Street, Mokelumme Hill, Calif. 95245
Head: R. G. Wilborn, President. *Format:* PB. *Forms:* BK; RP. *Titles:* 100–299. *Subjects:* Health, physical education, & recreation; homeopathy; astrology; occultism; Freemasonry. *Comments:* Mail order sales only; issue some limited editions. No further information supplied.

H5 HEATH-RAYTHEON. *See* Russell and Russell.

H54 WALLACE HEBBERD, PUBLISHER, P.O. Box 180, Santa Barbara, Calif. 93102

Type: COMM. *Subjects:* History— U.S.–California; humor. *Comments:* No further information supplied.

H58 WILLIAM S. HEIN & CO., INC., 369–379 Niagara Street, Buffalo, N.Y. 14201

Subjects: Law. *Comments:* Law book publishers; no further information supplied.

H62 HENNESSEY & INGALLS, INC., 8419 Lincoln Boulevard, Los Angeles, Calif. 90045

Head: R. G. Hennessey, President; David K. Ingalls, Vice-President. *Type:* BKSL. *Format:* HC. *Forms:* BK. *Subjects:* Art–World–20th Century; architecture & decorative arts; rare books & manuscripts; art history & reference. *Comments:* Sell imported reprints. Tentative plans to publish reprints reported in 1970. *ISBN:* 0–912158

H66 HERALDIC PUBLISHING CO., INC., 305 West End Avenue, New York, N.Y. 10023

Head: Louis R. Sosnow, Publisher. *Founded:* 1955 (R 1962). *Type:* COMM. *Format:* HC. *Forms:* BK. *Titles:* Fewer than 10. *Subjects:* Heraldry; genealogy; history. *Comments:* All titles are reprints. *ISBN:* 0–910716

H7 HERMON PRESS, 10 East 40th Street, New York, N.Y. 10016

Head: Samuel Gross, Editor-Manager. *Founded:* 1964 (R 1965). *Type:* COMM. *Format:* HC. *Forms:* BK. *Titles:* 10–49. *Subjects:* Judaica & Hebraica; religion & theology. *ISBN:* 0–87203

H72 HIGH DENSITY SYSTEMS, INC. *See* University Music Editions.

H74 HILLIARY HOUSE PUBLISHERS. *See* Humanities Press, Inc.

*THE HISTORICAL SOCIETY SOCIETY OF PENNSYLVANIA

H78 HOOVER INSTITUTION ON WAR, REVOLUTION, AND PEACE, Stanford, Calif. 94305

Head: Dr. W. Glenn Campbell, Director; Brien Benson, Hd., Publications. *Founded:* 1919 (R 1963). *Type:* MICR; FNDT. *Format:* MF. *Forms:* JL; NP. *Titles:* 50– 99. *Subjects:* International affairs; history–World–20th Century; periodicals; newspapers. *Comments:* Microfilming of individual material is an adjunct operation to the Hoover Institution Press, which publishes about 20 titles annually. *ISBN:* 0–8179

H82 HOPE FARM PRESS AND BOOKSHOP, Strong Road, Cornwallville, N.Y. 12418

Head: Charles E. Dornbusch, Owner. *Founded:* 1959. *Type:* BKSL. *Format:* HC; PB. *Forms:* BK; RP. *Titles:* Fewer than 10. *Subjects:* Military history; history– U.S.–New York; history–U.S.–regional. *Comments:* "Professional book service for the Catskill Mountain area." *ISBN:* 0–910746

H86 CALVIN HORN, PUBLISHER, INC., P.O. Box 4204, Albuquerque, N.M. 87106

Founded: 1967. *Type:* COMM. *Format:* HC; PB. *Forms:* BK. *Titles:* 10–49. *Subjects:* Americana; history–U.S.–Southwest; history– U.S.–New Mexico. *Comments:* Formerly Horn and Wallace Publishers, Inc. No further information supplied. *ISBN:* 0–910750

H9 HOWELL-NORTH BOOKS, 1050 Parker Street, Berkeley, Calif. 94710

Head: Mrs. Flora D. North, President. *Founded:* 1956. *Type:* COMM; PRTR. *Format:* HC; PB.

Forms: BK. *Titles:* 50–99. *Subjects:* Railroadiana; maritime history & sciences; Americana–Western. *Comments:* Books manufactured in company's own plant. Information from catalogs. No further information supplied. *ISBN:* 0–8310

H94 HUMANITIES PRESS, INC., 303 Park Avenue South, New York, N.Y. 10010

Head: Simon Silverman, President; Lothar Simon, Sales Manager. *Founded:* 1950 (R 1958). *Type:* COMM. *Format:* HC. *Forms:* BK. *Titles:* 10–49. *Subjects:* Social sciences; philosophy; history; sociology; literature; anthropology. *Comments:* U.S. distributor for anthropological publications, Holland, reprint specialists. Reprints are a very small part of firm's publishing program. *ISBN:* 0–391

I1 IBEG, LTD. *See* University of California Press.

*INDIANA UNIVERSITY PRESS

I18 INSILCO. *See* Kennikat Press.

I26 INSTITUTE OF MEDIAEVAL MUSIC, LTD., THE, 1653 W. 8th Street, Brooklyn, N.Y. 11223

Head: Dr. Luther A. Dittmer, Director. *Founded:* 1957. *Type:* COMM. *Format:* HC; MF. *Forms:* BK; MS. *Titles:* Fewer than 10. *Subjects:* Music; music–Medieval. *Comments:* Institute is inc. in U.S.; communications & prices in German. *ISBN:* 0–912024

I34 INSTITUTE OF PAPER CHEMISTRY, Lawrence College, East South River Street, Appleton, Wisc. 54911

Head: John G. Strange, President. *Founded:* 1929. *Type:* UNIV. *Format:* MF. *Comments:* No further information supplied. *ISBN:* 0–87010

I42 INTERNATIONAL BOOK CORPORATION. *See* International Book Reprints, Inc.

I5 INTERNATIONAL BOOK REPRINTS, INC., P.O. Box 3063, Norland Station, Miami, Fla. 33169

Head: Hernando Maya, President and General Manager. *Founded:* 1969. *Type:* BKSL. *Format:* HC. *Forms:* BK. *Titles:* 10–49. *Subjects:* History; literature; Spanish language; Latin American studies. *Comments:* Primarily import, rebind and sell books from Latin America and Spain. Reprints mostly in Spanish. Subsidiary of International Book Corporation.

I55 INTERNATIONAL MARINE PUBLISHING CO., Camden, Me. 04843

I56 INTERNATIONAL HOUSE LIBRARY, P.O. Box 52020, New Orleans, La. 70150

Head: Paul A. Fabry, Managing Director. *Comments:* No further information requested.

I58 INTERNATIONAL MICROFILM PRESS. *See* 3M/IM Press.

I66 INTERNATIONAL PUBLISHERS, 381 Park Avenue South, New York, N.Y. 10016

Head: James S. Allen, President and Editor. *Founded:* 1924. *Type:* COMM. *Format:* HC; PB. *Forms:* AN; BK. *Subjects:* Political science; history; Marxism; Black studies; Russian studies. *Comments:* New World Paperback is a series imprint, including reprints of "Source Books of Marxism." *ISBN:* 0–7178

I7 INTERNATIONAL TELEPHONE & TELEGRAPH (ITT). *See* G. K. Hall & Co.

I74 INTERNATIONAL UNIVERSITY BOOKSELLERS, INC. *See* Africana Publishing Corporation.

I82   INTEXT   (INTERNATIONAL TEXTBOOK CO.). *See* Chandler Publishing Co.

I9   IONE PRESS, INC. *See* E. C. Schirmer Music Company.

I95   IRISH UNIVERSITY PRESS, INC., 1508 Pennsylvania Ave., Wilmington, Del. 19806

Comments: No further information requested.

I98   I-TEX PUBLISHING COMPANY, INC., P.O. Box 63, Ames, Iowa 50010

Head: Richard Beck, President; Robert D. Greenlee, Vice President. *Founded:* 1968 (R 1969). *Type:* COMM. *Format:* HC. *Forms:* BK. *Titles:* Fewer than 10. *Subjects:* Horses.

J1   J BAR M PUBLISHERS, INC. *See* James F. Carr.

J12   JENKINS PUBLISHING COMPANY, 6925 Interregional Hwy., Austin, Texas 78703

Head: John H. Jenkins, publisher. *Comments:* Pemberton Press is an imprint. No further information supplied. *ISBN:* 0–8363

°THE JOHANNES PRESS, THE GALERIE ST. ETIENNE

J2   JOHN HARVARD LIBRARY. *See* Harvard University Press.

J3   JOHNSEN PUBLISHING COMPANY, 1135 R Street, Lincoln, Neb. 68508

Subjects: History—U.S.—Nebraska; education. *Comments:* No further information supplied. *IBSN:* 0–910814

J4   JOHNSON PUBLISHING COMPANY, P.O. Box 217, Murfreesboro, N.C. 27855

Head: F. Roy Johnson, Proprietor. *Founded:* 1963 (R 1968). *Type:* PRTR. *Format:* HC. *Forms:* BK.

Titles: Fewer than 10. *Subjects:* History—U.S.—regional; folklore; Americana. *ISBN:* 0–87335

J5   JOHNSON PUBLISHING COMPANY, INC., BOOK DIVISION, 1820 South Michigan Avenue, Chicago, Ill. 60616

Head: John H. Johnson, President. *Founded:* 1962. *Type:* COMM. *Format:* HC; PB. *Forms:* AN; BK. *Titles:* 10–49. *Subjects:* Black studies; social history. *Comments:* Primarily publish original works. Issue Ebony Classics and redesigned reprints of works of early Black writers. *ISBN:* 0–87485

J6   JOHNSON REPRINT CORPORATION, 111 Fifth Avenue, New York, N.Y. 10003

Head: Walter J. Johnson, President; Fred Rappaport, Vice President. *Founded:* 1946. *Type:* COMM. *Format:* HC; MI; PB. *Forms:* BK; GD; JL. *Titles:* 1000–1499. *Subjects:* Anthropology; literature—English; Germanic studies; American studies; science; periodicals; general; government documents; history—Canada; newspapers; history; history—Australia; music; science—history; bibliography & reference; mathematics; zoology; religion & theology; African studies; Shakespeare. *Comments:* Publish many titles in foreign languages. Subsidiary of Academic Press, Inc., acquired by Harcourt Brace & World, Inc. in 1969 (Now Harcourt Brace Jovanovich, Inc.) *ISBN:* 0–384. CIP

J7   JULIAN PRESS, INC., 150 Fifth Avenue, New York, N.Y. 10011

Comments: No further information supplied. *ISBN:* 0–87097

K1   EDWIN F. KALMUS, P.O. Box 1007, Comack, N.Y. 11725

Head: Edwin F. Kalmus, Publisher. *Founded:* 1927. *Type:* COMM. *Format:* PB. *Forms:* BK.

Titles: 3000–5000. *Subjects:* Music. *Comments:* All titles are reprints.

K2 AUGUSTUS M. KELLEY, PUB-LISHERS, 305 Allwood Road, Clifton, N.J. 07012

Head: Augustus M. Kelley, Publisher. *Founded:* 1947 (R 1949). *Type:* COMM. *Format:* HC. *Forms:* BK. *Titles:* 500–999. *Subjects:* Economics; archeology–industrial; law; history–Gt. Britain; social history; periodicals. *Comments:* Some joint ventures with Rothman Reprints, Inc.; also co-publish with firms in Great Britain. *ISBN:* 0–678

K3 KENNEDY GALLERIES, INC. *See* Da Capo Press.

K4 KENNIKAT PRESS, INC., P.O. Box 270, 215 Main Street, Port Washington, N.Y. 11050

Head: Cornell Jaray, President. *Founded:* 1961. *Type:* COMM. *Format:* HC. *Forms:* BK. *Titles:* 500–999. *Subjects:* Black studies; philosophy; art history & reference; history; literary history & criticism; religion & theology; history–U.S.–New York; history–U.S.–Pennsylvania. *Comments:* Subsidiary of Taylor Publishing Co., a division of INSILCO (International Silver Company); Ira J. Friedman, Inc., an affiliate, issues the Empire State & Keystone State Historical Publications series. *ISBN:* 0–8046

K5 N. A. KOVACH, Microfilm Dept., 4801–09 Second Avenue, Los Angeles, Calif. 90043

Format: MF. *Comments:* No further information supplied.

K6 KRAUS REPRINT COMPANY, 16 East 46th Street, New York, N.Y. 10017

Head: James Warren, President; Frederick Altman, Executive Vice President; Herbert Gstalder, Manager. *Founded:* 1957. *Type:*

COMM. *Format:* HC; PB. *Forms:* BK; GD; JL; NP; RP. *Titles:* 1000–1499. *Subjects:* Humanities; social sciences; government documents; periodicals; little magazines; general; periodicals–indexes; bibliography & reference; rare books & manuscripts; newspapers; Judaica & Hebraica; science–history; Latin American studies; education; Germanic studies; French studies; Spanish language. *Comments:* Division of Kraus-Thomson Organization, Ltd.; Liechtenstein. *ISBN:* 0–527. CIP

K7 KRAUS-THOMSON ORGANIZATION, LTD. *See* Kraus Reprint Company.

K8 KREGEL PUBLICATIONS, 525 Eastern Avenue, S.E., Grand Rapids, Mich. 49503

Head: Robert L. Kregel, President. *Founded:* 1910 (R 1949). *Type:* BKSL. *Format:* HC; PB. *Forms:* BK. *Titles:* 100–299. *Subjects:* Religion & theology. *Comments:* Also stock 75,000 used books; Grand Rapids International Publications is an imprint. *ISBN:* 0–8254

K81 KREIGER PUBLISHING COMPANY, P.O. Box 542, Huntington, N.Y. 11743

Founded: 1971. *Subjects:* Science; technology. *Comments:* No further information requested.

K9 KTAV PUBLISHING HOUSE, INC., 120 E. Broadway, New York, N.Y. 10002

Head: Asher Scharfstein, President. *Founded:* 1924. *Type:* COMM. *Format:* HC. *Forms:* BK; JL. *Subjects:* Judaica & Hebraica; religion & theology. *Comments:* No further information supplied. *ISBN:* 0–87068. CIP

L1 LAKESIDE CLASSICS. *See* R. R. Donnelly & Sons Company.

L15 LANEWOOD PRESS, INC., 729 Boylston Street, Boston, Mass. 02116

Head: R. M. Levy, President. *Founded:* 1969. *Type:* COMM. *Format:* HC. *Forms:* BK. *Titles:* Fewer than 10. *Subjects:* General. *Comments:* Lanewood Largetype Editions is imprint of books for the visually handicapped. *ISBN:* 0-912120

L17 LANSDOWNE PRESS. *See* Folcroft Press

L2 LARGEPRINT PUBLICATIONS, P.O. Box 711, San Marcos, Calif. 92069

Head: William Carroll, Managing Director. *Founded:* 1963 (R 1964). *Type:* COMM. *Format:* PB. *Forms:* BK; GD. *Titles:* Fewer than 10. *Subjects:* Automobiles—history & technology; business & finance; police; general. *Comments:* CODA Publications and Auto Book Press are imprints. Expansion in technical book field planned. *ISBN:* 0-87209

L25 LA SIESTA PRESS, P.O. Box 406, Glendale, Calif. 91209

Head: Walt Wheelock, Publisher. *Founded:* 1960 (R 1961). *Type:* COMM. *Format:* HC; PB. *Forms:* BK. *Titles:* 10–49. *Subjects:* History—U.S.–California; mining. *Comments:* Reprints, mostly paperbound, constitute about 75% of publishing program.

L3 LAWYERS CO-OPERATIVE PUBLISHING COMPANY, THE, Aqueduct Building, Rochester, N.Y. 14603

Head: Thomas H. Gosnell, President. *Founded:* 1882. *Type:* COMM. *Format:* MF. *Subjects:* Law. *Comments:* No further information supplied.

L33 LEEKLEY BOOKSTORE, 711 Sheridan Road, Winthrop Harbor, Ill.

Comments: No further information requested.

L35 LEMMA PUBLISHING CORPORATION, 509 Fifth Avenue, New York, N.Y. 10017

Comments: No further information supplied. *ISBN:* 0-87696

L36 LENOX HILL PUBLISHING & DISTRIBUTING CORPORATION, 235 East 44th Street, New York, N.Y. 10017

Head: Burt Franklin, Publisher. *Founded:* 1949. *Type:* COMM. *Format:* HC. *Forms:* BK; JL; MS: RP. *Titles:* 1500–2999. *Subjects:* Art; humanities; social sciences; bibliography & reference; rare books & manuscripts; general; exploration & travels. *Comments:* Burt Franklin, Publisher became an imprint in 1971. *ISBN:* 0-8337

L38 LIBRARY EDITIONS LTD., 200 W. 72nd Street, New York, N.Y. 10023

Head: Dr. Sol Lewis, President & General Ed.; J. T. Claiborne, Jr., Chrmn.; David Glotzer, Prod. Mgr. *Founded:* 1970. *Type:* COMM. *Format:* HC. *Forms:* BK. *Titles:* 10–49. *Subjects:* Art; bibliography & reference; biography; history—U.S.–West; literature; maritime history & sciences; military history; Americana. *Comments:* First titles due late 1970. *ISBN:* 0-8432

*THE LIBRARY OF CONGRESS

L4 LIBRARY REPRINTS, LTD., P.O. Box 68, New York, N.Y. 10002

Head: I. Smith, President. *Founded:* 1967. *Type:* COMM. *Format:* HC. *Forms:* BK; GD; JL. *Titles:* 100–299. *Subjects:* Literature—English; literature—U.S.; history—U.S.; history—Europe; history—Gt. Britain; history—World. *Comments:* All titles are reprints.

L45 LIBRARY REPRODUCTION SERVICE. *See* Microfilm Company of California.

L48 LIBRARY RESOURCES, INC. 301 E. Erie Street, Chicago, Ill. 60610

Head: Treadwell Ruml, President. *Type:* MICR. *Comments:* Subsidiary of Encyclopaedia Britannica; vast "Microbook" publishing projects in progress were announced too late for inclusion in this survey.

L49 LIBRARY SERVICES, INC. *See* Folcroft Press.

L5 ELIZABETH LICHT, PUBLISHER, 360 Fountain Street, New Haven, Conn. 06515

Head: Elizabeth Licht, Publisher. *Founded:* 1952 (R 1960). *Type:* COMM. *Format:* HC; PB. *Forms:* BK. *Titles:* Fewer than 10. *Subjects:* Medicine. *Comments:* Reprints constitute a very small part of publishing program. *ISBN:* 0–910888

L55 JOHN LILBURNE COMPANY, Green River Road, Williamstown, Mass. 01267

Head: Richard M. Schneer; Maurice Filler, Partners. *Founded:* 1967. *Type:* COMM. *Subjects:* History. *Comments:* No further information supplied.

L6 LITERATURE HOUSE. *See* Gregg Press, The.

L61 LITTLEFIELD, ADAMS & COMPANY. *See* Rowman & Littlefield.

L65 LIVERIGHT PUBLISHING CORPORATION, 386 Park Avenue South, New York, N.Y. 10016

Head: Sam Melner, President. *Founded:* 1917. *Type:* COMM. *Format:* HC. *Forms:* BK. *Titles:* 50–99. *Subjects:* General. *Comments:* Black & Gold Library is

imprint of reprint series. *ISBN:* 0–87140

L7 LONG'S COLLEGE BOOK COMPANY, 1836 N. High Street, Columbus, Ohio 43201

Head: F. C. Long, Jr., President. *Type:* BKSL. *Format:* HC; PB. *Subjects:* History; sociology; education; botany; agriculture. *Comments:* Primarily booksellers of used books and remainders. "Basic Western Classics" is imprint for series of limited edition reprints. Information from catalogs; no further information supplied. *ISBN:* 0–910906

L75 LOST CAUSE PRESS, 1141 Starks Bldg., Louisville, Ky. 40202

Head: Charles P. Farnsley, President. *Founded:* 1955. *Type:* MICR. *Format:* MC; MI. *Forms:* BK; JL. *Titles:* More than 5000. *Subjects:* Black studies; history—U.S.; fiction; literature—U.S.; exploration & travels; Americana. *Comments:* All titles are reprints.

L8 GREGORY LOUNZ, BOOKS, 501 Fifth Avenue, New York, N.Y. 10017

Format: HC; PB. *Titles:* Fewer than 10. *Subjects:* Russian Studies; philosophy & religion; bibliography & reference. *Comments:* Information from secondary sources; no further information supplied. *ISBN:* 0–910910

L85 ERIC LUNDBERG, Ashton, Md. 20702

Head: Eric Lundberg, Proprietor. *Founded:* 1937 (R 1959). *Type:* BKSL. *Format:* HC. *Forms:* BK. *Titles:* Fewer than 10. *Subjects:* Botany; zoology; natural history. *Comments:* Primarily antiquarian bookseller. *ISBN:* 0–910914

L9 LYLE STUART, INC. *See* Citadel Press, Inc.

M1   McCLAIN PRINTING COM-
PANY, Parsons, W. Va. 26287

Head: Ken McClain, Publisher.
Type: PRTR. *Format:* HC; PB.
Forms: AN; BK; MS; RP. *Titles:*
Fewer than 10. *Subjects:* History—
U.S.—West Virginia; mining. *Com-
ments:* Primarily book printers.
Issue occasional reprint editions
under own imprint. No further
information supplied. *ISBN:*
0–87012

M13   McGRATH PUBLISHING COM-
PANY, 5932 Westchester Park
Drive, College Park, Md. 20740

Head: Dr. Daniel F. McGrath,
President. *Founded:* 1968. *Type:*
COMM. *Format:* HC. *Forms:* BK.
Titles: 10–49. *Subjects:* Black
Studies; education; fiction; litera-
ture—U.S. *Comments:* Titles in
series available individually or as a
collection. *ISBN:* 0–8434. CIP

M16   McNALLY & LOFTIN, PUB-
LISHERS, 111 East De La Guerra
Street, P.O. Box 1316, Santa Bar-
bara, Calif. 93102

Head: William J. McNally, Presi-
dent. *Founded:* 1956. *Comments:*
No further information supplied.
ISBN: 0–87461

M18   M & S PRESS, INC., P.O. Box 311,
Weston, Mass. 02193

Comments: No further information
requested. *ISBN:* 0–87730

ISBN: 0–87730

M19   MACOY PUBLISHING & MA-
SONIC SUPPLY COMPANY,
INC., 3011 Dumbarton Rd., Rich-
mond, Va. 23228

Head: V. Hansen, Secretary and
Treasurer. *Founded:* 1849. *Type:*
BKSL. *Format:* HC; PB. *Forms:*
BK. *Titles:* 10–49. *Subjects:* Freemasonry; astrology. *Comments:*
New or corrected data sometimes
added; reprints are about 50% of
publishing program. *ISBN:*
0–910928

*MAGNA CARTA BOOK COM-
PANY

M22   MANAGEMENT INFORMA-
TION SERVICES. *See* Scholarly
Press, Inc.

M25   MANESSIER PUBLISHING
COMPANY, P.O. Box 5517, Riverside, Calif. 92507

Type: COMM. *Format:* HC.
Forms: BK. *Titles:* Fewer than 10.
Subjects: Natural history; natural
resources; anthropology; maritime
history & sciences. *Comments:* No
further information supplied. *ISBN:*
0–910950

M28   MANSELL INFORMATION/
PUBLISHING, LTD., 360 North
Michigan Avenue, Chicago, Ill.
60601

Founded: 1966. *Type:* COMM.
Format: HC. *Comments:* U.S.
Division of British firm formed to
publish pre-1956 National Union
Catalog. No further information
supplied.

*MASSACHUSETTS HISTORI-
CAL SOCIETY

M31   MAXWELL REPRINT COM-
PANY, Fairview Park, Elmsford,
N.Y. 10523

Head: Dr. Edward Gray, President;
Albert Henderson, General Manager. *Founded:* 1968. *Type:*
COMM. *Format:* HC; MF; PB.
Forms: BK; GD; JL. *Titles:* 10–49.
Subjects: Business & finance; economics; political science; mathematics; chemistry; sex education &
hygiene; physics; periodicals; government documents. *Comments:*
Division of Maxwell Scientific International, Inc. *ISBN:* 0–8277

M33   MELLIFONT PRESS, INC., 1508
Pennsylvania Avenue, Wilmington,
Del. 19806

Comments: No further information
requested. *ISBN:* 0–8420

ISBN: 0–8420

M34 MERIDIAN BOOKS. *See* World Publishing Company.

M37 MERIT PUBLISHERS, P.O. Box 1344, Beverly Hills, Calif. 90213
Format: HC. *Forms:* BK. *Subjects:* Labor history; Socialism. *Comments:* No further information supplied. *ISBN:* 0–910962

M4 MICHIE COMPANY, THE, P.O. Box 57, Charlottesville, Va. 22902
Head: David W. Parrish, President; J. G. Gilbert, Sales Manager. *Founded:* 1897 (R 1900). *Type:* BKSL; PRTR. *Format:* HC; PB. *Forms:* BK; JL; RP. *Titles:* 100–299. *Subjects:* Law. *Comments:* Reprints, primarily of state law reports & excerpts from state codes, are a very small part of publishing-printing-bookselling programs. *ISBN:* 0–87215

M43 MICROCAN, INC., 618 Parker Street, Boston, Mass. 02120
Head: Marshall Libowitz, General Manager. *Founded:* 1949. *Type:* MICR. *Format:* MC. *Forms:* JL. *Subjects:* General. *Comments:* Affiliated with J. S. Canner & Company, Inc. Produce periodical sets on microcard. Also sell microcard editions of titles issued by other publishers.

M46 MICROCARD CORPORATION. *See* NCR Microcard Editions.

M49 MICROCARD EDITIONS. *See* NCR Microcard Editions.

M52 MICRO-CLIPS. *See* Microfacts Corporation.

M55 MICROFACTS CORPORATION, 13815 W. Eighth Mile Road, Detroit, Mich. 48235
Head: Monroe P. Molner, President. *Founded:* 1967. *Type:* MICR. *Format:* EL; MF; MI. *Forms:* JL; NP. *Titles:* 10–49. *Subjects:* Advertising & advertisements; underground press; protest literature.

Comments: Micro-Clips is an imprint.

M58 MICROFILM COMPANY OF CALIFORNIA (THE), 1977 South Los Angeles Street, Los Angeles, Calif. 90011
Comments: Library Reproduction Service is a division. No further information supplied.

*MICROFILMING CORPORATION OF AMERICA

M61 MICROFORM DATA SYSTEMS, INC. *See* Microform Publishing Corporation.

M64 MICROFORM PUBLISHING CORPORATION, 1518 K Street, N.W., Washington, D.C. 20005
Head: George A. Hoy, Jr., President. *Founded:* 1969 (R 1970). *Type:* MICR. *Format:* MI. *Forms:* BK; GD. *Titles:* 500–999. *Subjects:* General. *Comments:* Publishing subsidiary of Microform Data Systems, Inc., Calif.; "Essential Reference Collections" is imprint. Firm plans to organize research information into indexed microfiche collections primarily for high schools, small & medium-sized public libraries.

M67 MICRO PHOTO DIVISION, Bell & Howell Company, Old Mansfield Road, Wooster, Ohio 44691
Head: John C. Marken, General Manager; Larry E. Block, Manager, Project Operations. *Founded:* 1947. *Type:* COMM. *Format:* EL; HC; MF; MI; PB. *Forms:* BK; JL; MS; NP. *Titles:* More than 5000. *Subjects:* Russian studies; Black studies; folklore; religion & theology; mathematics; history–U.S.; genealogy; periodicals; underground press; newspapers. *Comments:* Acquired by Bell & Howell Company in 1962. Hard copy book reproductions issued on demand as Duopage books; firm's catalog,

"Newspapers on Microfilm" lists current & back files.

M7   MICRO-RESEARCH CORPORATION, C/O American Antiquarian Society, 185 Salisbury Street, Worcester, Mass. 01609

Comments: No further information supplied.

M73 MICROTECH PRESS, 9655 West Colfax Avenue, Denver, Colo. 80215

Head: Wynn D. Crew, President. *Founded:* 1969 (R 1971). *Type:* MICR. *Format:* UM. *Comments:* Newly organized subsidiary corporation of Dakota. Plans in progress for a "Microaperture" publishing system. System and product line not yet available.

M75 MIKRO-BUK, INC., 150 Fifth Avenue, New York, N.Y. 10010

Head: Larry Hower, President; Marvin Lipper, V. P., Publishing. *Founded:* 1969 (R 1970). *Type:* MICR. *Format:* MI. *Forms:* BK. *Titles:* 300–499. *Subjects:* History; Black studies; humanities; sociology; anthropology; philosophy; psychology; religion & theology. *Comments:* Individual titles are for sale.

M76 MILFORD HOUSE, 21 Walnut St., Boston, Mass. 02108

Comments: No further information supplied. *ISBN:* 0–87821. CIP

M79 MINI-PRINT CORPORATION. *See* Scarecrow Press, Inc.

M82 MINNESOTA HISTORICAL SOCIETY, 690 Cedar Street, St. Paul, Minn. 55101

Head: Russell W. Fridley, Director; Mrs. June D. Holmquist, Managing Editor. *Founded:* 1849 (R 1890). *Type:* ASSN. *Format:* HC; MF; PB. *Forms:* BK; NP; SH. *Titles:* Fewer than 10. *Subjects:* History—U.S.; history—U.S.—Minnesota; his-

tory—U.S.—Midwest; rare books & manuscripts; newspapers. *Comments:* Microfilms of some titles, primarily newspapers, not included in title count. Also excluded are many older, often rare titles reprinted from Society's own backlist. *ISBN:* 0–87351

M85 MNEMOSYNE, 54 S.W. 7th Street, Miami, Fla. 33130

Head: Frank Wills, President. *Founded:* 1968. *Type:* COMM. *Format:* HC; PB. *Subjects:* Black Studies; Americana. *Comments:* No further information requested.

M88 MONTHLY REVIEW PRESS, 116 West 14th Street, New York, N.Y. 10011

Head: Harry Braverman, President; Susan Lowes, Managing Editor. *Founded:* 1949. *Type:* COMM. *Format:* HC; PB. *Forms:* BK. *Titles:* 10–49. *Subjects:* Economics; political science; history. *Comments:* Reprints constitute small part of general trade list. *ISBN:* 0–85345

M91 MONUMENT EDITIONS. *See* Bald Eagle Press.

M94 W. M. MORRISON, BOOKS, P.O. Box 3277, Waco, Texas 76707

Head: W. M. Morrison, Owner. *Founded:* 1952 (R 1956). *Type:* BKSL. *Format:* HC. *Forms:* BK. *Titles:* 10–49. *Subjects:* History—U.S.—Texas.

N1   NATIONAL CASH REGISTER COMPANY. *See* NCR Microcard Editions.

N18 NCR MICROCARD EDITIONS, 901 26th Street, N.W., Washington, D.C. 20037

Head: Albert J. Diaz, Executive Director. *Founded:* 1960 (R 1969). *Type:* COMM. *Format:* HC; MF; MI; MP; PB; UM. *Forms:* BK; GD; JL; NP. *Subjects:* History—U.S.; history—Gt. Britain; government documents; botany; chemistry; Russian studies; periodicals; newspapers; medicine; general; Spanish language. *Comments:* Part of Industrial Products Division, National Cash Register Company, Dayton, Ohio. Publish "Guide to Reprints" and other reprint bibliographies. About 80% of reprints are on microfiche. Hardcopy reprinting begun in 1969. *ISBN:* 0–910972

N26 NEGRO HISTORY PRESS. *See* Scholarly Press, Inc.

N34 NEGRO UNIVERSITIES PRESS. *See* Greenwood Publishing Corp.

N35 THE NEW HAMPSHIRE PUBLISHING COMPANY, Somersworth, N.H. 03878

Comments: No further information requested.

N38 NEW WORLD PRESS, INC. *See* Books For Libraries, Inc.

N42 NEWBERRY LIBRARY, THE, 60 West Walton Street, Chicago, Ill. 60610

Head: Lawrence W. Towner, Director and Librarian; J. M. Wells, Associate Director. *Founded:* 1887. *Type:* LIBY. *Format:* ES; HC; MF; PB. *Forms:* BK. *Titles:* 10–49. *Subjects:* History; literature; music —early; rare books & manuscripts. *Comments:* Titles published with Northwestern University Press; Chicago, Sansoni and Micro Photo Division, Bell & Howell. *ISBN:* 0–911028

N5 NEWBY BOOK ROOM, Rt. 1, P.O. Box 296, Noblesville, Ind. 46060

Head: J. Edwin Newby, Owner. *Founded:* 1950 (R 1951). *Type:* BKSL. *Format:* HC; PB. *Forms:* BK. *Titles:* 10–49. *Subjects:* Bible studies; church history; sermons. *Comments:* Primarily booksellers. *ISBN:* 0–87748

N58 NEW JERSEY HISTORICAL SOCIETY, 230 Broadway, Newark, N.J. 07104

Comments: No further information supplied. *ISBN:* 0–911020

N66 NEW WORLD PAPERBACKS. *See* International Publishers.

N74 NEW YORK TIMES/ARNO PRESS. *See* Arno Press.

N82 NORTHLAND PRESS, P.O. Box N, Flagstaff, Ariz. 86001

Head: Paul E. Weaver, Jr., Editor. *Type:* COMM. *Format:* HC. *Forms:* AN; BK. *Comments:* No further information supplied. *ISBN:* 0–87358

N9 NOTABLE BOOKS ON PREACHING SERIES. *See* Baker Book House.

O1 OAK PUBLICATIONS, 33 West 60th Street, New York, N.Y. 10023

Head: Paul Gewirtz, President. *Founded:* 1960. *Type:* COMM. *Format:* HC; PB. *Forms:* AN; BK; SH. *Titles:* 50–99. *Subjects:* Music-folk; musicology; music–scores. *Comments:* Sales and shipping handled by Music Sales Corp., New York. *ISBN:* 0–8256

O2 OCEANA PUBLICATIONS, INC., 75 Main Street, Dobbs Ferry, N.Y. 10522

Head: Philip F. Cohen, President. *Founded:* 1945 (R 1950). *Type:* COMM. *Format:* HC; MC; MF. *Forms:* BK; JL. *Titles:* 10–49. *Subjects:* Law; international law; international affairs; international relations. *Comments:* Publish "Reprint Bulletin," (including reprint reviews as of 1971); Glanville Publishers, Inc. is a subsidiary. *ISBN:* 0–379. CIP

O3 OCTAGON BOOKS, INC., 19 Union Square West, New York, N.Y. 10003

Head: Henry G. Schlanger, Editor-in-Chief. *Founded:* 1963. *Type:*

COMM. *Format:* HC. *Forms:* BK. *Titles:* 300–499. *Subjects:* History; literary history & criticism; sociology; psychology; Black studies. *Comments:* Division of Farrar, Straus & Giroux, Inc. since 1968. *ISBN:* 0–374. CIP

O4 OLD HICKORY BOOKSHOP, Brinklow, Md. 20727

Type: BKSL. *Format:* HC. *Forms:* BK. *Titles:* Fewer than 10. *Subjects:* Medicine. *Comments:* No further information supplied. *ISBN:* 0–911064

O5 OLD-WEST PUBLISHING CO., THE, 1228 E. Colfax Avenue, Denver, Colo. 80218

Head: Fred A. Rosenstock, Owner. *Type:* BKSL. *Format:* HC. *Forms:* BK. *Titles:* Fewer than 10. *Subjects:* History–U.S.–West. *Comments:* No further information supplied. *ISBN:* 0–912904

°OXFORD UNIVERSITY PRESS

P1 PACIFIC BOOKS, PUBLISHERS, P.O. Box 558, Palo Alto, Calif. 94302

Head: Henry Ponleithner, Publisher. *Founded:* 1945 (R 1962). *Type:* COMM. *Format:* HC; PB. *Forms:* BK. *Titles:* 10–49. *Subjects:* General. *Comments:* Reprints of non-fiction titles account for about 25% of firm's publishing program. *ISBN:* 0–87015

P15 PAISANO PRESS, INC., P.O. Box 85, Balboa Island, Calif. 92662

Head: Dr. Horace Parker, Editor and Publisher. *Founded:* 1957 (R 1959). *Type:* BKSL. *Format:* HC; PB. *Forms:* BK; JL; SH. *Titles:* 500–999. *Subjects:* Americana–Western. *Comments:* Publish no fiction or poetry. *ISBN:* 0–911102

P2 PALADIN PRESS. *See* AMS Press, Inc.

P25 PANTHER PUBLICATIONS, INC., P.O. Box 1307, Boulder, Colo. 80302

Type: BKSL. *Format:* HC; PB. *Forms:* AN; BK; RP. *Titles:* Fewer than 10. *Subjects:* Unconventional warfare; espionage; counterinsurgency; arms & armament. *Comments:* Information from secondary sources. No further information supplied. *ISBN:* 0–87364

P3 PARAGON BOOK REPRINT CORP., 14 East 38th Street, New York, N.Y. 10016

Head: Max Faerber, President. *Founded:* 1962. *Type:* COMM. *Format:* HC; PB. *Forms:* BK. *Titles:* 100–299. *Subjects:* Asian studies; Chinese studies. *Comments:* Distributors of foreign publications; affiliated with Paragon Book Gallery, Ltd. *ISBN:* 0–8188

P35 PEMBERTON PRESS. *See* Jenkins Publishing Company.

P4 PEQUOT LIBRARY, Southport, Conn. 06490

Head: Stanley Crane, Librarian. *Type:* LIBY. *Format:* PB. *Forms:* MS. *Titles:* Fewer than 10. *Subjects:* Americana–New England. *Comments:* A very small reprint program.

P45 PERCEPTUAL AND MOTOR SKILLS, P.O. Box 1441, Missoula, Mont. 59801

Type: COMM. *Format:* MP. *Comments:* No further information supplied.

P5 PHAETON PRESS, INC. *See* Gordian Press, Inc.

P55 PHAIDON PRESS. *See* Frederick A. Praeger.

P6 PLENUM PUBLISHING CORP. *See* J. S. Canner & Company and Da Capo Press.

P65 RICHARD L. POLESE, PUB-LISHERS, P.O. Box 1295, Santa Fe, N.M. 87501

Comments: No further information supplied.

P7 FREDERICK A. PRAEGER, 111 Fourth Avenue, New York, N.Y. 10003

Head: George Aldor, President; Jerry Strand, Manager, Sales Dept. *Founded*: 1950 (R 1966). *Type*: COMM. *Format*: HC. *Forms*: BK. *Titles*: 50–99. *Subjects*: Rare books & manuscripts; art; graphic arts; Latin America—history & politics; Pacific Area studies. *Comments*: Subsidiary of Encyclopaedia Britannica since 1966; acquired Phaidon Press, London, 1967; Eugrammia is an imprint. *ISBN*: 0–275

P75 PRINCETON MICROFILM COR-PORATION, P.O. Box 235, Princeton Junction, N.J. 08550

Head: Franklin Crawford, Managing Director. *Type*: MICR. *Format*: MF. *Comments*: No further information supplied.

P8 PRO MUSICA PRESS, 2962 N. Prospect, Milwaukee, Wisc. 53211

Head: Edward V. Foreman, General Editor. *Founded*: 1965. *Format*: HC; PB. *Forms*: BK. *Titles*: Fewer than 10. *Subjects*: Music; singing; education–singing; literature—translations into English. *Comments*: Most titles issued in hardcover. Also publish original books on vocal pedagogy.

P85 PUBLISHERS COMPANY, INC. *See* United Publishing Corp.

P9 PYNE PRESS, THE, Lower Pyne Bldg. at Nassau Street, Princeton, N.J. 08540

Head: Bernard M. Barenholtz. *Founded*: 1970. *Subjects*: Antiques; art—American. *Comments*: No further information requested. *ISBN*: 0–87861

Q4 QUALITY BOOKS. *See* Folcroft Press.

Q8 QUEST BOOKS. *See* Theosophical Publishing House.

R1 R AND E RESEARCH ASSOCI-ATES, 4843 Mission Street, San Francisco, Calif. 94112

Head: Adam S. Eterovich, Editor. *Founded*: 1966 (R 1967). *Type*: BKSL; PRTR. *Format*: HC; MF; PB. *Forms*: BK; NP. *Titles*: 500–999. *Subjects*: Black studies; ethnic studies; sociology; immigration. *Comments*: Reprints are about 25% of the publishing program.

R16 RACE RELATIONS INFORMA-TION CENTER, P.O. Box 6156, Nashville, Tenn. 37212

Head: Robert F. Campbell, Executive Director. *Founded*: 1969. *Type*: MICR. *Format*: MF. *Forms*: JL. *Titles*: More than 5000. *Subjects*: Race relations; Black studies; education; social history. *Comments*: Successor to Southern Education Reporting Service, founded in 1954; "Facts on Film" is an imprint; Tennessee Microfilms is sole sales agent. All titles are reprints.

R22 READEX MICROPRINT COR-PORATION, 5 Union Square, New York, N.Y. 10003

Head: Albert Boni, President. *Founded*: 1950. *Type*: COMM; MICR. *Format*: HC; MP; UM. *Forms*: BK; GD; JL; MS; NP; RP. *Titles*: More than 5000. *Subjects*: General; bibliography & reference; government documents; drama & dramatics; science—history; Slavic studies; newspapers; technology—history; government documents—United Nations; periodicals—indexes; Latin American studies. *Comments*: Also publish hardcover

"Compact Editions" with reduced-sized, eye legible text.

R25 REDGRAVE INFORMATION RESOURCES CORP. 67 Wilton Road, Westport, Conn. 06880

Head: Herbert C. Cohen, President; Jeffrey Heynan, Exec. V.P. *Founded:* 1972. *Type:* MICR. *Comments:* Firm to publish original and retrospective microform collections for reference and research, with first titles announced spring 1972.

R28 REGIONAL PUBLISHING CO. *See* Genealogical Publishing Company, Inc.

R34 RENAISSANCE ENGLISH TEXT SOCIETY. *See* Newberry Library.

R4 RENZI'S COLLEGE BOOK STORE, INC., 36 Spring Street, Williamstown, Mass. 01267

Head: Ralph R. Renzi, President. *Founded:* 1968 (R 1969). *Type:* BKSL. *Format:* PB. *Forms:* BK. *Titles:* Fewer than 10. *Subjects:* Education; humanities. *Comments:* Publish "Williams Tracts," reprinting materials from Williams College, but not only from that collection.

R46 REPRINT COMPANY, THE, P.O. Box 5401, Spartanburg, S.C. 29303

Head: Thomas E. Smith, Owner. *Founded:* 1959. *Type:* COMM. *Format:* HC. *Forms:* BK. *Titles:* 50–99. *Subjects:* History—U.S.—Colonial; history—Revolutionary War. *Comments:* "Specializing in the reproduction of rare old books." *ISBN:* 0–87152

R52 RESEARCH AND MICROFILM PUBLICATIONS, INC. *See* CCM Information.

R58 RESEARCH PUBLICATIONS, INC., 254 College Street, New Haven, Conn. 06510

Head: Samuel B. Freedman, President; Paul Ferster, Executive Editor. *Founded:* 1966. *Type:* MICR. *Format:* ES; MF; MI. *Forms:* AN; BK; JL; MS; NP; RP. *Titles:* More than 5000. *Subjects:* Business & finance; business & finance–directories; histories–Canada; history–U.S.–Pacific Northwest; literature; Asian studies; history–U.S.; government documents —League of Nations; bibliography & reference. *Comments:* Specialize in micropublishing "quality resource publications for scholars."

R64 RESEARCH REPRINTS, INC., 135 E. 50th Street, New York, N.Y. 10022

Head: Jo-Ann Jacobs, Publisher. *Founded:* 1970. *Type:* COMM. *Format:* HC. *Forms:* BK. *Titles:* 50–99. *Subjects:* Economics; African studies; Americana. *Comments:* 150 titles due for publication in 1970. *ISBN:* 0–87803

R68 RHISTORIC PUBLICATIONS, 302 N. 13th Street, Philadelphia, Pa. 19107.

Comments: Publish Afro-American historical series. No further information requested.

R69 RIDGEWAY BOOKS, P.O. Box 6431, Philadelphia, Pa. 19145

See Folcroft Press.

R7 THE RIO GRANDE PRESS, INC., Glorieta, N.M. 87535

Head: Robert B. McCoy, President. *Founded:* 1962. *Type:* COMM. *Format:* HC. *Forms:* BK; SH. *Titles:* 50–99. *Subjects:* History; Americana—Western; exploration & travels. *Comments:* Beautiful Rio Grande Classics is a series imprint. *ISBN:* 0–87380

R76 ROSS & HAINES, INC., 314 WCCO Bldg., Minneapolis, Minn. 55402

Head: B. J. Ghostley, President; Harlow Ross, V. P. and Editor.

Founded: 1926 (R 1953). *Type:* COMM. *Format:* HC. *Forms:* BK. *Titles:* 50–99. *Subjects:* American Indian—history & culture; exploration & travels; Americana—Western; literature—U.S.—local authors. *Comments:* Reprints constitute about 75% of publishing program. *ISBN:* 0–87018

R82 ROTHMAN REPRINTS, INC., 57 Leuning Street, South Hackensack, N.J. 07606

Head: Fred B. Rothman, President. *Founded:* 1945 (R 1955). *Type:* BKSL. *Format:* HC; PB. *Forms:* BK; JL. *Titles:* 100–299. *Subjects:* Social sciences; international law; periodicals; law. *Comments:* Continental Legal History series; Modern Legal Philosophy series. Also publish original books under Fred B. Rothman & Company imprint. *ISBN:* 0–8377

R85 ROWMAN & LITTLEFIELD, 87 Adams Drive, Totowa, N.J. 07512

Head: John Mladinich, Managing Director. *Founded:* 1957. *Type:* COMM. *Format:* HC. *Forms:* BK. *Titles:* 50–99. *Subjects:* Bibliography & reference; history; library catalogs; literature; literary history & criticism.

R88 RUSSELL & RUSSELL, 122 East 42nd Street, New York, N.Y. 10017

Head: Sidney A. Russell, Managing Editor. *Founded:* 1953. *Type:* COMM. *Format:* HC. *Forms:* BK. *Titles:* 1000–1499. *Subjects:* Political science; philosophy; logic; social sciences; Black studies. *Comments:* A division of Atheneum Publishers.

S1 SAGE BOOKS. *See* Swallow Press, Inc.

S12 ALBERT SAIFER, PUBLISHER, P.O. Box 56, Town Center, West Orange, N.J. 07052

Type: BKSL. *Subjects:* Bibliography & reference; language; military history; science–history. *Comments:* Primarily bookseller. Publisher is also editor of "TAAB." No further information supplied. *ISBN:* 0–87556

S14 WILLIAM SALLOCH, Pinebridge Road, Ossining, N.Y. 10562

Head: William Salloch, Owner. *Founded:* 1939 (R 1956) *Type:* BKSL. *Format:* HC. *Forms:* BK. *Titles:* Fewer than 10. *Subjects:* Music; art history & reference; bibliography & reference. *Comments:* Reprints are small part of antiquarian bookselling business. *ISBN:* 0–911702

S16 SAVILE BOOK SHOP, 3236 P Street, N.W., Washington, D.C. 20007

Type: BKSL. *Format:* HC. *Forms:* BK. *Titles:* Fewer than 10. *Subjects:* Latin America–history & politics. *Comments:* Also sell original and reprinted titles of other publishers. No further information supplied. *ISBN:* 0–87384

S18 SCARECROW PRESS, INC., 52 Liberty Street, P.O. Box 656, Metuchen, N.J. 08840

Head: Eric Moon, President; Albert W. Daub, Vice President. *Founded:* 1950 (R 1967). *Type:* COMM. *Format:* HC. *Forms:* BK. *Titles:* 10–49. *Subjects:* Bibliography & reference; libraries & librarianship. *Comment:* Wholly-owned subsidiary of Grolier, Inc.; publish mostly original works. Reprints issued under imprints, Scarecrow Reprint Corporation and Mini-Print Corporation. Mini-print reprints are photographically reduced and printed two or more original pages on one. *ISBN:* 0–8108. CIP

S2 SCARECROW REPRINT CORP. *See* Scarecrow Press, Inc.

S22 E. C. SCHIRMER MUSIC COM-
PANY, 600 Washington Street,
Boston, Mass. 02111

Head: Robert MacWilliams, President. *Founded:* 1921. *Type:*
COMM. *Format:* HC; PB. *Forms:*
BK; MS; SH. *Titles:* 3000–5000.
Subjects: Music; music–choral;
music–modern. *Comments:* Ione
Press, Inc. is an imprint; reprints
constitute about 50% of publishing
program. *ISBN:* 0–911318

S24 ANNEMARIE SCHNASE, Reprint
Department, 120 Brown Road, P.O.
Box 119, Scarsdale, N.Y. 10583

Head: Mrs. Annemarie Schnase,
Owner. *Founded:* 1950 (R 1960).
Type: BKSL. *Format:* HC; PB.
Forms: JL. *Titles:* 10–49. *Subjects:*
Periodicals; music. *Comments:* All
publications are reprints.

S26 SCHOCKEN BOOKS, INC., 67
Park Avenue, New York, N.Y.
10016

Head: Theodore Schocken, President; Hanna Gunther, Managing
Editor. *Founded:* 1945 (R 1961).
Type: COMM. *Format:* HC; PB.
Forms: BK. *Titles:* 100–299. *Subjects:* Black studies; art; literature;
sociology; philosophy; history; political science; psychology; education; literary history & criticism;
art history & reference; religion &
theology. *Comments:* Large non-
fiction original trade publishing list;
"Schocken Paperbacks" constitute
about 60% of reprint list. *ISBN:*
0–8052

S28 SCHOLARLY PRESS, INC., 22929
Industrial Drive East, St. Clair
Shores, Mich. 48080

Head: Frank H. Gille, President;
R. John Oliver, V.P., Assistant to
the President. *Founded:* 1968.
Type: COMM. *Format:* HC.
Forms: BK. *Titles:* 500–999. *Subjects:* Literature; history; Black
studies; American Indian–history

& culture. *Comments:* Negro History Press is an imprint; affiliated
with Management Information Services until May 1, 1969. All titles
are reprints. *ISBN:* 0–403

S3 SCHOLARS' FACSIMILES & RE-
PRINTS, P.O. Box 344, Delmar,
N.Y. 12054

Founded: 1936. *Type:* COMM.
Format: HC. *Forms:* BK; JL.
Titles: 100–299. *Subjects:* Psychology; rare books & manuscripts; history–U.S.; literature–English; literature–U.S.; history–Gt. Britain.
ISBN: 0–8201. CIP

S32 SCHOOL OF HEALTH, PHYSI-
CAL EDUCATION, AND REC-
REATION. *See* University of Ore-
gon.

S34 ABNER SCHRAM, 1860 Broadway, New York, N.Y. 10023

Head: Abner Schram, President.
Founded: 1967. *Type:* COMM.
Format: HC; PB. *Forms:* BK.
Titles: 10–49. *Subjects:* Graphic
arts; calligraphy; art history & ref-
erence. *Comments:* Publishing
Division of Schram Enterprises.
ISBN: 0–8390

S36 SHERWIN & FREUTEL, PUB-
LISHERS, 1017 N. La Cienega
Blvd., Los Angeles, Calif. 90069.

Founded: 1970. *Comments:* No
further information requested.
ISBN: 0–8404

S38 SHOE STRING PRESS, INC.,
THE, 955 Sherman Avenue, Hamden, Conn. 06514

Head: Mrs. Frances T. Ottemiller
Rudder, President; Lewis N. Wiggin, Director of Sales. *Founded:*
1952. *Type:* COMM. *Format:* HC.
Forms: BK. *Titles:* 500–999. *Subjects:* History; literary history &
criticism; bibliography & reference;
libraries & librarianship. *Comments:*
Archon Books is an imprint. Company also publishes many original
titles. *ISBN:* 0–208. CIP

S4 SHOREY BOOK STORE, 815 3rd Avenue, Seattle, Wash. 98104

Head: John W. Todd, Jr., Owner-Manager. *Founded:* 1890 (R 1964). *Type:* BKSL. *Format:* PB. *Forms:* BK; MS; RP. *Titles:* 100–299. *Subjects:* Americana; history—U.S.—Northwest. *Comments:* Book store established in 1890. Publish "limited facsimile editions of scarce and rare materials." Information from secondary sources. No further information supplied.

S42 GEORGE SHUMWAY, PUBLISHER, R.D. 7, York, Pa. 17402

Head: George Shumway, Publisher. *Founded:* 1962 (R 1966). *Type:* COMM. *Format:* HC; PB. *Forms:* BK; SH. *Titles:* Fewer than 10. *Subjects:* Arms & armament; Americana. *Comments:* About 25% of list are reprints. *ISBN:* 0–87387

S44 SINGING TREE PRESS. *See* Gale Research Co.

S46 PATTERSON SMITH PUBLISHING CORP., 23 Prospect Terrace, Montclair, N.J. 07042

Head: Patterson Smith, President; Thomas Kelley, Sales Manager. *Founded:* 1954 (R 1968). *Type:* BKSL. *Format:* HC. *Forms:* BK. *Titles:* 100–299. *Subjects:* Criminology; law enforcement; sociology. *Comments:* Firm has long specialized in selling books related to the subjects it reprints. *ISBN:* 0–87585. CIP

S48 PETER SMITH, PUBLISHER, INC., 6 Lexington Avenue, Gloucester, Mass. 01930

Head: Peter Smith, President. *Founded:* 1929. *Type:* COMM. *Format:* HC. *Forms:* BK. *Titles:* 3000–5000. *Subjects:* History; humanities; literature; bibliography & reference; general. *Comments:* Firm also rebinds paperbacks for library use. *ISBN:* 0–667

S5 SOCIETY PRESS, THE. *See* The State Historical Society of Wisconsin.

S52 SOURCE BOOK PRESS. *See* Collectors Editions Ltd.

S54 SOUTHERN EDUCATION REPORTING SERVICE. *See* Race Relations Information Center.

S56 SOUTHERN ILLINOIS UNIVERSITY PRESS, Carbondale, Ill. 62901

Head: Vernon Sternberg, Director. *Founded:* 1953. *Type:* UNIV. *Comments:* No further information supplied. *ISBN:* 0–8093. CIP

S58 SOUTHERN METHODIST UNIVERSITY PRESS, Dallas, Texas 75222

Head: B. D. Kornmann, Sales Manager. *Founded:* 1937. *Type:* UNIV. *Format:* HC; PB. *Forms:* BK; JL; MS; RP. *Titles:* 100–299. *Comments:* Primarily publish original works. No further information supplied. *ISBN:* 0–87074

S6 STAGECOACH PRESS, P.O. Box 4422, Albuquerque, N.M. 87106

Head: Jack Rittenhouse, Owner. *Founded:* 1949. *Type:* COMM. *Format:* HC; PB. *Forms:* BK; GD; JL; SH. *Titles:* 10–49. *Subjects:* History; Americana—Western. *Comments:* Most titles produced by letterpress from new type. *ISBN:* 0–87238

S62 STANFORD UNIVERSITY PRESS, Stanford, Calif. 94305

Head: James W. Torrence, Jr., Sales Manager. *Founded:* 1923 (R 1969). *Type:* UNIV. *Format:* HC. *Forms:* BK. *Titles:* Fewer than 10. *Subjects:* Asian studies; political science; Russian studies; history. *Comments:* Reprints constitute a very small part of the list. Press has own complete manufacturing and binding plant. *ISBN:* 0–8047

S64 STATE HISTORICAL SOCIETY OF WISCONSIN, 816 State Street, Madison, Wisc. 53706

Head: Richard A. Erney, Acting Director; Paul H. Hass, Editor. *Founded:* 1854 (R 1900). *Type:* ASSN. *Format:* HC; PB. *Forms:* BK. *Titles:* 10–49. *Subjects:* History—U.S.; history—U.S.—Wisconsin. *Comments:* Reprints constitute a small part of the business of the Society's press. *ISBN:* 0–87020

S66 STECHERT-HAFNER, INC. *See* Hafner Publishing Company.

S68 STORMJADE BOOKS, Stormjade Mt. Mines, Chiariaco Summit, Indio, Calif. 92201

Subjects: History—U.S.—regional; mining. *Comments:* No further information supplied. *ISBN:* 0–9600304

S7 SUPERIOR PUBLISHING COMPANY, 708 Sixth Avenue North, P.O. Box 1710, Seattle, Wash. 98111

Head: Albert P. Salisbury, President. *Subjects:* Americana—Western; photography; art; history—U.S.—regional. *Comments:* Hardcover reprints of Superior's out-of-print titles are published by Bramhall House and Bonanza Books. Hangman Press is an imprint; information from secondary sources; no further information supplied. *ISBN:* 0–87564

S72 SWALLOW PRESS, INC., THE, 1139 S. Wabash Avenue, Chicago, Ill. 60605

Head: Morton Weisman, President. *Founded:* 1942 (R 1946). *Type:* COMM. *Format:* HC; PB. *Forms:* BK. *Titles:* 50–99. *Subjects:* Fiction; poetry; literary history & criticism; American Indian—history & culture; Americana. *Comments:* Primarily publishers of original works. Reprints are a small part of the firm's list. *ISBN:* 0–8040

S74 SWEDISH PIONEER HISTORICAL SOCIETY, 5125 North Spaulding Avenue, Chicago, Ill. 60625

Comments: No further information requested.

T1 TALISMAN PRESS, THE, P.O. Box 455, Georgetown, Calif. 95634

Comments: No further information supplied. *ISBN:* 0–87399

T17 TAYLOR PUBLISHING COMPANY. *See* Kennikat Press.

T24 TENNESSEE MICROFILMS, P.O. Box 1096, Nashville, Tenn. 37202

Comments: Producer of microforms for Race Relations Information Center. No further information supplied.

*TERRITORIAL PRESS OF ARIZONA

T31 TEXAS FOLKLORE SOCIETY BOOKS. *See* Southern Methodist University Press.

T38 TEXIAN PRESS, 1301 Jefferson Street, Waco, Texas 76702

Head: Robert E. Davis; Frank Jasek, Partners. *Founded:* 1961 (R 1964). *Type:* COMM. *Format:* HC. *Forms:* BK. *Subjects:* History—U.S.—Texas. *Comments:* Reprints constitute about 25% of the list. Also produce filmstrips and issue journal, *Texana. ISBN:* 0–87244

T45 THEOSOPHICAL PUBLISHING HOUSE, THE, P.O. Box 270, Wheaton, Ill. 60187

Head: Stephen E. Kellogg, Manager. *Founded:* 1875 (R 1902). *Type:* COMM; BKSL. *Format:* HC; PB. *Forms:* BK; MS. *Titles:* 100–299. *Subjects:* Theosophy; occultism; religion & theology; Sanskrit texts; Pali texts. *Comments:* Affiliate of Theosophical Publishing Houses of London and Adyar, India. Quest Books is an imprint. *ISBN:* 0–8356

T5 THEOSOPHICAL UNIVERSITY PRESS, P.O. Bin C, Pasadena, Calif. 91109

Type: COMM. *Format:* HC; PB. *Forms:* AN; BK; MS. *Titles:* 10–49. *Subjects:* Occultism; theosophy. *Comments:* Issue "Standard Occult Books." No further information supplied. *ISBN:* 0–911500

T55 3M/IM PRESS, P.O. Box 720, New York, N.Y. 10036

Head: J. Donald Furlong, Editorial Supervisor. *Founded:* 1967. *Type:* MICR. *Format:* MF; MI. *Forms:* BK; JL; NP. *Titles:* 1500–2999. *Subjects:* History; social sciences; Black studies; newspapers. *Comments:* Microform publisher of materials in New York Public Library and other research collections. Division of the 3M Company.

T57 TIDEWATER PUBLISHERS, P.O. Box 109, Cambridge, Md. 21613

Head: Robert F. Cornell. *Subjects:* History—U.S.—Maryland; maritime history & sciences. *Comments:* Division of Cornell Maritime Press, Inc.; no further information requested.

T6 TIMES MIRROR CO., THE. *See* World Publishing Company.

T61 TOWER BOOKS. *See* Gale Research Company.

T65 TRADITION PRESS. *See* Gale Research Company.

T7 TUDOR PUBLISHING COMPANY, 572 Fifth Avenue, New York, N.Y. 10036

Head: L. Amiel, President; Norman Blaustein, Vice President and Editor. *Founded:* 1929 (R 1931). *Type:* COMM. *Format:* HC. *Forms:*

BK. *Titles:* 300–499. *Subjects:* Art; history, rare books & manuscripts. *Comments:* Reprints constitute about 25% of list and are issued in editions of over 2000 copies. A division of Computer Applications, Inc.; also distributes reprints via Harlem Book Company, Inc. *ISBN:* 0–8148

T8 CHARLES E. TUTTLE CO., INC., 28 S. Main Street, Rutland, Vt. 05701

Head: Charles E. Tuttle, President. *Founded:* 1832. *Type:* COMM. *Format:* HC; PB. *Forms:* BK. *Titles:* 100–299. *Subjects:* Asian studies; Hawaii; genealogy; general; Japan; religion & theology; art; graphic arts; folklore; history—Canada; Americana; hobbies; Oriental languages. *Comments:* Also publish about 200 reprinted Asian editions of current U.S. titles, and many original works. Address in Japan: Suido 1-chome, 2–6, Bunkyo-ku Toyko. *ISBN:* 0–8048

T9 TWIN BROOKS SERIES. *See* Baker Book House.

U1 FREDERICK UNGAR PUBLISHING CO., INC., 250 Park Avenue South, New York, N.Y. 10003

Head: Frederick Ungar, President. *Founded:* 1940. *Type:* COMM. *Format:* HC; PB. *Subjects:* Political history; economic history; history; social history; literary history & criticism. *Comments:* Publish reprints in the "American Classics" series. Also publish many original works. Information from catalogs. No further information supplied. *ISBN:* 0–8044

U15 UNITED PUBLISHING CORPORATION, 5530 Wisconsin Avenue, Washington, D.C. 20015

Head: Leonard Klingsberg, President. *Founded:* 1969. *Type:* COMM. *Format:* HC; PB. *Forms:* BK; JL. *Titles:* Fewer than 10.

Subjects: Black studies; ethnic studies; periodicals. *Comments:* First major reprint program is 54 volumes of the Journal of Negro History; subsidiary of Publishers Company, Inc. *ISBN:* 0–87781

U18 UNITED STATES HISTORICAL DOCUMENTS INSTITUTE, 3701 Leland Street, Washington, D.C. 20015

Head: William Buchanan, President; Franklin Crawford, Co-Founder. *Founded:* 1970. *Type:* COMM. *Format:* HC; MF. *Forms:* BK; GD; RP. *Subjects:* Government documents; history. *Comments:* Joint venture of the owners of Carrollton Press and The Princeton Microfilm Corp. CIP

U2 UNIVERSAL MICROFILM CORPORATION, 141 Pierpont Avenue, Salt Lake City, Utah 84101

Type: MIR. *Format:* MF. *Comments:* No further information supplied.

U25 UNIVERSITY BOOKS, INC., 1615 Hillside Avenue, New Hyde Park, N.Y. 11040

Head: Lyle Stuart, Chairman of the Board; Robert N. Salmon, President. *Founded:* 1955. *Type:* COMM. *Format:* HC. *Forms:* AN; BK. *Subjects:* Occultism. *Comments:* Mystic Arts Book Society is a division. No further information supplied. *ISBN:* 0–8216

U3 UNIVERSITY MICROFILMS, 300 N. Zeeb Road, Ann Arbor, Mich. 48106

Head: Robert F. Asleson, President. *Founded:* 1938. *Type:* MICR. *Format:* ES; HC; MF; MI; PB. *Forms:* BK; JL; NP; RP. *Titles:* More than 5000. *Subjects:* General; history; literature; Americana; periodicals; bibliography & reference; Slavic Studies; Latin American Studies. *Comments:* Unit of Xerox Education Group; will reprint any out-of-print title "On Demand." *ISBN:* 0–8357

U35 UNIVERSITY MUSIC EDITIONS, P.O. Box 192, Ft. George Station, New York, N.Y. 10040

Head: Donald K. Leinbach, President; Christopher Pavlakis, Vice-President. *Founded:* 1967 (R 1968). *Type:* MICR. *Format:* MI. *Forms:* BK. *Titles:* 10–49. *Subjects:* Music. *Comments:* Microfiche reprint series of complete collected composer editions (Gesamtausgaben) of some 400 volumes, in indexed, hardcover "Micro-Book Form." Division of High Density Systems, Inc.

°UNIVERSITY OF ALASKA

U45 UNIVERSITY OF CALIFORNIA PRESS, 2223 Fulton Street, Berkeley, Calif. 94720

Head: August Fruge, Director; Lloyd G. Lyman, Assistant Director. *Founded:* 1893 (R 1956). *Type:* UNIV. *Format:* HC; PB. *Forms:* BK. *Titles:* 100–299. *Subjects:* Political science; sociology; anthropology; history; literature; Classical studies. *Comments:* University of California Press Ltd., London is a wholly-owned subsidiary that partially controls Ibeg Ltd., distributor in Europe, Africa and the Near East. Most reprints are from own backlist. Reprints are a very small part of the list. *ISBN:* 0–520

U48 UNIVERSITY OF CHICAGO PRESS, 5801 Ellis Avenue, Chicago, Ill. 60637

Head: Morris Philipson, Director; Philip D. Jones, Editor-in-Chief. *Founded:* 1892. *Type:* UNIV. *Format:* HC. *Forms:* BK. *Titles:* 10–49. *Subjects:* Anthropology; biological sciences; education; history; law; sociology. *Comments:* Print in double-page format. Most reprints are from own backlist. *ISBN:* 0–226

*UNIVERSITY OF FLORIDA PRESS

U55 UNIVERSITY OF ILLINOIS, Graduate School of Library Science, 435 Library, Urbana, Ill. 61801

Head: Herbert Goldhor, Managing Editor. *Founded:* 1952 (R 1968). *Type:* UNIV. *Format:* HC. *Forms:* BK. *Titles:* Fewer than 10. *Subjects:* Libraries & librarianship. *Comments:* Small reprint program of titles for library science history and education. *ISBN:* 0–87845

U58 UNIVERSITY OF NEBRASKA PRESS, Lincoln, Nebr. 68508

Head: Bruce M. Nicoli, Director. *Founded:* 1941 (R 1961). *Type:* UNIV. *Format:* HC; PB. *Forms:* BK. *Titles:* 100–299. *Subjects:* History—U.S.; literature—U.S.; literature—English; history—U.S.—Nebraska. *Comments:* Additional reprinted titles are published as Bison Books, a paperback imprint. Information from secondary sources. No further information supplied. *ISBN:* 0–8032

U6 UNIVERSITY OF NEW MEXICO PRESS, Journalism Bldg., Albuquerque, N.M. 87106

Head: Roger W. Shugg, Director; Jack D. Rittenhouse, Editor. *Founded:* 1930. *Type:* UNIV. *Format:* HC; PB. *Forms:* BK. *Titles:* 10–49. *Subjects:* History—U.S.—New Mexico; Americana—Western. *Comments:* Reprints constitute about 10% of publishing program. *ISBN:* 0–8263

U63 UNIVERSITY OF OKLAHOMA PRESS, 1005 Asp Avenue, Norman, Okla. 73069

Head: Edward A. Shaw, Director. *Founded:* 1928 (R 1950). *Type:* UNIV. *Format:* HC. *Forms:* BK. *Titles:* 10–49. *Subjects:* Exploration & travels; American Indian—history

& culture; literary history & criticism; history—U.S.—West. *Comments:* Reprints constitute a very small part of the list. *ISBN:* 0–8061. CIP

U65 UNIVERSITY OF OREGON, School of Health, Physical Education, and Recreation, Eugene, Oreg. 97403

Head: H. Harrison Clarke, Director. *Founded:* 1949. *Type:* UNIV. *Format:* MC. *Forms:* JL; RP. *Subjects:* Health, physical education, & recreation; education—tests. *Comments:* Cost of microcards includes library catalog cards. No further information supplied.

U68 UNIVERSITY OF ROCHESTER PRESS, Rush Rhees Library, River Campus Station, Rochester, N.Y. 14627

Comments: No further information supplied.

U7 UNIVERSITY OF SOUTH CAROLINA PRESS, Columbia, S.C. 29208

Head: Robert T. King, Director. *Founded:* 1945 (R 1950). *Type:* UNIV. *Format:* HC; PB. *Forms:* BK. *Titles:* Fewer than 10. *Subjects:* Humanities; bibliography & reference; Americana. *Comments:* Reprints constitute a small part of the list. Press is a department of the University. *ISBN:* 0–87249. CIP

U73 UNIVERSITY OF UTAH PRESS, University of Utah, Bldg. 513, Salt Lake City, Utah 84112

Head: Richard Thurman, Director. *Founded:* 1960 (R 1964). *Type:* UNIV. *Format:* HC; PB. *Forms:* BK. *Titles:* Fewer than 10. *Subjects:* Anthropology; literature—U.S.; Americana—Western. *Comments:* Reprint program to be expanded. *ISBN:* 0–87480

U75 UNIVERSITY OF WASHINGTON PRESS, Seattle, Wash. 98105

Head: Donald R. Ellegood, Director. *Founded:* 1909. *Type:* UNIV. *Subjects:* Music; Asian studies. *Comments:* Also distribute University of Alaska Press books. No further information supplied. *ISBN:* 0–295. CIP

U78 UNIVERSITY OF WISCONSIN PRESS, THE, P.O. Box 1379, Madison, Wisc. 53701

Head: Thompson Webb, Jr., Director. *Founded:* 1937. *Type:* UNIV. *Format:* HC; MC; PB. *Forms:* BK. *Titles:* 10–49. *Subjects:* General. *Comments:* Reprints constitute a very small part of publishing program. *ISBN:* 0–299. CIP

U8 UNIVERSITY PLACE BOOK SHOP, 840 Broadway, New York, N.Y. 10003

Head: Walter Goldwater, Owner. *Founded:* 1932 (R 1962). *Type:* BKSL. *Format:* HC; PB. *Forms:* BK. *Titles:* 10–49. *Subjects:* Black studies; African studies; West Indian studies; chess & checkers; ethnic studies. *Comments:* University Place Press is an imprint. *ISBN:* 0–911556

U85 UNIVERSITY PRINTS AND REPRINTS. *See* Academic International.

V2 LAWRENCE VERRY, INC., 16 Holmes Street, Mystic, Conn. 06355

Head: Lawrence Ian Verry, President. *Founded:* 1963 (R 1965). *Type:* BKSL. *Format:* HC. *Forms:* BK. *Titles:* 10–49. *Subjects:* History; literature; education; sociology. *Comments:* Mostly imports for which firm is sole, official, or designated agent. *ISBN:* 0–8426

V4 VESTAL PRESS, THE, 3533 Stratford Drive, Vestal, N.Y. 13850

Head: Harvey N. Roehl, Owner. *Founded:* 1961. *Type:* COMM; BKSL. *Format:* HC; PB. *Forms:* BK; SH. *Titles:* 50–99. *Subjects:* Music–automatic; pipe organs. *Comments:* Reprints music company catalogs and pamphlets. About 50% of titles issued are reprints. *ISBN:* 0–911572

V5 VIENNA HOUSE, INC., 342 Madison Avenue, New York, N.Y. 10017

Head: Ronald Shakerdge, Philip F. Winters, Co-Directors. *Founded:* 1970. *Type:* COMM. *Format:* HC. *Forms:* BK. *Subjects:* Music–history; literary history & criticism. *Comments:* First titles due 1971. *ISBN:* 0–8443

V6 VIKING PRESS, INC., THE, 625 Madison Avenue, New York, N.Y. 10022

Head: Thomas H. Guinzburg, President. *Founded:* 1925. *Type:* COMM. *Format:* HC; PB. *Comments:* Trade Publisher. Issue Compass reprints and Viking Large-Type books. No further information supplied. *ISBN:* 0–670

V8 VIRGINIA BOOK COMPANY, Berryville, Va. 22611

Head: Stuart E. Brown, Jr., President. *Founded:* 1947 (R 1962). *Type:* BKSL. *Format:* ES; HC. *Forms:* BK. *Titles:* 10–49. *Subjects:* Americana; history—U.S.—Virginia. *Comments:* Chesapeake Book Company is an imprint. *ISBN:* 0–911578

*WALKER AND COMPANY

*WASHINGTON SQUARE PRESS, DIVISION OF SIMON & SCHUSTER, INC.

W1 WEST BOOKS. *See* Folcroft Press.

W2 WESTERNLORE PRESS, Publishers, P.O. Box 41073, Eagle Rock Station, Los Angeles, Calif. 90041

Head: Paul D. Bailey, Owner. *Founded:* 1943. *Type:* COMM. *Format:* HC. *Forms:* BK. *Titles:* 10–49. *Subjects:* Americana—Western. *Comments:* "Books of the West . . . from the West." *ISBN:* 0–87026

W3 THE BOND WHEELRIGHT COMPANY, Porter's Landing, Freeport, Me. 04032

Head: Bond Wheelright, President; Thea Wheelright, Editor. *Founded:* 1949 (R 1960). *Type:* COMM. *Format:* HC; PB. *Forms:* BK. *Titles:* 10–49. *Subjects*: History—U.S.—regional. *Comments:* Cumberland Press is an imprint. In 1969, publisher opened "The Country Store" selling Maine books, and non-fiction titles from other publishers. Reprinting is a small part of publishing program. *ISBN:* 87027

W4 WILLIAMHOUSE-REGENCY. *See* Greenwood Press, Inc.

W6 WILLO INSTITUTE OF GENEALOGY, P.O. Box 523, Handsboro, Miss.

Subjects: Genealogy. *Comments:* No further information supplied.

W65 WINCHESTER PRESS, 460 Park Avenue, New York, N.Y. 10022

Subjects: Horses, health, physical education and recreation. *Comments:* No further information requested. ISBN: 0–87691

W7 WORLD PUBLISHING COMPANY, 110 East 59th Street, New York, N.Y. 10022

Head: Christopher Shaw, President; Peter Ritner, Vice-President and Editorial Director. *Founded:* 1906. *Type:* COMM. *Format:* HC; PB. *Forms:* BK. *Subjects:* General. *Comments:* Subsidiary of the Times Mirror Co.; Meridian Books is an imprint. No further information supplied. *ISBN:* 0–529

W8 WORLDWIDE BOOKS, INC., 250 West 57th Street, New York, N.Y. 10019

Head: Eva Kroy Wisbar, Publisher. *Comments:* No further information supplied. *ISBN:* 0–87115

X1 XEROX EDUCATION DIVISION, XEROX CORP. *See* R. R. Bowker Company and University Microfilms.

Y1 YE GALLEON PRESS, P.O. Box 400, Fairfield, Wash. 99012

Head: Glen C. Adams, Owner. *Founded:* 1937 (R 1964). *Type:* COMM; PRTR. *Format:* HC; PB. *Forms:* BK; RP. *Titles:* 10–49. *Subjects:* History—U.S.—Pacific Northwest; Americana; rare books & manuscripts. *Comments:* Firm specializes in reprints of "rare works of historic importance." Publisher does own letterpress printing. All titles are reprints. *ISBN:* 0–87770

Appendix F

Index to Subject Specialties

Black studies, A24, A28, A64, B49, C46, G7, H42, I66, J5, K4, L75, M13, M67, M75, M85, O3, R1, R16, R88, S26, S28, T55, U15, U8

Book industries & trade, B85

Books about books. *See* Bibliography & reference

Botany, B79, H14, L7, L85, N18

Business & finance, A64, F76, L2, M31, R58
  directories, R58

Calligraphy, S34. *See also* Graphic arts

Canadiana. *See* History–Canada

Chemistry, A3, D3, M31, N18. *See also* Science

Chess & checkers, U8. *See also* Hobbies

Children's books, A34, C28, D18, D82

Chinese studies, C24, C42, P3. *See also* Asian studies

Church history, N5. *See also* Religion & theology

Classic literature. *See* Literature–classical

Classical studies, A58, C66, U45. *See also* Literature–Classical

Communism, C58

Counterinsurgency, P25

Criminology, A26, S46

Dance, D26

Decorative arts. *See* Architecture & decorative arts

Drama & dramatics, B61, F22, R22

Ecology. *See* Environmental studies

Economic history, U1

Economics, A26, A68, C58, F76, K2, M31, M88, R64

Education, A26, B28, C22, C3, D18, D66, J3, K6, L7, M13, R16, R4, S26, U48, V2
  Montessori method, B43
  singing, P8
  tests, U65

Engineering, A68, D3

English history. *See* History–Gt. Britain

English literature. *See* Literature–English

Entomology, A32, E7

Environmental studies, A64

Espionage, P25

Ethnic studies, A24, R1, U15, U8

Etiquette, D58

European history. *See* History–Europe

Exploration & travels, A1, A48, A66, B22, F22, F7, G3, G7, L75, R7, R76, U63

Fascism, F34

Fiction, B46, B7, G2, G75, L75, M13, S72

Financial history. *See* Business & finance

Folk music. *See* Music–folk

Folklore, A58, E8, G1, G3, J4, M67, T8

Freemasonry, H46, M19

French studies, K6

Genealogy, B19, G1, G25, G45, H42, H66, M67, T8, W6

General, B61, C12, C3, C8, D18, D82, F7, G1, G3, G7, H18, J6, K6, L15, L2, L65, M43, M64, N18, P1, R22, S48, T8, U3, U78, W7

Germanic studies, A48, J6, K6

Government documents, C18, C22, C26, C34, C58, G25, G7, J6, K6, M31, N18, R22, U18
  League of Nations, R22, R58
  U.S.–state, F22
  United Nations, R22

Government–U.S., C34

Graphic arts, B7, D1, G65, S34, T8

Hawaii, T8

Health, physical education, & recreation, A1, H46, U65, W65

Heraldry, G25, H66

History, A4, A48, A6, A68, A8, B22, B28, B49, B52, B73, C12, C66, D82, F34, G1, G5, G7, G75, H42, H66, H94, I5, I66, J6, K4, L55, L7, M75, M88, N42, O3, R7, R71, S26, S28, S38, S48, S6, S62, T55, T7, U1, U18, U3, U45, U48, V2
  American. *See* History–U.S.

Notes

CHAPTER 1

1. "Bibliographical Control of Reprints," *Library Resources & Technical Services,* Fall 1967, pp. 415–435. See also *Library Trends,* January 1970; and articles by Frederick Freedman, "Perspective—Music Reprint Industry," *Choice,* October 1969, pp. 977–85, and Lewis M. Wiggin, "Aspects of Reprinting," *Scholarly Publishing,* January 1971, pp. 149–61. Mr. Freedman, librarian, Vassar College, is general editor of the DaCapo Press Music Reprint Series. Mr. Wiggin, director of sales, Shoe String Press, has long experience in the reprint industry.
2. Helen Welch Tuttle, "Library-Book Trade Relations," *Library Trends,* January 1970, p. 403.
3. Sol M. Malkin, "The Specialist Reprint Trade," in the 1969 *AB Bookman's Year-book,* Part 1, p. 3.
4. S. A. Belzer, "Remarks on Reprinting," *Reprint Expediting Service Bulletin,* Spring 1964, p. 2.
5. "Report of the Out-of-Print Book Survey," conducted by G. William Bergquist (Chicago: American Library Association, 1951); see also Malcolm M. Hutton, "Retention 'in print' of titles by five large publishers," report of a thesis prepared for Kent State University, Department of Library Science, under the direction of Dr. Guy Marco (Kent, Ohio: University of Kentucky Press, 1962; Kentucky Microcards, Series B. Library Series, Number 55).
6. Lawrence S. Thompson, "The Microfacsimile in American Research Libraries," *Libri* 8 (1958): 209. *See also Manual on Methods of Reproducing Materials,* a survey made for the Joint Committee on Materials for Research of the Social Science Research Council and the American Council of Learned Societies by Robert C. Brinkley and others. (Ann Arbor, Mich.: Edwards Brothers, 1936).
7. Robert C. Sullivan, "Developments in Reproduction of Library Materials and Graphic Communication, 1968," *Library Resources & Technical Services,* Summer 1969, pp. 391–421. See also Allen B. Veaner's 1967 review, Spring 1968, pp. 203–214, in which 1967 is called "the year of the micropublication."
8. Helen Welch Tuttle, "Library-Book Trade Relations," *Library Trends,* January 1970, p. 403.

219

9. Chester Kerr, "The Kerr Report Revisited," *Scholarly Publishing*, October 1969, pp. 5–30. See also Gene R. Hawes, *To Advance Knowledge* (New York: American University Press Services, 1967).

10. *Publishers' Weekly*, February 8, 1971, and earlier *Bowker Annuals*.

11. Personal letter from Carole Collins, then managing editor, *The Bowker Annual*, dated February 4, 1970.

12. If others share the quest for these factual data, there might be reliable figures forthcoming from the Library of Congress' MARC tapes and from the Cataloging in Publication program.

13. "12,000 Books O–P Every Year," *Publishers' Weekly*, August 25, 1958.

14. Burt Franklin, "Ten Years of the Hard Cover Scholarly Reprint: A Retrospective View and a Proposal for Improvements in Processing Orders" (an address before the New Jersey Library Association, Atlantic City, May 2, 1968), in *The Reprint Bulletin*, July–August 1968, pp. 1–9; *Publishers' Weekly*, December 30, 1968, states that Franklin estimated that 30 million titles have been produced since the invention of movable type, but reprinters haven't touched more than 1 percent of the publishing output of the past.

15. J. H. Pafford, "Principles of Reprint Publishing," *Times Literary Supplement*, March 6, 1969.

16. Francis Sweeney, ed., *The Knowledge Explosion: Liberation and Limitation* (New York: Farrar, Straus & Giroux, 1966), p. 31.

17. Abigail Dahl-Hansen and Richard M. Dougherty, "Acquisition Trends—1968," *Library Resources & Technical Services*, Summer 1969, p. 373.

18. Felix Reichmann, "The Purchase of Out-of-Print Material in American University Libraries," *Library Trends*, January 1970, p. 328.

19. Personal letter, dated September 15, 1969.

20. Burt Franklin, "The Antiquarian Reprint 1966: A Glance Backward and Forward. Part I," *The Reprint Bulletin*, May–June 1967, p. 3.

21. Louis R. Wilson and Maurice F. Tauber, *The University Library: Its Organization, Administration, and Functions* (Chicago, University of Chicago Press, 1956), pp. 348 ff.

22. Harry M. Lydenberg, "Publishing as a Librarian Sees it," *Publishers' Weekly*, February 23, 1935.

CHAPTER 2

1. Personal interview, January 14, 1969.

2. Felix Reichmann, "Bibliographical Control of Reprints," Fall 1967, p. 419.

3. Rolland E. Stevens. "The Microform Revolution," *Library Trends*, January 1971, pp. 379–395.

4. "Microforms: Where Do They Fit?" *Library Resources & Technical Services*, Winter 1971, pp. 57–62. Revised text of talk delivered at the Joint Sections Program meeting of the Resources and Technical Services Division, ALA, Detroit, July 2, 1970.

5. The ARL Microform Project, Cornell University Libraries, Ithaca, New York. (Personal letter from Felix Reichmann dated October 29, 1969, and subsequent conversations.)

6. Periodicals helpful for current awareness of developments and changes in the printing industries are: *Book Production Industry, Reproduction Methods* and *Printing Impressions*. Shortrun printing and small-edition binding are topics discussed in the Bookmaking section of *Publishers' Weekly*.

7. Hawken, William R. *Copying Methods Manual* (Chicago: American Library Association, 1966).

8. See "Microfiche 1969—A User Survey," conducted at the request of the Committee on Scientific and Technical Information (COSATI) by Harold Wooster, director of Information Sciences, U.S. Air Force Office of Scientific Research, July 1969. (Contains a brief history and discussion of standardization of fiche size.)

9. "What is Microprint? A Guide for Scholars and Librarians," booklet prepared by Readex, April 1969; various microforms are also explained in "The Microfilm Technology Primer on Scholarly Journals," booklet prepared by the Library Service Division, Princeton Microfilm Corporation of New Jersey, September 1969.

10. Dan Lacy, in "Alleged Price Fixing of Library Books," *Hearings before the Subcommittee on Antitrust and Monopoly*, U.S. Senate, 89th Congress, 2nd Session, Committee on the Judiciary (Washington, D.C.: Government Printing Office, 1966), p. 133.

11. Personal interview, April 28, 1969.

12. Reichmann, *op. cit.*

13. See "Progress Report VI, January 1970," prepared by Julian G. Plante, or request further details directly from the project.

14. Charles Scribner's Sons announced a new series "to make Scribner's popular contemporary classics accessible to the visually handicapped, reluctant readers, senior citizens and readers to whom English is a second language," in an advertising brochure mailed October 1968.

15. The study was conducted by the Subcommittee on Large Type of the Commission on Blind and Visually Handicapped, under a grant from the U.S. Department of Health, Education and Welfare and a private funding source. The recommendations, including a standard of a minimum of 16 point type or larger and other standards dealing with opacity and overall size, and special features for creating and handling large type books were published in 1970 by the National Accreditation Council for Agencies Serving the Blind and Visually Handicapped, New York City.

16. Robert A. Landau and Judith S. Nyren, eds., *Large Type Books in Print* (New York: Bowker, 1970). The first edition lists some 1,500 currently available titles from 38 publishers, and includes a directory.

17. A. J. A. Symons, "Edition and Impression," *The Book Collector's Quarterly* 6, January–March, 1932, pp. 1ff.

18. Frederick Freedman, "Perspective—Music Reprint Industry," *Choice,* October 1969, p. 978.

19. Harold J. Mason, "The Periodical Reprinting Business" (Unpublished typescript prepared for the School of Library Service, Columbia University, January 1961), p. 2.

20. T. L. Rowland, "An Outline and Notes Towards the Planning of a Survey of the Scholarly Reprint Publishing Trade" (Xerox copy of an unpublished paper submitted to the School of Library Service, Columbia University, 1968). The writer is grateful to Mr. Rowland for providing a copy of his paper.

21. Chandler B. Grannis, ed., *What Happens in Book Publishing* (New York: Columbia University Press, 1957), p. 1.

22. Frederick Freedman, *op. cit.,* p. 979.

23. C. Sumner Spalding, general editor, North American text, *Anglo-American Cataloging Rules* (Chicago: American Library Association, 1967).

CHAPTER 3

1. Isaac Taylor, *History of the Transmission of Ancient Books to Modern Times* (London: printed for B. J. Holdsworth, St. Paul's Churchyard, 1827), p. 68.
2. Frank Arthur Mumby, *Publishing and Bookselling: A History from the Earliest Times to the Present Day*, 4th ed. (London: Jonathan Cape, 1956), p. 15.
3. John Mathew Gutch, *Observations or Notes upon the Writings of the Ancients* (Bristol: printed by J. M. Gutch at the Office of Felix Farley's *Bristol Journal*, 1827), p. 64.
4. Beatrice White, "Philobiblon: The Love of Books in Life and in Literature" (London: The Library Association, 1967), p. 7. (Arundel Esdaile Memorial Lecture.)
5. Ernest Cushing Richardson, *Some Old Egyptian Librarians* (New York: Charles Scribner's Sons, 1911), p. 13.
6. Raymond Irwin, *The English Library: Sources and History* (London: George Allen & Unwin, 1966), p. 30.
7. Alfred Gudeman, "The Alexandrian Library and Museum," *The Columbia Literary Monthly*, December 1895, p. 100. See also the more recent book by Edward A. Parsons, *The Alexandrian Library, Glory of the Hellenic World; Its Rise, Antiquities, and Destructions*. (Amsterdam: Elsevier Press, 1952).
8. Rudolph Hirsch, *Printing, Selling and Reading* (Wiesbaden: Otto Harrassowitz, 1967), quoting C. Wehmer, p. 19, n. 21.
9. James M. Wells, "Introduction," *The Scholar Printers: A Catalog of Two Exhibitions at the Newberry Library, Chicago, May 31, 1964* (Chicago: University of Chicago Press, 1964), p. 1.
10. Hirsch, *op. cit.*, p. 27.
11. Curtis G. Benjamin, "Book Publishing's Hidden Bonanza," *Saturday Review*, April 18, 1970, pp. 19 ff.
12. *Medieval Texts and Their First Appearance in Print* (London: printed for the Bibliographical Society at the University Press, Oxford, 1943; reprinted with corrections, Hain, 1965), p. 13.
13. Hellmut Lehman-Haupt, "A New Look at Old Books," *The New York Times Book Review*, December 1, 1968, p. 50.
14. R. A. B. Mynors, "A Fifteenth-Century Scribe: T. Werken," *Transactions of the Cambridge Bibliographical Society* I, Part 2 (1950): p. 103.
15. Marjorie Plant, *The English Book Trade*, 2nd ed. (London: George Allen & Unwin, 1965), p. 16.
16. Roberts, *op. cit.*, p. 35.
17. Plant, *op. cit.*, pp. 23–24.
18. Alfred W. Pollard, *Shakespeare's Fight With the Pirates and the Problems of the Transmission of His Text*, Sandars Reader in Bibliography, 1915 (London: Alexander Moring Ltd., 1917), p. 21.
19. *Ibid.*, pp. 46–47.
20. David Kaser, *Book Pirating in Taiwan* (Philadelphia: University of Pennsylvania Press, 1969), p. 5.
21. Joyce H. Brodowski, "Statement of Proposed Dissertation" entitled "Literary Piracies in England in the Restoration and Early Eighteenth Century" (Proposal for a doctoral thesis submitted to Columbia University School of Library Science, 1967.)
22. Ellen B. Shaffer, lecture to the Seminar in the History of Books and Printing, October 1967, Columbia University School of Library Service.

23. Henry Walcott Boynton, *Annals of American Bookselling: 1638–1850* (New York: John Wiley & Sons, 1932), p. 37.
24. Eugene Exman, *The House of Harper* (New York: Harper & Row, 1967), p. 52.
25. Boynton, *op. cit.*, p. 154.
26. "The Distribution of Reprint Books: A Survey of the Market and the Means of Reaching It," *Publishers' Weekly*, March 30, 1935, pp. 1313–1317.
27. Charles A. Madison, *Book Publishing in America* (New York: McGraw-Hill, 1966), Part II, pp. 50–153.
28. Kaser, *op. cit.*, p. 3.

CHAPTER 4

1. Robert O. Ballou, *A History of the Council of Books in Wartime,* from a working draft prepared by Irene Rakowsky (New York: Country Life Press, 1946).
2. "Withdrawal by the Custodian from the Periodical Republication Program," Memorandum from Eugene A. Tilleux to Howland H. Sargeant (Washington, D.C.: U.S. Office of the Alien Property Custodian, May 25, 1945), 39 pp. and Exhibits A-P, p. 1 (copy in Columbia University Libraries).
3. Thomas P. Fleming, head, Medical Sciences Division, Columbia University Libraries, personal interview March 19, 1969.
4. U.S. Office of the Alien Property Custodian, "Report on Periodical Republication Program," mimeographed (Washington, D.C.: November 1945), p. 2.
5. "Keeping Back List Titles in Print Under the Paper Shortage," *Publishers' Weekly*, July 31, 1943, pp. 320–326. See also *Publishers' Weekly*, April 3, 1943, for descriptions of wartime bookmaking problems.
6. U.S. Office of the Alien Property Custodian, Annual Report No. 2, for the period ending June 30, 1944, (copy in Business Library, Columbia University Libraries).
7. "Photographic Books in Threatened Libraries," *New York Times*, May, 26, 1940, pp. 2, 3. This article discusses librarians' concern over the destruction of Old World cultural treasures and plans to microfilm books and manuscripts in England, France, and in the Vatican Library.
8. The series of announcements were entitled "Book Republication Program Titles suggested for Republication . . ." and "Periodical Republication Program. List . . ." (See bibliography under "U.S. Office of the Alien Property Custodian.")
9. Quoted by Reuben Peiss, in "European Wartime Acquisitions and the Library of Congress Mission," *Library Journal,* June 15, 1946.
10. By Executive Order No. 9182, June 13, 1942, certain functions of the Office of Coordinator of Information were merged with those of the short-lived Office of Facts and Figures, the Office of Government Reports, and the Division of Information of the Office for Emergency Management, to form the Office of War Information. Tilleux Report, p. 2.
11. U.S. Office of the Alien Property Custodian, Annual Report No. 1, for the period March 11, 1942–June 30, 1943.
12. Advisory Council members were: Dr. E. J. Crane, editor, Chemical Abstracts; Watson Davis, president, American Documentation Institute; Luther H. Evans, Chief Assistant Librarian of Congress; Thomas P. Fleming, chairman, Joint Committee on Importations; Sarah A. Jones, librarian, Bureau of Standards; W. H. Kenerson, executive secretary, National Research Council; Frederick B. Kilgour, executive secretary, Interdepartmental Committee for the Acquisition of Foreign Periodicals; Waldo G. Leland, director, American Council of Learned Societies; Keyes D. Metcalf, president, American Library Association; Paul North Rice, executive secretary, Association of Research Libraries; E. Wilder Spaulding, chief,

Division of Research and Publication, Department of State; Donald Young, executive director, Social Science Research Council; and George F. Zook, president, American Council on Education.

13. U.S. Office of the Alien Property Custodian, Terminal Report, transmitted to President Harry S Truman by James A. Markham, Alien Property Custodian, mimeographed (Washington, D.C.: October 14, 1946).

14. U.S. "Report on Periodical Republication Program," Office of the Alien Property Custodian (Washington, D.C., November 1945) (copy in Columbia University Libraries).

15. "Periodical Republication Program. List 1," *op. cit.*

16. *Ibid.,* p. 10.

17. Howland H. Sargeant to J. W. Edwards, president of Edwards Brothers, Inc., March 23, 1943, and reply. Reproduced as Exhibits N and O in Tilleux Report.

18. Sargeant to Dr. B. A. Uhlendorf, senior editor, Edwards Brothers, May 9, 1944. Quoted by Tilleux, p. 37, and reproduced as Exhibit P in the Tilleux Report.

19. Tilleux Report, p. 35.

20. U.S. Office of the Alien Property Custodian, Annual Report No. 1, 1942/43, p. 63.

21. U.S. Office of the Alien Property Custodian, Report 1943, *op. cit.,* p. 7.

22. Tilleux Report, p. 14.

23. Johnson Reprint Corporation, *Newsletter,* March–April 1970.

24. Information extracted from Luther H. Evans' "Report on Important Developments," Nos. 59, 61 and 65, January 14, 1942, January 16, 1942, and January 21, 1942, respectively, is presented here with Dr. Evans' kind permission.

25. Thomas P. Fleming, personal interview March 19, 1969.

26. Joseph Edwards, president of Edwards Brothers, Inc., personal interview March 12, 1960.

27. Report of the Alien Property Custodian, 1945, pp. 6–7.

28. "Reports on the Destruction of Leipzig's Book Center," *Publishers' Weekly,* August 19, 1944. Copy in Tilleux Report, Exhibit F. See also Reuben Peiss, "European Wartime Acquisitions and the Library of Congress Mission," *Library Journal,* June 15, 1946.

29. Dr. Charles H. Brown (then librarian, Iowa State College), a member of the Advisory Committee of the Association of Research Libraries, was chairman. Members attending were: Dr. Carl M. White, director of libraries, Columbia University; Keyes D. Metcalf, director, Harvard College Library; Dr. Ralph Beals, director, University of Chicago Libraries; Dr. Paul North Rice, director, New York Public Library; Dr. Carl Vitz, librarian, Minneapolis Public Library (and president of the ALA); Dr. Harry M. Lydenberg, chairman, International Relations Office, ALA; Thomas P. Fleming, assistant librarian, Columbia University Libraries (and consultant on the Periodical Republication Program); and J. W. Edwards, president, Edwards Brothers, Inc., as guest.

30. Tilleux Report, p. 15.

31. *Ibid.*

32. Luther H. Evans, personal conversation, August 24, 1970.

33. Tilleux Report, p. 7.

34. At this meeting were: Howland H. Sargeant; Edward A. Chapman; Carl H. Milam, executive Secretary of ALA; Keyes D. Metcalf, librarian, Harvard University and president of the ALA; Miss Sarah A. Jones, librarian, Bureau of Standards; Frederick G. Kilgour, executive secretary, Interdepartmental Committee for the Acquisition of Foreign Publications, Office of Strategic Services; Thomas P. Fleming, Columbia University and chairman of the Joint Committee on Importations; Luther H. Evans, Chief Assistant Librarian of Congress; and Harry M. Lydenburg, director, International Relations Office, ALA.

35. Attending the December 2, 1943 meeting were: Keyes D. Metcalf, librarian, Harvard University, and advisory member of the Joint Committee on Importations; Paul North Rice, head of Reference Department, New York Public Library, and secretary of the Association of Research Libraries; Miss Eleanor S. Cavanaugh, librarian, Standard and Poor's, and president of the Special Libraries Association; Edward G. Freehafer, head of the Acquisitions Department, New York Public Library, and executive Member of the Joint Committee on Importations; Harrison W. Craver, director, Engineering Societies Library; Lawrence Heyl, associate librarian, Princeton University, and executive member of the Joint Committee on Importations; and Thomas P. Fleming, medical librarian, Columbia University, chairman of the Joint Committee on Importations. (Affiliations are those at the time of the meeting.)
36. Tilleux Report, p. 7.
37. Markham, "Terminal Report," pp. 3–13.
38. Report of the U.S. Office of the Alien Property Custodian, 1945, *op. cit.*, p. 6.

CHAPTER 5

1. R. E. Kingery, "Some Solved and Unsolved Problems of Reprinting," *The Reprint Expediting Service Bulletin,* June 1959, p. 3.
2. Peter P. Muirhead, former Deputy Commissioner for Higher Education, quoted in "Report on the Seventy-Third meeting of the Association of Research Libraries," Washington, D.C., January 1969, in College & Research Library *News,* May 1969, p. 155.
3. "A Statistical Look at American Education 1970," *American Education,* October 1969, pp. 24–25.
4. Neil A. Radford, doctoral candidate at the University of Chicago. (Personal letter, July 30, 1971). Mr. Radford is studying the role of the Carnegie Corporation in the development of American academic libraries between 1928 and 1943.
5. The 1960 statistics are from the 1962 *American Library Directory* (ALD) 23rd edition. Later figures are from the 1970–1971 *ALD,* 27th edition, edited by Eleanor F. Steiner-Prag (New York: Bowker, September 1970). Neither *ALD* nor *The Bowker Annual* (which reports statistics from *ALD*) specifies which year is reported. For this research study, it has been assumed that the *ALD,* issued biennially, reports the state of the library world for some time during the two years prior to its publication.
6. Statistics on elementary and secondary schools are available in "Projections of Educational Statistics," U.S. Office of Education 1969 edition (Washington, D.C.: Government Printing Office, 1970). See also the "Third Annual Report, Fiscal Year 1968, Title II, Elementary and Secondary Education Act of 1965; School Library Resources, Textbooks, and other Instructional Materials," issued by the U.S. Office of Education, and other annual reports of education enabling legislation.
7. See, for example, Alan Caruba, "Building a New Library for a New College," *Publishers' Weekly,* October 26, 1970. Ramapo College of New Jersey, a new four-year state college, had a library budget of $125,000 for fiscal year 1970–1971. This was expected to double by the next year. An opening day collection of 16–20,000 volumes was planned.
8. *Publishers' Weekly,* November 4, 1969. Discussion of the Book Manufactures Institute (BMI) annual meeting.
9. According to E. Alden Dunham, "What Is the Junior College All About?," *PMLA,* June 1968, p. 530, there were 8 junior colleges in 1900 with 100 students; 650

with 818,000 students in 1960; and 900 with 1.6 million enrolled at the end of 1967; and about 50 new junior colleges opening yearly.

10. Review of *Junior College Libraries: Development, Needs and Perspectives,* edited by Everett LeRoy Moore (Chicago: American Library Association, 1969; ACRL Monograph Number 30), in *Library Journal,* November 15, 1969.

11. "Statistics in Trends in Education," prepared by the National Center for Educational Statistics (Washington, D.C.: Government Printing Office, 1970), OE–10068.

12. *Publishers' Weekly, op. cit.,* quoting Howard M. Warrington, president of the College Books Division, Prentice-Hall.

13. *ALD, op. cit.* These figures include public libraries, and branch libraries of city, county and regional systems, as well as branch libraries maintained by public libraries. The library categories listed in the 1970 *ALD* differ somewhat from earlier editions, but the types of public libraries included appear to be the same.

14. Sol Lewis, "A Plea for More Scholarship and Creativity in Reprints," *Reprint Expediting Service Bulletin,* November–December 1966, p. 6. Dr. Lewis was then general editor of Argonaut Press, Ltd., whose books were distributed through University Microfilms. Lewis was president of Antiquarian Press, Ltd. from 1960–1963, and Argosy-Antiquarian Press, Ltd., 1963–1965. Later he directed the Paladin program for AMS Press, and in 1970 became president of a newly formed company, Library Editions, Ltd. (personal interview, August 20, 1970).

15. Telephone communication, September 2, 1969; and personal note from Mr. Smith, dated October 26, 1969.

16. Personal interview, Albert J. Diaz, executive director, NCR Microcard Editions, January 28, 1969.

17. *The Reprint Bulletin,* January–April 1965, pp. 3–10.

18. Dobbs Ferry, New York: Oceana, 1969, pp. 208–220.

19. "Reprints of Books and Journals on Africa," 11, No. 3, pp. 329–362. Miss Ells is associated with the Foreign Area Materials Center, the State University of New York, State Education Department. The center compiles lists of reprints in specific fields (Asian and African studies) in order to "inform scholars about what is available." The center also compiles a series of five bibliographies on Asia, Africa, and the Middle East, "to be used as buying guides for undergraduate libraries," The center includes reprints on these lists in the hopes of making the OP titles attractive to reprinters. (Letter from Edith Ehrman, manager, dated November 21, 1969.)

20. Vol. 13, Supplement No. 1, September 1968. The issue is devoted to "Reprints and Microform Materials in Asian Studies."

21. Subtitle: *Current List of Available Reproductions (Microforms and Reprints),* prepared by Odette Paoletti and Odile Daniel (Paris: Maison des Sciences de l'Homme, July 1966). A 1967–1968 supplement is available.

22. *Two Kinds of Power: An Essay on Bibliographical Control* (Berkeley and Los Angeles: University of California Press, 1968), p. 60.

23. Personal interview, John Mladinich, then vice-president, Barnes & Noble, August 20, 1969.

24. "The Antiquarian Reprint Trade," *Antiquarian Bookman,* April 19, 1965.

25. Personal interview, Bernard M. Rosenthal, owner, April 4, 1969. Bernard M. Rosenthal, Bookseller, has since moved from New York City to San Francisco.

26. *See* Rush Welter's *Problems of Scholarly Publication in the Humanities and Social Sciences* (New York: American Council of Learned Societies, 1959).

27. Personal interview, Nachman Halberstadt, president, October 14, 1969.

28. Promotional leaflet, n.d., but received by mail, October 1970.

29. See, for example, "Facsimile Reprint: The Newest Revolution," *Publishers' Weekly*, December 30, 1968, in which it is stated that "Statistically, there are some 200 U.S. reprinters active today, about 40 of which could be considered 'major.'"
30. Geographical distribution of the general book publishing industry is noted in *U.S. Industrial Outlook 1970*, issued by the Business and Defense Services Administration, U.S. Department of Commerce (Washington, D.C.: Government Printing Office, 1970), p. 66. See also an excellent and much needed "Historical Analysis of U.S. Book Publishing Statistics," by William S. Lofquist, in "Printing and Publishing," *BSDA Quarterly Industry Report*, 2, No. 8 (July 1970), 13024 (Washington, D.C.: Government Printing Office, 1970).
31. Personal letter date April 28, 1970. Mr. Adams was the winner of the Special Commendation Award for Printers sponsored by the Washington State Library Commission and the State Arts Commission on April 19, 1970.
32. Personal interview, January 14, 1969.

CHAPTER 6

1. Personal interview, November 24, 1969. See also "Book Forum: Letters from Readers," *Saturday Review*, March 28, 1970.
2. "Books on Demand: A Catalog of OP Titles," 1971 edition, produced by Microfilm Xerography (Ann Arbor, Michigan, n.d.).
3. Personal interview, Larry Block, manager, Project Operations, October 9, 1969.
4. Assisted by funding from the Council on Library Resources, the *Core Collection* project was developed in collaboration with the Association of College and Research Libraries. In 1969 Melville J. Ruggles, then CLR program officer, kindly described the early states of this "packaged program" designed to assign each title to one of four categories representing relative urgency of need. The *Core Collection* is intended to help newly established libraries and librarians strengthening their collections. (Personal interview, July 8, 1969.)
5. Personal interview, May 14, 1969.
6. Telephone communication, Harry Lubrecht, July 1969.
7. Personal interview, President, Howard Fertig, Inc., August 22, 1969.
8. Personal interview, February 1, 1969.
9. Personal interview, August 28, 1969. Mr. Schlanger is editor-in-chief, Octagon Books, a division of Farrar, Straus & Giroux, Inc.
10. Personal interview, July 18, 1969. Mr. Mladinich was then vice-president, Barnes & Noble. In 1971 he became general manager, Rowman & Littlefield.
11. "Book Selection for Reprints," *Reprint Expediting Service Bulletin*, Winter 1964–1965), pp. 1–2.
12. See "The Ethics of Reprint Publishing," *LRTS*, Winter 1971, pp. 53–56, for the text of Mr. Garrett's speech; see also Lewis M. Wiggin, "Aspects of Reprinting," *Scholarly Publishing*, January 1971, pp. 149–161.
13. See Robert M. Orton, *Catalog of Reprints in Series*, 20th ed., 1965 and supplements (Metuchen, N.J.: Scarecrow, 1965, 1967); see also Sam P. Williams, comp. and ed., *Reprints in Print—Serials; 1966* (Dobbs Ferry, N.Y.: Oceana, 1967).

CHAPTER 7

1. *The Art and Science of Book Publishing* (New York: Harper & Row, 1970), p. 2.
2. Personal interview, April 24, 1969.
3. Personal interview, February 25, 1969.

4. Personal interview, May 26, 1969.
5. Personal interview, May 14, 1969.
6. "The Future Isn't What It Used To Be," text of a paper by Gardner, president of Technical Information, Inc., Los Angeles, given at the COMPRINT 90 Conference, New York City, October 12, 1970, in *Proceedings of the ASIS Workshop on Computer Composition* (Washington, D.C.: American Society for Information Science, 1971), p. 5.
7. *Graphic Communications Weekly*, July 8, 1969.
8. Personal interview, Melville J. Ruggles, then program officer, Council on Library Resources, Inc., July 8, 1969; and telephone communication with Carl B. Hansen, assistant director, Columbia University Press, April 13, 1971.
9. "The Ethics of Reprint Publishing," *Library Resources & Technical Services*, Winter 1971, p. 55; see also the discussion of printruns and pricing considerations provided by Fred Rappaport, vice-president, Johnson Reprint Corp., in "The Changing Philosophy of Reprint Publishers," and Robert F. Asleson's "Microforms: Where Do They Fit?" in this same issue.
10. See various years of *The Bowker Annual* for the Materials Price Indexes that provide the averages for nonreprint titles.
11. U.S. Copyright Office, "International Copyright Protection," Circular 38 (Washington, D.C.: Library of Congress, June 1969), p. 1.
12. There is an extensive literature on the subject of copyright laws and legislation. One report (though no longer of recent date) that specifically treats attitudes of copying practices is: U.S. Office of Education, Bureau of Research, "The Determination of Legal Facts and Economic Guideposts with Respect to the Dissemination of Scientific and Educational Information as it is Affected by Copyright—A Status Report," by Gerald J. Sophar and Lawrence B. Heilprin (for) the Committee to Investigate Copyright Problems . . . (Washington, D.C.: December 1967) (Final Report, Project No. 70793, Contract No. OEC 1–7–070793–3559).

CHAPTER 8

1. Dan Lacy, senior vice-president, McGraw-Hill, Inc., quoted in "The Publishing Decision—The Relative Influence of the Bookseller and the Library," by Simon Michael Bessie, president, Atheneum Publishers, in *The Future of General Adult Books and Reading in America*, ed. by Peter S. Jennison and Robert N. Sheridan (Chicago: American Library Association, 1970), p. 82.
2. Edwin Castagna, "A Librarian Looks at American Publishing," in *Trends in American Publishing*. Papers presented at an Institute . . . November 5–8, 1967, University of Illinois Graduate School of Library Science, edited by Katheryn Luther Henderson (Champaign, Illinois: 1968; Allerton Park Institute, No. 14), pp. 75–88.
3. Howard Mumford Jones, "Modern Scholarship and the Data of Greatness," in *The Knowledge Explosion: Liberation and Limitation*, ed. by Francis Sweeney (New York: Farrar, Strauss & Giroux, 1966), p. 29.
4. Title output figures for 1955 are taken from *The American Library Annual 1957* (New York: Bowker, 1957). The 1970 figures are reported in *Publishers' Weekly*, February 8, 1971.
5. Jerrold Orne, "The Renaissance of Academic Library Building 1967–1971," *Library Journal*, December 1, 1971.
6. Daniel Bell, Harvard University professor of sociology, and chairman of the Commission on the Year 2000 of the American Academy of Arts and Sciences, describes the fantastic explosion of knowledge in his "Introduction" to *The

Future of General Adult Books and Reading in America, ed. by Peter S. Jennison and Robert N. Sheridan (Chicago: American Library Association, 1970), p. 82.

7. Margit Kraft, "An Argument for Selectivity in the Acquisition of Materials for Research Libraries," *Library Quarterly* 37, July 1967, p. 285.

8. Lawrence S. Thompson, "The Dogma of Book Selection in University Libraries," *College & Research Libraries,* November 1960, pp. 444–445.

9. J. R. Blanchard, "Planning the Conversion of a College to a University Library," *College & Research Libraries,* July 1968, pp. 207–302. See also John Emmett Burke, *The Rising Tide—More Research Libraries* (Commerce: East Texas State University, 1966), for a careful discussion of how the growth in graduate education affects the nature of library collections.

10. "Historians and Reprint Publishing," edited text of paper delivered at the 1965 annual meeting of the American Historical Association, San Francisco in *The Reprint Expediting Service Bulletin,* September–October 1966, p. 1.

11. "The Professional Historian and His Readers," *Scholarly Publishing,* April 1970, p. 278.

12. Connie R. Dunlap, "Reprinting: Problems, Directions, Challenges," with an "Introduction," *Library Resources & Technical Services,* Winter 1971, pp. 34–75.

13. Alfred H. Lane, "Reprints in the Preservation Picture—and a Drift Aside," *Antiquarian Bookman,* December 7, 1970.

14. James H. Hoover, "Pitfalls in Purchasing Reprints," *LLA Bulletin* (Louisiana Library Association), Fall 1967, pp. 109–110. See also Nicholas Dewey, "The Reprint Business," letter to the editor, *Times Literary Supplement,* September 28, 1967.

15. 3rd ed. (New York: McGraw-Hill, 1966), p. 179.

16. "Retailing: Direct Sales of Books in America," *Publishers' Weekly,* June 15, 1970. See also previous issue under "Retailing."

17. Telephone communication from Lyman Newlin, assistant to the president, September 30, 1970.

18. "Richard's Reference. No. 1," cited in *American Libraries,* October 1970, p. 916, is available from the OP Department, Richard Abel & Company, Inc., Portland, Oregon.

19. Personal interview with Harold L. Roth, then vice-president, Library & Institutional Relations, the Baker & Taylor Company, March 20, 1969.

20. Copy of promotional letter, with accompanying personal letter of explanation, from Herbert M. Johnson, September 16, 1970.

21. Advertisement in *Publishers' Weekly,* April 19, 1971, p. 11.

22. "Approaching the Librarian: What Really Happens to Those Circulars After They Leave the Post Office," *Scholarly Publishing,* January 1971, p. 179.

23. Personal interview, November 24, 1969.

24. Telephone communication, December 9, 1969.

CHAPTER 9

1. Frank Cremonesi, "Knowledge—of Machines and Men," in *Proceedings* of the ASIS Workshop on Computer Composition, ed. by Robert M. Landau (Washington, D.C.: American Society for Information Science, 1971), p. 120.

2. J. Periam Danton, *Book Selection and Collections* (New York: Columbia University Press, 1963), p. 136. See also Mary D. Carter and Wallace J. Bonk, *Building Library Collections* (New York: Scarecrow Press, 1959); and Gertrude Wulfekoetter, *Acquisition Work: Processes Involved in Building Library Collections* (Seattle: University of Washington Press, 1962).

230 Scholarly Reprint Publishing in the United States

3. Robert P. Haro, "Some Problems in the Conversion of a College to a University Library," *College & Research Libraries*, May 1969, pp. 260.
4. Harold Wooster, "Microfiche 1969—A User Survey," U.S. Air Force, Office of Scientific Research (Arlington, Va.: Clearinghouse for Federal Scientific and Technical Information, July 1969), p. 12 (AD 695 049).
5. *The Evaluation of Micropublications: A Handbook for Librarians* (Chicago: American Library Association, 1971).
6. "Microtext and the Management of Book Collections: A Symposium," *College & Research Libraries*, July 1953, pp. 292–302. See also Robert C. Sullivan, "Developments in Reproduction of Library Materials and Graphic Communication, 1968," *Library Resources & Technical Services*, Summer 1969, pp. 391–421, and, for an excellent description of dissertations in microform with much helpful background information, see Robert Flanders Clarke, "The Impact of Photocopying on Scholarly Publishing" (Ph.D. diss., Rutgers, The State University, 1963; Microfilm Number F2717).
7. The hardware for processing and utilizing microforms is described in *Guide to Microproduction Equipment* by Hubbard W. Ballou (Silver Spring, Md.: National Microfilm Association, 1969). A 1970 Supplement lists 137 new items and 40 new manufacturers and distributors.
8. John G. Veenstra, in *Library Journal*, October 15, 1970.
9. Ray Astbury, *Bibliography and Book Production* (New York: Pergamon Press, 1967). See also *Esdaile's Manual of Bibliography*, 4th ed., rev. by Roy Stokes (New York: Barnes & Noble, 1967), and Derek Williamson, *Historical Bibliography* (Hamdem, Conn.: Archon Books, 1967).
10. Manfred Kochen and A. Bertrand Segur, "Effects of Cataloging Volume at the Library of Congress on Total Cataloging Costs of American Research Libraries," *Journal of the American Society for Information Science*, March–April 1970, p. 138.
11. Personal interview, April 22, 1969.
12. Telephone communication, Glen A. Zimmerman, assistant to the chief, Descriptive Cataloging Division, Library of Congress, November 16, 1971.
13. On January 1, 1956, the *Library of Congress Catalog—Books: Authors* was expanded to include not only LC printed cards but also entries and locations of titles with imprints of 1956 or later, reported to NUC by other North American libraries. The July 1956 issue bore the new name, *The National Union Catalog: A Cumulative Author List*. In 1968, publication of the retrospective NUC, Pre-1956 Imprints Publication was begun by Mansell. See also Gale Research Company's catalog for a description of their reprinting of LC Author Lists (which their jolly staff calls "Nucal" and "Supernucal"); Edwards Brothers reprints of LC Catalogs; Rowman and Littlefield's LC Catalogs; and NCR's microfiche republication of selected LC Catalogs.
14. Much information about the National Union Catalog and other matters relating to reprinting was kindly provided by Dr. George Schwegmann, then chief, Union Catalog Division, and Mary E. Kahler, then assistant chief, in personal interviews. Other members of the staff who graciously gave of their time and talents are Mr. Richard Angell, chief, Technical Processes Research Office; Jean B. Metz, selection officer, Processing Department; Dr. Roy P. Basler, chief, Manuscripts Division; Paul W. Winkler, Principal Cataloger, Descriptive Catalog Division; Nathalie B. Wells, head, Pre-Assigned Numbers, Card Division; and John Cole, technical assistant to the assistant director for the Development of the Collections, Reference Division. (All interviews were conducted April 22 and 23, 1969.)
15. NCR Guides include the *Guide to Reprints, Guide to Microforms in Print, Subject Guide to Microforms in Print* and *Announced Reprints*. This latter title began

publication in February 1969. It is a quarterly, intended to list forthcoming titles from reprinters. Each issue cumulates all previous ones, until November when titles that have been published are dropped. Only about 125 of the 218 publishers listed in the alphabetical listing of publishers in an early issue supplied titles. It is too early to judge the success of this journal, or to know whether or not publishers will be reticent to submit their information for listing. Librarians who follow the listings will be able to judge publishers' reliability regarding the "announced but not published" practices.

16. Oceana issues *The Reprint Bulletin,* "published as a bibliographic and reference service for libraries." With its November 1970 issue the scope changed to become primarily a review journal for reprints.

17. For more on this topic, which warrants a separate study, see Thomas William Huck, "The Birth of the Various Book–Trade Catalogues," *The Librarian* (London), 1 (August 1910–July 1911), pp. 98–101ff. Huck notes that the earliest printers acted as their own booksellers; that modern publishers' lists evolved from early book advertisements; and that the earliest known book advertisements were issued by Schoefer, one in about the year 1469. See also "The Book Catalogue and How It Should Be Printed," reprinted by the Southworth Press, Portland, Maine (n.d.), from an article by George S. Sargent in *Direct Advertising* (1924). This is a charming account of the "appalling typographical atrocities" committed by booksellers, which cannot be neglected by collectors who may find the very title which has been searched for years; and Jacob Zeitlin, "Bookselling Among the Sciences," *College & Research Libraries* (November 1960, pp. 453–457.

18. "Selected Statistics based on L.C. MARC Bibliographic Records: Cumulated . . . for v. 1, no. 1–54, March 1969–March 1970, Technical Note No. 2" (New York: Columbia University Libraries, Systems Office, September 1970. Unpublished copy of computer printout.) The writer is indebted to Mr. Swanson for permission to review the data and to mention the project here.

19. Felix Reichmann, "Appendix" to "Bibliographical Control of Reprints," *Library Resources & Technical Services,* Fall 1967, p. 427.

20. Mary D. Carter and Wallace J. Bonk, *Building Library Collections* (New York: Scarecrow Press, 1959), p. 146.

21. Alex Jackinson, *The Barnum–Cinderella World of Publishing.* (New York: Impact Press, 1971).

22. Columbia University, 1970, p. 79.

23. *Library Response to Urban Change: A Study of the Chicago Public Library* (Chicago: American Library Association, 1969), p. 144.

CHAPTER 10

1. "The American Library Association and the Field of Reprint Publishing, 1924–1965, Some Aspects of History: Part I: First Attempts," *Reprint Bulletin* September–October 1967, pp. 2–11; "Part II: The Bergquist Report and After," *Reprint Bulletin* November–December 1967, pp. 1–7.

2. ALA Reprinting Committee/American Book Publishers Council invitational meeting, Roosevelt Hotel, New York City, April 23, 1970.

3. For further references see the bibliography in "Permanence/Durability of the Book–V: Strength and Other Characteristics of Book Papers, 1800–1899" (Richmond, Va.: W. J. Barrow Research Laboratory, 1967), pp. 114–115. See also the informative "Annual Reports" of the CLR and a good review of "The Librarian as Conservator," by James W. Henderson and Robert G. Krupp, in *Library Quarterly* 40, No. 1 (January 1970), pp. 176–178. A 69-item bibliography is provided. The entire issue is devoted to preservation topics.

4. Hannah B. Friedman, "Preservation Programs in New York State: Existent and Non-Existent," *Special Libraries* 60, No. 9 (November 1969): p. 579.
5. Gordon R. Williams, "The Preservation of Deteriorating Material," *Library Journal,* January 1 and January 15, 1961. Williams, director of the Midwest Inter-Library Center, Chicago (later renamed the Center for Research Libraries), reports on a study to determine the size and nature of the preservation problems conducted for the Association of Research Library's Committee on the Preservation of Research Materials.
6. *Annual Report of the Librarian of Congress for Fiscal Year Ending June 30, 1969* (Washington, D.C.: 1970), pp. 8, 78.
7. Personal letter from Norman J. Shaffer, preservation microfilming officer, Library of Congress, dated May 6, 1969.
8. Hannah B. Friedman, in the Annual Report of the Preservations Office prepared for the 1970 Annual Report of the NYPL noted that 836 items were requested during fiscal year 1969–1970, almost double that of the previous year: 294 requests were rejected; 542 were fulfilled.
9. Personal letter from John P. Baker, then executive assistant, The Research Libraries, November 14, 1969.
10. Personal interview, Warren J. Haas, director of libraries, Columbia University, June 22, 1970.
11. Association of Research Libraries, Committee on Availability of Resources, "Reprinting Library Resources," questionnaire with accompanying cover letter dated March 13, 1970 (Richard E. Chapin, director of libraries, Michigan State University, East Lansing, chairman). Unpublished xerographic copy of typescript distributed to members of the ALA Reprinting Committee by its chairman, Alfred H. Lane, with the permission of the ARL committee.
12. Ralph E. Ellsworth, "The Contribution of the Library to Improving Instruction," *Library Journal,* May 15, 1969.
13. Personal interview, Eileen Rowland, librarian, New Books Section, Assistant Superintendent of Acquisitions, Queens Borough Public Library, May 7, 1969.
14. Eldred Smith, "Out-of-Print Booksearching," *College & Research Libraries,* July 1968, pp. 303–09; Patterson Smith, "Reprinting Hokum," letter to the editor, *Library Journal,* April 1, 1968; and Peter Smith, "Securing Out of Print Books," *ALA Bulletin,* November 1948, pp. 511–512.
15. Shirley Heppel, "A Survey of OP Buying Practices," *Library Resources & Technical Services,* Winter 1966, pp. 28–30. See also Margit Kraft, "An Argument for Selectivity in the Acquisition of Materials for Research Libraries," *Library Quarterly* 37 (July 1967), p. 284.
16. See Lewis M. Wiggin, "Aspects of Reprinting," *Scholarly Publishing,* January 1971, pp. 149–161.

Bibliography

ABELE, JOHN J. "Take-Overs Shake Business," *New York Times,* March 9, 1969, p. 1.

ALTMAN, FREDERICK. "The Antiquarian Reprint Dealer Looks at Acquisitions." *Library Resources & Technical Services,* Spring 1967, pp. 207–211.

AMERICAN BOOK PUBLISHERS COUNCIL, INC. *The Buck Hill Falls Report: The Changing Nature and Scope of the School and Library Market. A Conference sponsored by the School and Library Promotion and Marketing Committee, April 27–29, 1966, Buck Hill Falls, Pa.* New York: the Council, 1967.

AMERICAN LIBRARY ASSOCIATION. Out-of-Print-Books Committee. *Report of the Out-of-Print Book Survey.* Conducted by G. William Bergquist, under the auspices of the Out-of-Print Books Committee. Edith A. Busby, Chairman. Chicago: American Library Association, 1951.

ANDERSON, DONALD M. *The Art of Written Forms.* New York: Holt, Rinehart & Winston, 1969.

"Arno Press: Reprinting Is a Creative Event." *Publishers' Weekly,* November 4, 1968, pp. 25–27.

ASH, LEE. "Education Needed for Building Large Library and Specialized Collections." In *Library School Teaching Methods: Courses in the Selection of Adult Materials,* ed. by Larry Earl Bone. Proceedings of a Conference on Library School Teaching Methods held at the University of Illinois, September 8–11, 1968. Urbana: University of Illinois. Graduate School of Library Science, 1969.

———. "Out-of-Print Titles Recommended for Purchase, Toronto." *Antiquarian Bookman,* July 4–11, 1966, pp. 68–69.

ASLESON, ROBERT F. Letter to the editor, *Publishers' Weekly,* July 29, 1968. About on-demand and reprint publishing.

———. "Microforms: Where Do They Fit?" *Library Resources & Technical Services,* Winter 1971, pp. 57–62.

ASTBURY, RAY. *Bibliography and Book Production.* Oxford: Pergamon Press, 1967.

AVEDON, DON M., ed. *Glossary of Micrographics.* Silver Spring, Md.: National Microfilm Association, 1971.

233

234   *Scholarly Reprint Publishing in the United States*

BAATZ, WILMER H. "Microcards, Microprint, and Microfilms for Medical Libraries." *Bulletin of the Medical Library Association,* April 1957, pp. 139–148.

BAILEY, HERBERT S., JR. *The Art and Science of Publishing.* New York: Harper & Row, 1970.

BANCROFT, HUBERT HOWE. *Literary Industries: A Memoir.* New York: Harper & Brothers, 1891.

BELL & HOWELL COMPANY. Micro Photo Division. *Newspapers on Microfilm,* 1953–, 11th ed. Cleveland: 1968–1969.

———. *Out-of-Print Books from the John G. White Folklore Collection at the Cleveland Public Library.* Reproduced by the Duopage Process. Cleveland: 1966.

BELL, J. G. "The Proper Domain of Scholarly Publishing." *Scholarly Publishing,* October 1970, pp. 11–18.

BELZER, S. A. "Remarks on Reprinting." Part I, *Reprint Expediting Service Bulletin,* Spring 1964, pp. 1–4: Part II, Fall 1964, pp. 1–4: Part III, *Reprint Bulletin,* April 1965, pp. 1–6. Includes "Informal Directory of Reprinters."

———. "Reprints Attract University Presses." *New York Times,* July 11, 1965.

BENNETT, JOSIAH Q. "The Cataloguing Requirements of the Book Division of a Rare Book Library." Occasional Paper No. 3. Kent, Ohio: Kent State University Libraries, 1969.

BENNETT, PAUL A., ed. *Books and Printing: A Treasury for Typophiles,* rev. ed. Cleveland: World Publishing Co., 1963.

BERRY, W. TURNER, and POOLE, H. EDMUND. *Annals of Printing: A Chronological Encyclopaedia from the Earliest Times to 1950.* Toronto: University of Toronto Press, 1966.

Bibliographia Anastatica: a BiMonthly Bibliography of Photomechanical Reprints. Edited by P. Schippers, A. M. Hakkert and B. R. Güner. Amsterdam: Niewve Herengracht 31, Vol. 1, 1964– (issued in fascicles).

"The Big Boom in Instant Printing." *Book Production Industry,* June 1968, pp. 67–69.

"The Big Story in Books Is Financial." *Business Week,* May 16, 1970, pp. 68–74.

BLANCHARD, J. R. "Planning the Conversion of a College to a University Library." *College & University Libraries,* July 1968, pp. 297–302.

BLANCK, JACOB, comp. *Bibliography of American Literature,* vol. I. Prepared for the Bibliographic Society of America. New Haven: Yale University Press, 1955.

BLUM, FRED, comp. "Music Serials in Microform and Reprint Editions." *Notes: The Quarterly Journal of the Music Library Association,* 24, June 1968, pp. 670–679.

BONI, ALBERT. "Letters from Readers." *Saturday Review,* March 28, 1970 (reply to David Dempsey).

BOYNTON, HENRY WALCOTT. *Annals of American Bookselling: 1638–1850.* New York: John Wiley & Sons, 1932.

Breaking Into Print: Being a Compilation of Papers wherein each of a Select Group of Authors tells of the Difficulties of Authorship & How such Trials are met together with Biographical Notes and Comment by an editor of The Colophon, Elmer Adler. New York: Simon and Schuster, 1937.

BROADUS, ROBERT N. "The Problem of Dates in Bibliographic Citations." *College & Research Libraries,* September 1968, pp. 387–392.

BRUBAKER, ROBERT L. "The Publication of Historical Sources: Recent Projects in the United States." *The Library Quarterly* 37, April 1967, pp. 193–225.

BÜHLER, CURT F. *The Fifteenth Century Book and the Twentieth Century.* New York: Grolier Club, 1952.

BURKE, JOHN EMMETT. *The Rising Tide—More Research Libraries.* Commerce: East Texas State University, 1966.

CARLEN, SISTER M. CLAUDIA. "Expanding Resources: The Explosion of the Sixties." *Library Trends,* July 1969, pp. 48–56.

CARROLL, MARK. "The Belknap Press of Harvard University Press." *Harvard Library Bulletin,* July 1970, pp. 248–253.

CARTER, MARY D., and BONK, WALLACE J. *Building Library Collections.* New York: Scarecrow Press, 1959.

CAZDEN, ROBERT E. *German Exile Literature in America: 1933–1950: A History of the Free German Press and Book Trade.* Chicago: American Library Association, 1970 (c. 1965).

CHANCELLOR, E. BERESFORD. *Literary Diversions.* London: Dulau & Co., 1925.

CHAPMAN, R. W. "Oxford Type Facsimiles." *The Library,* 4th Series, 1926, pp. 317–321.

CHARVAT, WILLIAM. *Literary Publishing in America: 1790–1850.* Philadelphia: University of Pennsylvania Press, 1959.

CHENEY, O. H. *Economic Survey of the Book Industry, 1930–1931,* as prepared for the National Association of Book Publishers, introduction by Robert W. Frase. New York: Bowker, c. 1931, repr. c. 1960.

CHICOREL, MARIETTA. "Acquisitions in an Age of Plenty." *Library Resources & Technical Services,* Winter 1966, pp. 19–27.

CIRKER, HAYWARD. "In Print, Out of Print: Conflicting Information." Letter to the editor. *Publishers' Weekly,* July 22, 1968, p. 23.

———. "More About 'Demand' and Reprint Publishing." *Publishers' Weekly,* August 26, 1968, pp. 189–190.

———. "The Scientific Paperback Revolution." *Science,* May 10, 1963, pp. 591–594.

CLAIR, COLIN. *A Chronology of Printing.* New York: Frederick A. Praeger, 1969.

CLAPP, VERNER W. "Copyright—A Librarian's View." Prepared for the National Advisory Commission on Libraries. Washington, D.C.: Copyright Committee, Association of Research Libraries, August 1968.

———. "The Greatest Invention Since the Title Page? Autobibliography from Incipit to Cataloging-in-Publication." *Wilson Library Bulletin.* December 1971, pp. 348–359.

CLARIDGE, P. R. P. "What the User Needs from Microforms." In Micropublishing for Learned Societies. Prepared by the National Reprographic Centre for Documentation, Hatfield College of Technology. Hatfield, England: Hertis, 1968.

CLARKE, ROBERT FLANDERS. "The Impact of Photo-Copying on Scholarly Publishing." Ph.D. diss., New Brunswick: Rutgers, The State University, 1963.

CLIFFORD, W. G. *Books in Bottles: The Curious in Literature.* New York: Lincoln Macveagh, Dial Press, n.d.

CUNHA, GEORGE and MARTIN, DANIEL. *Conservation of Library Materials.* Metuchen, N.J.: Scarecrow Press, 1967.

DANTON, J. PERIAM. *Book Selection and Collections.* New York: Columbia University Press, 1963.

DAVIS, JO-ANN, BOONE, ROBERTA, and HOADLEY, IRENE BRADEN. "Of Making Many Books: A Library Publication Program." *College & Research Libraries,* January 1971, pp. 31–35.

DEMPSEY, DAVID. "The Publishing Scene." *Saturday Review,* February 21, 1970, p. 39.

DERBY, J. C. *Fifty Years Among Authors, Books and Publishers.* New York: G. W. Carleton & Co., 1884.

DEWEY, NICHOLAS. "The Reprint Business." *Times Literary Supplement,* September 28, 1967, p. 888.

DEWTON, JOHANNES L., comp. "A Tentative List of Catalogs of Microforms." Washington, D.C.: Union Catalog Division, Library of Congress, n.d.

DOEBLER, PAUL D. and LEVY, NANCY S. "A New Look at Publishing and Printing." *Book Production Industry,* June 1968, pp. 47–66.

DOIRON, PETER M. "Choice: Fair Comment." *Missouri Library Association Quarterly* 36, March 1968, pp. 3–8.

DUFFUS, R. L. "Printing and Publishing." In the *Encyclopaedia of the Social Sciences,* vol. 6. New York: Macmillan, 1934, pp. 406–415.

DUNCAN, JOHN E. "Mansell Information/Publishing Ltd." *RQ,* Summer 1968, pp. 159–162. Quarterly publication of the Reference Services Division, American Library Association.

DUNHAM, E. ALDEN. "What Is the Junior College All About?" *PMLA,* June 1968, pp. 530–533.

DUNLAP, CONNIE R. "Reprinting: Problems, Directions, Challenges," *Library Resources & Technical Services,* Winter 1971, pp. 34–35.

DUNN, O. C., Seibert, W. F., and Scheuneman, Janice. *The Past and Likely Future of 58 Research Libraries, 1951–1980: A Statistical Study of Growth and Change.* Lafayette, Indiana: University Libraries and Audio Visual Center, Purdue University, 1965. See also later, revised printings.

ECKMAN, JAMES. *The Heritage of the Printer,* vol. I. Philadelphia: North American Publishing Co., 1965.

EDELSTEIN, DAVID SIMEON. *Joel Munsell: Printer and Antiquarian.* New York: Columbia University Press, 1950.

ELDRIDGE, HERBERT G. "The American Republication of Thomas Moore's 'Epistles, Odes, and Other Poems': An Early Version of the Reprint 'Game.'" *Papers of the Bibliographic Society of America* 62, 2nd quarter 1968, pp. 199–205.

ELLSWORTH, RALPH E. "The Contribution of the Library to Improving Instruction." *Library Journal,* May 15, 1969, pp. 1955–1957.

ESHELMAN, WILLIAM R. "The Behemoths and the Book Publishers." *Library Trends,* July 1970, pp. 106–114.

EXMAN, EUGENE. *The House of Harper: One Hundred and Fifty Years of Publishing.* New York: Harper & Row, 1967.

"Facsimile Reprinting: The Newest Revolution." *Publishers' Weekly,* December 30, 1968, pp. 31–36.

"Facsimile Reprints: Making Money on Limited Editions." *Printing Impressions,* April 1971, pp. 18ff.

FEINBERG, HILDA. "Publishing in the Electronics Era." Unpublished typescript, submitted to the School of Library Service, Columbia University, May 5, 1968.

FELLER, SIEGFRIED. "Antiquarian Reprint Trade." *Antiquarian Bookman,* January 17, 1966, p. 138.

FERSTER, PAUL. Letter to the editor. *Publishers' Weekly,* July 29, 1968. About on-demand and reprint publishing.

FLEMING, THOMAS P., and SHANK, RUSSELL. "Scientific and Technical Book Publishing." *Library Trends,* July 1968, pp. 197–209.

FORMAN, SIDNEY. "Innovative Practices in College Libraries." *College & Research Libraries,* November 1968, pp. 486–492.

FORSTER, H. C., comp. *From Xylographs to Lead Molds: AD1440–AD1921.* Cincinnati: Rapid Electrotype Company, 1921.

FRANKLIN, BURT. "The Antiquarian Reprint 1966: A Glance Backward and Forward." Part I. *Reprint Bulletin,* pp. 1–4. Part II, July–August 1967, pp. 1–5.

———. "Reprint Publishing in the United States." Paper presented at the annual New Jersey Library Association Conference, 1968. In *New Jersey Libraries,* Summer 1968, pp. 23–24.

———. "Ten Years of the Hard Cover Scholarly Reprint: A Retrospective View and a Proposal for Improvements in Processing Orders." Address before the New Jersey Library Association, Atlantic City, May 2, 1968. In *The Reprint Bulletin,* July–August 1968, pp. 1–9.

FREE, OPAL M. "Commercial Reprints of Federal Documents: Their Significance and Acquisition." *Special Libraries,* March 1969, pp. 126–131.

FREEDMAN, FREDERICK. "Perspective—Music Reprint Industry." *Choice,* October 1969, pp. 977–985.

FRIEDMAN, HANNAH B. "Preservation of Library Materials: The State of the Art." *Special Libraries,* October 1968, pp. 608–613.

"From Shoestring to Archon: The Story of the Ottemiller Publishing Enterprise." The *1968 AB Bookman's Yearbook.* 20th anniversary ed., pp. 29–31.

"The Future of the Humanities." *Daedalus: Journal of the American Academy of Arts and Sciences,* Summer 1969. Entire issue devoted to this topic. See also Ong, Walter J., and Whitman, Cedric H.

GARRETT, DANIEL C. "The Ethics of Reprint Publishing." *Library Resources & Technical Services,* Winter 1971, pp. 53–56.

"General Description of UNESCO's Project for Reproduction of Out-of-Print Periodicals," *College & Research Libraries,* July 1949, p. 260.

GINGRICH, ARNOLD. "Communications, Media, and People." Address given at the meeting of the Illinois Library Trustee Association, October 18, 1968. In *Illinois Libraries,* February 1969, pp. 132–147.

GLICKMAN, ART. "A Company Prospers by Reprinting Weird, Scholarly Old Books." *Wall Street Journal,* April 14, 1969, p. 1. About Gale Research Company.

GOFF, FREDERICK R. "Incunabula and Sixteenth Century Imprints." *Library Trends,* January 1967, pp. 446–458. Issue entitled "Bibliography: Current State and Future Trends, Part I." Ed. by Robert B. Downs and Frances B. Jenkins.

GOLDSCHMIDT, E. Ph. *Medieval Texts and Their First Appearance in Print.* London: Printed for the Bibliographical Society at the University Press, Oxford, 1943. Repr. with corrections. Meisenheim, Germany: Hain, 1965.

GREG, R. W. "Type Facsimiles and Others." *The Library.* 4th Series. 1926, pp. 321–326.

GUDEMAN, ALFRED. "The Alexandrian Library and Museum." The *Columbia Literary Monthly,* December 1895, pp. 97–107. Photocopy in Columbia University Libraries.

GUTCH, JOHN MATHEW. *Observations or Notes upon The Writings of the Ancients: upon the Materials Which They Used, and upon the Introduction of the Art of Printing; being Four Papers read before The Philosophical and Literary Society, annexed to the Bristol Institution, at their evening meeting in 1827*. Bristol: Printed by J. M. Gutch at the Office of Felix Farley's *Bristol Journal*, 1827. Copy in special collections, Columbia University Libraries.

GUTHRIE, HUGH. "Without a Million! The Century House Story." In *The American Life: A Collectors Annual*. Ed. by John Crosby Freeman. Watkins Glen, N.Y.: The American Life Foundation, 1964, pp. 9–14.

HALE, RICHARD W. ed. *Guide to Photocopied Historical Materials in the United States and Canada*. Ithaca, N.Y.: Published for the American Historical Association (by) Cornell University Press, 1961.

HALL, DONALD. *Editions of One: Eugene B. Power and Publication on Demand: the Biography of a Man and an Idea*. Ann Arbor: Mich., 1969. Xerographic copy of unpublished typewritten manuscript, kindly loaned by the author.

HARKINS, WILLIAM G., DIMOCK, FRED L., and HANSON, MARY ELIZABETH. "Microfilm in University Libraries: A Report." *College & Research Libraries*, July 1953, pp. 307–316.

HARMAN, ELEANOR, ed. *The University as Publisher*. Toronto: The University of Toronto Press, 1961.

HARRIS, G. EDWARD. "The Antiquarian Bookman." in *Progress in Library Science: 1967*, ed. by Robert L. Collison. Hamden, Conn.: Archon, 1967, pp. 171–181.

HARRIS, JESSICA L. "Offset Printing from Typescript as a Substitute for Microfilming of Dissertations." *American Documentation*, January 1968, pp. 60–65.

HARRISON, G. B. "Facsimile Reprints: Being a Paper read before the Anglo-American Conference of Historians, July 13–18, 1931." Produced by Percy Lund, Humphries & Co. Ltd., Proprietors of the Replica Process . . . London, 1931. Microfilm of copy in Folger Library, Washington, D.C.

HART, HORACE. *Bibliotheca Typographica: A List of Books about Books*. Rochester, N.Y.: The Printing House of Leo Hart, 1933.

HATTERY, LOWELL H. and BUSH, GEORGE P. eds. *Automotion and Electronics in Publishing*. Washington, D.C. Spartan Books, 1965. The American University Technology of Management Series, vol. 3.

HAWES, GENE R. *To Advance Knowledge: A Handbook on American University Press Publishing*. Published for the Association of American University Press Services, Inc., 1967.

HAWKEN, WILLIAM R. *Copying Methods Manual*. Chicago: American Library Association, 1966. Library Technology Project, No. 11.

HAYNES, MERRITT WAY. *A Student's History of Printing giving the Principal Dates, Personages and Events in the Development of the Typographic Art from the Earliest Times to the Present in Chronological Order*. New York: McGraw-Hill Book Co., 1930. OP, available from University Microfilms, No. 44, 355.

HAZEN, A(LLEN) T. "J. Sturt, Facsimilist." *The Library*. 4th Series, 1944, pp. 72–79.

———. "Type-Facsimiles." *Modern Philology*, May 1947, pp. 209–217.

HEBERT, HUGH. "The Reprint Industry." *Manchester Guardian Weekly*, June 19, 1969, p. 14.

HINZE, FRANZ. *Book Market Research and Its Application to Bookselling and Marketing Problems in Europe*. New York: R. R. Bowker, 1966; Hamburg: Verlag für Buchmarkt-Forschung, 1966. Reports of the Institut für Buchmarkt-Forschung.

HIRSCH, RUDOLF. *Printing, Selling and Reading*. Wiesbaden: Otto Harrassowitz, 1967.

A *History of the Council on Books in Wartime: 1942–1946.* New York: The Council, 1946. Written by Robert O. Ballou from a working draft prepared by Irene Rakosky.

HIXSON, RICHARD F. *Isaac Collins: A Quaker Printer in 18th Century America.* New Brunswick, N.J.: Rutgers University Press, 1968.

HOLLEY, EDWARD G. *Charles Evans, American Bibliographer.* Urbana: University of Illinois Press, 1963. Illinois Contributions to Librarianship, No. 7.

HOOVER, JAMES H. "Pitfalls in Purchasing Reprints." *LLA Bulletin* (Louisiana Library Association), Fall 1967, pp. 109ff.

HOUSEHOLDER, FRED W. "The First Pirate." *The Library.* 4th Series, 1943, pp. 39–46.

International Association of Printing House Craftsmen, Inc. *Printing Progress: A Mid-Century Report.* Cincinnati: The Association, 1959.

IRWIN, RAYMOND. *The English Library: Sources and History.* London: George Allen & Unwin, 1966.

JACKSON, ISABEL H., ed. *Acquisition of Special Materials.* San Francisco: Bay Region Chapter, Special Libraries Association, 1966.

JEANNERET, MARSH. "Information Retrieval and the Decision to Publish." *Scholarly Publishing,* April 1970, pp. 229–243.

JUDGE, CYRIL BATHURST. *Elizabethan Book-Pirates.* Cambridge: Harvard University Press, 1934. Repr., New York: Johnson Reprint, 1970.

KASER, DAVID. *Book Pirating in Taiwan.* Philadelphia: University of Pennsylvania Press, 1957.

KATZ, NORMAN. Letter to the Editor. *Times Literary Supplement,* March 6, 1969, p. 241. About the Early English Text Society and reprints of their works.

KERR, CHESTER. *A Report on American University Presses.* New York: The Association of American University Presses, 1949.

KERR, WALTER B. "The Revolution in Printing." *Saturday Review,* August 10, 1968, pp. 54–55.

KONVITZ, MILTON R. Review of "The Nature and Tendency of Free Institutions," by Frederick Grimke. Cambridge: John Harvard Library of Harvard University Press, 1968. (First published, 1848.) In *Saturday Review,* October 5, 1968, pp. 29–30. Questions the need for reprinting.

LACY, DAN. "The Changing Face of Publishing." *NYLA Bulletin* (New York Library Association), November–December 1966, pp. 187–190.

————. "The © Quagmire," *Saturday Review,* November 27, 1971, pp. 24–28.

————. "Microfilming as a Major Acquisitions Tool: Policies, Plans and Problems," *Library of Congress Quarterly Journal of Current Acquisitions,* May 1949, pp. 8–17.

LANE, ALFRED H. "Reprints in the Preservation Picture—and a Drift Aside," Text of speech, NYLA Preservation of Library Materials, a Conference Within a Conference, New York, November 12, 1970. Reprinted in *AB Bookman's Weekly,* December 7, 1970.

LEHMANN-HAUPT, HELLMUT. *The Book in America: A History of the Making and Selling of Books in the United States,* in collaboration with Lawrence C. Wroth and Rollo G. Silver, 2nd ed. New York: R. R. Bowker, 1951.

————. "A New Look at Old Books." *New York Times Book Review,* December 1, 1968, pp. 50ff.

LEWIS, FREEMAN. "The Distribution of Reprint Books: A Survey of the Market and the Means of Reaching It." *Publishers' Weekly,* March 30, 1935, pp. 1313–1317.

LEWIS, SOL. "Book Selection for Reprints." *Reprint Expediting Service Bulletin,* Winter 1964/65, pp. 1–4.

———. "A Plea for More Scholarship and Creativity in Reprints." *The Reprint Bulletin,* November–December 1966, pp. 2–6.

———. "Why Reprints?" *The Reprint Bulletin,* January–February 1967, pp. 2–4.

LUTHER, FREDERICK. "The Earliest Experiments in Microphotography." *American Documentation,* August 1951, pp. 167–170.

McCLELLAN, A. W. "Library Developments Affecting the Book Trade." *Library Association Record,* January 1967, pp. 2–6.

McCROSSMAN, JOHN A. "Library Science Education and Its Relationship to Competence in Adult Book Selection in Public Libraries." Springfield: Illinois State Library, 1967. (Research Series No. 9.) Abridgement of a Ph.D. diss. submitted to the Graduate College, University of Illinois, 1966.

McMURTRIE, DOUGLAS C. "Some Facts Concerning the Invention of Printing; the five-hundredth anniversary of which will be celebrated internationally in 1940," 2nd ed. Chicago: Chicago Club of Printing House Craftsmen, 1939. "Issued in the interest of a wider and sounder knowledge of the beginnings of the world's most useful craft."

McREYNOLDS, HELEN. "Microforms of United States Government Publications." Urbana: University of Illinois Graduate School of Library Science, December 1963. (Occasional Papers, no. 69.)

MADISON, CHARLES A. *Book Publishing in America.* New York: McGraw-Hill, 1966.

MALKIN, SOL M. "The Antiquarian Reprint Trade." In "The Old and the New," *1967 AB Bookman's Yearbook,* Part II, pp. 2–4.

MANSBRIDGE, RONALD. "Reprints in America." Letter to the editor. *Times Literary Supplement,* May 8, 1969, p. 490.

MARKS, ALAN J. (executive editor, Da Capo Press). Letter to the associate editor (Mrs. Malkin). Quoted in *AB Bookman's Weekly,* August 5–12, 1968, p. 413. About Da Capo and Milford House.

MASSMAN, VIRGIL F., and OLSON, DAVID R. "Book Selection: A National Plan for Small Academic Libraries." *College and Research Libraries,* July 1971, pp. 271–279.

MELCHER, DANIEL. "Automation: Rosy Prospects and Cold Facts." *Library Journal,* March 15, 1968, pp. 1105–1109.

———. "Frankfurt, 1968: Many Issues Arise." *Publishers' Weekly,* October 21, 1968, pp. 25–28.

———. "New Techniques Permit the Reprinting of Book in Editions of 1 to 100 Copies," *American Library and Book Trade Annual: 1960.* New York: R. R. Bowker, 1961, pp. 101–102.

———. "When Is a Book Really OP?" *Library Journal,* October 1, 1966, pp. 4576–4578.

———. *Melcher on Acquisition.* Chicago: American Library Association, 1971.

MELCHER, DANIEL, and LARRICK, NANCY. *Printing and Promotion Handbook,* 3rd ed. New York: McGraw-Hill, 1966.

MELCHER, FREDERICK G. "12,000 Books O-P Every Year." *Publishers' Weekly,* August 25, 1958, p. 22.

Microfilm Norms: Recommended Standards for Libraries. Prepared by the Library Standards for Microfilm Committee of the Copying Methods Section, Resources and Technical Services Division. Peter R. Scott, committee chairman. Chicago: American Library Association, 1966.

"Microtext and the Management of Book Collections: A Symposium." Presented at the Conference of Eastern College Librarians, Columbia University, November 29, 1952. *College & University Libraries,* July 1953, pp. 292–302.

MILLER, ROBERT A. "The Improvement of Book Collections for Academic Libraries." In *Library Lectures,* edited by Sue B. Von Bodungen. Baton Rouge: Louisiana State University, 1968, pp. 43–54. LSU Library Lectures Nos. 5, 6, 7, and 8, November 1966–October 1967.

MOORE, EVERETT LEROY, ed. *Junior College Libraries: Development, Needs, Perspectives.* Chicago: American Library Association, 1969. (ACRL Monograph No. 30.)

MORAN, JAMES. "Warm-Blooded Presses." *Times Literary Supplement,* February 12, 1970, p. 180.

MYNORS, R. A. B. "A Fifteenth-Century Scribe: T. Werken." In *Transactions of the Cambridge Bibliographical Society,* 1, Part II, 1950, pp. 97–104.

MYRICK, FRANK B. "As Printers Specialize." *Publishers' Weekly,* April 7, 1969, p. 68.

NICHOLS, LEWIS. "Essentially a Second-Hand Bookstore." *New York Times Book Review,* December 31, 1967, pp. 8ff. About Peter Smith, Publisher.

OHMES, FRANCES. "Scarce and Desirable: An Essay on Peter Smith." Master's thesis, Graduate School, Florida State University, June 1961.

ONG, WALTER J. "Crisis and Understanding in the Humanities." *Daedalus,* Summer 1969, pp. 617–640.

OSTWALD, RENATE, comp. *Nachdruckverzeichnis von Enzelwerken, Serien und Zeitscriften aus allen Wissensgebieten* (Reprints). Wiesbaden: Nobis, 1965. Intended to be a kind of "Reprints in Print," with emphasis on European reprint houses. Ostwald includes some American firms.

PAFFORD, J. H. P. "Principles of Reprint Publishing." *Times Literary Supplement,* March 6, 1969, p. 247.

PARIS, BIBLIOTHEQUE NATIONALE. "Bibliographical Control of Microcopies." *UNESCO Bulletin for Libraries,* May–June 1965, pp. 136ff.

PARKER, JOHN. "The State of the Rare Book Market Today." *In Selection and Acquisition Procedures in Medium-Sized and Large Libraries,* edited by Herbert Goldhor. Champaign: Graduate School of Library Science, University of Illinois, 1962. (Allerton Park Institute, no. 9.)

PATTERSON, LYMAN RAY. *Copyright in Historical Perspective.* Nashville: Vanderbilt University Press, 1968.

"Photographing Books in Threatened Libraries." *New York Times,* May 26, 1940, p. 3.

POLLARD, ALFRED W. " 'Facsimile' Reprints of Old Books. Preliminary Survey." *The Library.* 4th Series, 1926, pp. 305–313.

PRESSER, HELMUT. "Gutenberg: Father of Printing." *International Nickel Magazine,* 1968/1969, pp. 14–19.

PRIEBISH, A., and SPEERS, G. "Book Prices 1968: A Survey." *The Australian Library Journal,* November 1969, pp. 339–343. The value and importance of reprints to retrospective buying for library collections.

"Producing and Marketing the High-Cost, Short-Run Book." *Publishers' Weekly,* April 15, 1968, pp. 65–72.

PUTNAM, GEORGE HAVEN. *Authors and Their Public in Ancient Times: A Sketch of Literary Conditions and of the Relations with the Public of Literary Producers, from the Earliest Times to the Fall of the Roman Empire.* 3rd ed. rev. New York: G. P. Putnam's Sons. The Knickerbocker Press, 1923.

———. *Books and Their Makers During the Middle Ages.* New York: G. P. Putnam's Sons, 1896.

RAPPAPORT, FRED. "The Changing Philosophy of Reprint Publishers." *Library Resources & Technical Services,* Winter 1971, pp. 48–52.

RAYMONT, H. "Book Trade Upset by Changes in Ownership, Size and Staff." *New York Times,* March 4, 1968, p. 28.

REDGRAVE, GILBERT R. "Photographic Facsimiles." *The Library.* 4th Series, 1926, pp. 313–317.

REICHMANN, FELIX. "Bibliographical Control of Reprints." *Library Resources & Technical Services,* Fall 1967, pp. 415–435.

———. "The Book Trade at the Time of the Roman Empire." *Library Quarterly,* January 1938, pp. 40–76.

REICHMANN, FELIX, and THORPE, JOSEPHINE M. *Determination of an Effective System of Bibliographic Control of Microform Publications.* Interim Report. Washington, D.C.: Association of Research Libraries, November 1970 (ED 046 404). [Final report due 1972.]

Report on the Application of Copyright on Computer Usage. Prepared by the National Academy of Sciences Panel on the Application of Copyright on Computer Usage. Washington, D.C.: National Academy of Sciences, December 1, 1967. (PB 178367.)

ROBERTS, MATT. "The Role of the Librarian in the Binding Process." *Special Libraries,* October 2, 1971, pp. 413–420.

ROSENTHAL, BERNARD M. "The Antiquarian Reprint Trade." *Antiquarian Bookman,* April 1, 1965, pp. 1667–1669.

SAMUELS, CHRISTOPHER J. "Reprint Publishers First Open Meeting." Special Report. *The Reprint Bulletin,* May–June 1970, pp. 1–11.

SCAL, MARJORIE. "Journal Separates." In *A Handbook of Scholarly Journal Publishing.* New York: Association of American University Presses, 1969. Offprint kindly provided by the author.

SCHICK, FRANK L. *The Paperbound Book in America: The History of Paperbacks and Their European Background.* New York: R. R. Bowker, 1958.

———. "The Recurring Emergence of American Paperbacks." In *Books in America's Past: Essays Honoring Rudolph Gjelsness,* edited by David Kaser. Charlottesville: The University Press of Virginia, 1966, pp. 196–202.

SHAFFER, NORMAN J. "Library of Congress Pilot Preservation Project." *College & Research Libraries,* January 1969, pp. 5–11.

SHATZKIN, LEONARD. "In-House Composition: Effects on Publishing." *Publishers' Weekly,* October 7, 1968, pp. 27–30.

SHUGG, ROGER W. "Publishing in Two Worlds." *Publishers' Weekly,* January 8, 1968, pp. 39–43.

SIMONTON, WESLEY. "The Bibliographical Control of Microforms." *Library Resources & Technical Services,* Winter 1962, pp. 29–40.

———. "Library Handling of Microforms." In *Proceedings* of the National Microfilm Association. Annapolis, Md., 1962.

"The Singing Tree Facsimiles." *Mankind,* April 1969, pp. 89–90. About Gale Research Company's subsidiary.

SMITH, PETER. "Out of Print Books." *Wilson Library Bulletin*, June 1945, pp. 690–691.

———. "Securing Out of Print Books." *ALA Bulletin*, November 1948, pp. 511–512.

" 'Spin-Off' Publishing." *Book Production Industry*, February 1968, pp 42–46.

STEINBERG, S. H. *Five Hundred Years of Printing*, 2nd ed. London: Penguin Books, 1961.

STEINER-PRAG, ELEANOR F., comp. *American Library Directory*, 26th and 27th eds. New York: R. R. Bowker, 1968, 1970.

STERNBERG, VERNON. "Multi-volume 'Definitive, Textual' Editions." Letter to the editor. *Publishers' Weekly*, August 26, 1969, pp. 191–193.

STEVENS, ROLLAND E., ed. "Problems of Acquisition for Research Libraries," *Library Trends*, January 1970. This journal is a quarterly publication of the University of Illinois Graduate School of Library Science, Urbana, Illinois.

STEWART, GEORGE R. "Twilight of the Printed Book." *Pacific Spectator* (Stanford, California), Winter 1949, pp. 32–39.

STILLWELL, MARGARET B. *Incunabula and Americana: 1450–1800: A Key to Bibliographical Study*. New York: Columbia University Press, 1931.

STRAUSS, VICTOR. "A Book Publishers' Guide to Color Printing—1." *Publishers' Weekly*, November 4, 1968, pp. 78–86.

———. "In-House Tape Composition: Basic Considerations." *Publishers' Weekly*, March 3, 1969, pp. 78–85.

———. "The New Composition Technology: Promises and Realities." *Publishers' Weekly*, May 5, 1969, pp. 62–65.

———. *The Printing Industry: An Introduction to Its Many Branches, Processes and Productions*. New York: Printing Industries of America, Inc., in association with R. R. Bowker, 1967.

SULLIVAN, ROBERT C. "Developments in Reproduction of Library Materials and Graphic Communication, 1968." *Library Resources & Technical Services*, Summer 1969, pp. 391–421.

TARSHISH, MANUEL B. "The 'Fourth Avenue' Book Trade." Part I, *Publishers' Weekly*, October 20, 1969, pp. 52–54; Part II, October 27, 1969, pp. 50–55; Part III, November 3, 1969, pp. 40ff.

TAUBER, MAURICE F., and associates. *Technical Services in Libraries: Acquisitions, Cataloging, Classification, Binding, Photographic Reproduction, and Circulation Operations*. New York: Columbia University Press, 1953. New ed. in preparation.

TAUBERT, SIGFRED. "Reprints: Some German Methods." *Times Literary Supplement*, March 6, 1969, pp. 248–249.

TAYLOR, ISAAC. *History of the Transmission of Ancient Books to Modern Times: or, A Concise Account of the Means by which the Genuineness and Authenticity of Ancient Historical Works are Ascertained: With an Estimate of the Comparative Value of the Evidence usually adduced in Support of the Claims of the Jewish and Christian Scriptures*. London: Printed for B. J. Holdsworth, St. Paul's Church-Yard, 1827.

TEPLITZ, ARTHUR. "Library Fiche: An Introduction and Explanation." Prepared by Systems Development Corporation. Arlington, Va.: Clearinghouse for Federal Scientific and Technical Information, October 9, 1967. AD 661 660.

THOMPSON, LAWRENCE S. "Facsimiles and the Antiquarian Trade." *Library Trends*, April 1961, pp. 437–445.

————. "The Microfacsimile in American Research Libraries." *Libri*, 1958, pp. 209–222.

TILTON, EVA MAUDE. "Microcards: A Brief Survey of their development and a Union List of Research materials in Opaque Microtext." Master's thesis, Kent State University, Kent, Ohio, 1957.

————, comp. *A Union List of Publications in Opaque Microforms*, 2nd ed. New York: Scarecrow Press, 1964. Twenty-six publishers are included.

TUTTLE, HELEN WELCH. "Library-Book Trade Relations." *Library Trends*, January 1970, pp. 398–411. This issue of *Library Trends*, edited by Rolland E. Stevens, is devoted to "Problems of Acquisition for Research Libraries."

UNDERWOOD, RICHARD G. *Production and Manufacturing Problems of American University Presses*. New York: Association of American University Press, 1960. University Microfilms OP 30507 96428.

UNION LIBRARY CATALOGUE OF THE PHILADELPHIA METROPOLITAN AREA. Committee on Microphotography. *Union List of Microfilms*. Cumulation, 1949–1959. 2 vols. Ann Arbor, Mich.: J. W. Edwards, 1961. Supplement to basic list, no longer published. Files transferred to the National Union Catalog, Library of Congress.

U.S. DEPARTMENT OF COMMERCE. BUSINESS AND DEFENSE SERVICES ADMINISTRATION. "Microforms: A Growth Industry." Washington, D.C.: Government Printing Office, February 1969.

————. National Bureau of Standards. *Electronic Composition in Printing*. Proceedings of a Symposium, National Bureau of Standards, June 15–16, 1967, edited by Richard W. Lee and Roy W. Worral. NBS Special Publication No. 295 Washington, D.C.: Government Printing Office, February 1968.

————. Quarterly Industry Report. "Printing and Publishing." Washington, D.C., Government Printing Office, July 1970. This special issue includes "Historical Analysis of Book Publishing Statistics" by William S. Lofquist, pp. 13–24, and "American Book Title Output—A Ninety-Year Overview" by Dorothy B. Hokkanen, pp. 24–28. *See also* January 1972, pp. 13–16.

U.S. *Government Publications. Acquisition, Processing, and Use: Proceedings of Three Workshops, May 1966*, edited by Elizabeth Howes and Marcha Schell. Sacramento: California State Library, Government Publications Section 1967, repr. 1969. (GPS Publication No. 2, mimeographed.)

U.S. LIBRARY OF CONGRESS. *Conversion of Retrospective Catalog Records to Machine-Readable Form: A Study of the Feasibility of a National Bibliographic Service*, edited by John C. Rather. Prepared by the RECON Working Task Force. Washington, D.C.: Library of Congress, 1969.

————. Geography and Map Division. "Facsimiles of Rare Historical Maps: A List of Reproductions for Sale by Various Publishers and Distributors," 3rd ed. rev. & enl., comp. by Walter W. Ristow, assisted by Mary E. Graziani. Washington, D.C.: Library of Congress, 1968.

————. Photoduplication Service. *Brittle Books Filmed by the Library of Congress*. Washington, D.C.: Library of Congress, 1965.

————. Processing Department. "Library of Congress Cataloging in Publication Programs," *Cataloging Service Bulletin*, November 1971.

U.S. OFFICE OF ALIEN PROPERTY CUSTODIAN. Annual Report. No. 1, 1942/1943.

————. Book Republication Program. List I. Washington, D.C.: n.d. Contains 68 items.

————. Book Republication Program. List II. Washington, D.C.: Government Printing Office, May 1944. Contains 279 items.

————. Book Republication Program. List III, Cumulative: Titles Licensed for Republication with a Subject Index and List of Names and Addresses of Licensed Publishers. Washington, D.C.: Government Printing Office, December 1944. Contains 539 items.

————. Book Republication Program. Titles Suggested for Republication. Current Foreign Imprints: 1940–1943, An Alphabetical List with a Subject Index. Washington, D.C.: Government Printing Office, June 1944. Contains 302 items.

————. Periodical Republication Program. List I: To Scientists, Libraries, Industrial and Research Organizations. Washington, D.C., n.d. Four unnumbered pages, mimeographed, over the signature of Leo T. Crowley, Alien Property Custodian.

————. Periodical Republication Program. List II: Supplement Announcing for Subscription the Back Volumes of Certain Enemy Scientific and Technical Periodicals. Washington, D.C., n.d. Two unnumbered pages, i.e. single sheet, over the signature of Howland H. Sargeant, Chief, Division of Patent Administration.

————. Periodical Republication Program. List III: Current Enemy Scientific and Technical Periodicals offered for Subscription, with a Cumulative List of All Titles Offered to date. Washington, D.C., September 1943. Six unnumbered pages, as above.

————. Periodical Republication Program. List IV: and Statement concerning Subscription to Reprints of Foreign Scientific Periodicals for 1944. Washington, D.C., February 1944. Two unnumbered pages, as above.

————. Periodical Republication Program. List V: Same as above, May 1944.

————. Periodical Republication Program. List VI: Same as above. November 1944, and including a "Cumulative List of All Titles Offered for Subscription." Contains 132 items.

————. Periodical Republication Program. Preliminary Announcement.. Washington, D.C., n.d. Four unnumbered pages, over the signature of Howland H. Sargeant.

————. Report on Periodical Republication Program. Washington, D.C., November 1945. Ten pages, mimeographed.

U.S. OFFICE OF ALIEN PROPERTY CUSTODIAN. Terminal Report, transmitted to President Harry S. Truman, by James E. Markham, Alien Property Custodian. Mimeographed. Washington, D.C., October 14, 1946.

————. Division of Patent Administration. Copyright Administration Section. "Withdrawal by the Custodian from the Periodical Republication Program: Some Elements of the Problems Involved." Memorandum from Eugene A. Tilleux, chief, Copyright Administration Section to Howland H. Sargeant, chief, Division of Patent Administration. Washington, D.C., May 25, 1945. Typewritten, signed copy, with mimeographed appendixes. 39 pp. and Exhibits A-P.

THE UNIVERSITY OF THE STATE OF NEW YORK. State Education Department. Office of State History. "The Challenge of Local History." A conference designed to broaden the interests of New York State local historians in scholarly history. Albany, 1968.

UPDIKE, DANIEL BERKELEY. *Printing Types: Their History, Forms and Use,* 3rd ed. Boston: Harvard University Press, 1951.

VEANER, ALLEN B. "Developments in Reproduction of Library Materials & Graphic Communication, 1967." *Library Resources & Technical Services,* Spring 1968, pp. 203–214.

————. *The Evaluation of Micropublications: A Handbook for Librarians.* Chicago: American Library Association, 1971. (Library Technology Program, No. 17.)

VEENSTRA, JOHN G. "Microimages and the Library." *Library Journal,* October 15, 1970, pp. 3443–3447.

"WAR ISSUES OF SERIAL PUBLICATIONS." *Special Libraries,* July–August 1948, pp. 200–201.

WASSERMAN, PAUL. "The Publishing Scene: Two Specialized Publishers." *RQ,* Summer 1968, pp. 155–158.

"What Happens When the Printer Turns Publisher." *Book Production Industry,* October 1968, pp. 69–71.

WHITMAN, ALDEN. "New Book Offers Bargains Galore—71 Years Too Late." *The New York Times,* August 8, 1968. About Sears Roebuck 1897 Catalogue repr. by Chelsea House.

WHITMAN, CEDRIC H. "Why Not the Classics? An Old-Fashioned View." *Daedalus,* Summer 1969, pp. 809–814.

WHITTEN, JOSEPH N., and FESSLER, AARON L. "Hard-cover Reprint Publishing." *Library Trends,* July 1958, pp. 82–92.

WIGGIN, LEWIS M. "Aspects of Reprinting." *Scholarly Publishing,* January 1971, pp. 149–161.

WILLIAMS, FRANKLIN B., Jr. "Photo-Facsimiles of STC Books: A Cautionary Check List." In *Studies in Bibliography: Papers of the Bibliographical Society of the University of Virginia,* vol. 21, edited by Fredson Bowers, 1968, pp. 109–130.

WILLIAMS, SAM P., comp. and ed. *Reprints in Print—Serials: 1966,* Dobbs Ferry, New York: Oceana Publications, 1967.

WILLIAMSON, DEREK. *Historical Bibliography.* Hampden, Conn.: Archon Books, Shoe String Press, 1967.

WILSON, LOUIS ROUND and TAUBER, MAURICE F. *The University Library: Its Organization, Administration, and Functions.* Chicago: University of Chicago Press, 1945. New edition in preparation.

ZEITLIN, JACOB I. *What Kind of a Business Is This? Reminiscences of the Book Trade and Book Collectors.* Lawrence: University of Kansas Libraries, 1959.

Index